Learning and Being
in
Person-Centred
Counselling

second edition

Learning and Being
in
Person-Centred
Counselling
second edition

Tony Merry

PCCS BOOKS
Ross-on-Wye

First edition published in 1999
Second edition published in 2002

PCCS BOOKS Ltd
Llangarron
Ross-on-Wye
Herefordshire
HR9 6PT
UK
Tel +44 (0)1989 77 07 07
enquiries@pccsbks.globalnet.co.uk
www.pccs-books.co.uk

**Learning and Being in Person-Centred Counselling
second edition**

A CIP catalogue record for this book is available from the British Library

ISBN 1 898059 53 5

Cover design by Denis Postle.
Printed by Bookcraft, Trowbridge, Wiltshire, UK

Contents

Acknowledgements   i

Preface   iii

1 Introducing person-centred counselling   1

2 Human nature, actualisation and the emerging self   16

3 Self and person   33

4 Towards a theory of person-centred counselling   47

5 Person-centred counselling in practice   72

6 Working at 'relational depth': the kid with the chips   101

7 Developing person-centred values, skills, attitudes and personal qualities   119

8 Training issues: client work and personal development   152

9 Supervision   170

10 Resources   189

References   203

Index of subjects   209

Index of checklists and exercises   212

Acknowledgements

Many people have contributed, either directly or indirectly, to this book, and I am grateful to all of them.

Firstly, Bob Lusty, a friend and colleague for twenty-five years, is co-author of the book from which this volume is a development, *What is Person-Centred Therapy?* (Gale Centre, 1993). His new ideas, suggestions and contributions have made a substantial and positive difference to this work.

I am particularly grateful to three experienced person-centred practitioners and theorists who made many useful comments on earlier drafts. Barbara Brodley kindly read every word I sent her. Her responses were swift, thoughtful and constructive. If I have succeeded in my aim of theoretical clarity and consistency, much of it is derived from her insightful criticisms of my attempts to provide concise descriptions of complex concepts. Though I doubt if she agrees with every word contained in this book, I took her constructive criticisms very seriously. Any inadvertent misrepresentation of Rogers' work is entirely my responsibility.

Thanks too to C.H. 'Pat' Patterson, a most respected and experienced exponent of the person-centred approach whose association with Rogers goes back to the very early days. His thoughtful suggestions and supportive comments meant a lot to me.

My heartfelt thanks also go to Godfrey Barrett-Lennard. Goff's work and writings have, over the years, been a source of great inspiration to me. He generously took time from a busy schedule to read sections of early drafts, and his comments enabled me to be clearer in my expression. He gently and with great skill corrected my tendency towards speculation where precision was called for. My admiration for his latest book, *Carl Rogers' Helping System: Journey and Substance*, will be evident to even the most casual reader of what follows.

I am indebted to two of my colleagues, Rowan Bayne and Ian Horton, at the University of East London. Their deep knowledge of counselling and counselling psychology provided criticism and feedback from perspectives other than the person-centred approach, and I think this book is the better for it.

Particular thanks and appreciation must go to Pete Sanders and

Maggie Taylor-Sanders at PCCS Books. Their unstinting encouragement provided energy when mine was flagging and Pete's additional thoughts on Rogers' nineteen propositions were especially welcome. I am fortunate to live close to them in the heart of the Herefordshire countryside, and I am glad to share its tranquillity and scenery with them.

My sincere appreciation and admiration is also extended to the many students, clients and supervisees I have met over the years both at the University of East London and through the Institute for Person-Centred Learning. In particular, I would like to thank Richard Baughan and Niru Williams, once students and now supervisees. The many discussions I have had with them taught me a great deal, and they kept me going during a difficult time.

I also want to thank Irene Fairhurst for putting up with me for nearly twenty years as a friend and colleague. I learn a lot from you, Irene.

Finally, I want to thank, and express my deepest love to, Jan, with whom I share my life. The beautiful sculptural forms you fashion from clay, your profound connection with nature, and your love, patience and infinite understanding make all the difference.

Tony Merry
July 1999

Preface to the second edition

This book is a development from an earlier work, *What is Person-Centred Therapy?* co-authored with Bob Lusty and published by the Gale Centre in 1993.

The first edition of *Learning and Being in Person-Centred Counselling* developed *What is Person-Centred Therapy?* from a brief, introductory guide into a much more comprehensive discussion of the theory and practice of the approach to counselling begun over fifty years ago by Carl Rogers and his colleagues. This second edition takes that development a significant stage further. It retains the essence, and much of the material of the first edition, but extends its vision into newer areas of theory, practice and underlying philosophy. For example, Garry Prouty's work with 'pre-therapy', and David Mearns' and Brian Thorne's work (both separately and together) on aspects of 'the self' and the theory of actualisation are introduced and discussed as examples of very new and still evolving perspectives. In the same spirit, I have included references to a wide range of contemporary theorists and practitioners in the person-centred counselling field to illustrate how the continuing debate on central issues like 'the necessary and sufficient conditions' have moved on even during the last three years or so.

I have, throughout this book, tried to engage you, the reader, as directly as is possible through the printed page. I have attempted to provide concise but accurate discussions of all the major theoretical and practical aspects of person-centred counselling, and I encourage you to involve yourself personally in experimenting with what they mean to you.

The essence of person-centred counselling is the meeting between us and our clients, and this makes it the hardest and most challenging approach to counselling that I know. Not being afraid to work at 'relational depth' or 'existential depth' demands so much of me as a person whenever I face the distress and confusion of another human being. The theory helps us to make sense of what we discover in ourselves and others, but this is of little value unless we can transform theoretical knowledge into a way of being that represents the best of our individuality in relation to others. Person-centred counselling provides no escape into techniques or strategies, but requires us to focus on the experiences of other living, breathing human beings without giving way to the temptation to rush in and fix things, however well intentioned we are. That is both the joy and the challenge of the person-centred way of being with others. The question is, 'If I can be myself, however hesitantly and imperfectly, will I be enough?'

I hope this book helps you to be yourself, but in particular kinds of ways. Being disciplined and self-aware enough to be non-judgemental, authentic and empathic is already part of your way of being. If we believe our clients have untapped, internal resources for change and growth, then we must believe in this for ourselves also.

Tony Merry
August 2002

Introducing person-centred counselling

1

This book is about the Person-Centred Approach (PCA) to counselling. It is for counsellors, therapists, and clinical psychologists either practising or in training, and for people who use counselling skills as part of their work, but who do not want to be full-time counsellors — nurses, teachers, social workers, personnel managers, and community workers, for example. It is based on the work of Carl Rogers (1902–1987), one of the leading counselling psychologists of the twentieth century, who was responsible for some of the most original research work ever undertaken into the factors that facilitate personal and social change (see, for example, Rogers, 1957a, 1959). Throughout a career that spanned more than fifty years as a writer, researcher, and practitioner, Rogers developed and refined an approach to counselling that is widely recognised as one of the most creative and effective ways of helping people in need.

Although this book is focused on person-centred counselling, I see it as useful for people exploring a range of different approaches before committing themselves to one in particular, and a valuable resource for counselling trainers, whether person-centred or not. It offers ideas and perspectives, perhaps even inspiration occasionally, and makes reference to some of the literature, both classical and recent.

I have tried to be careful about giving the sources for the material in this book, and I am indebted to the many authors I have referred to in writing it. The hundreds, perhaps thousands of hours spent discussing the person-centred approach to counselling with students and others, talking with practitioners and being with clients, have contributed to the content of this book.

The best-known books about the PCA were written by Carl Rogers, and perhaps the most familiar of these are *On Becoming a Person* (1961), and *A Way of Being* (1980), though the book *Client-Centered Therapy* (1951) is probably Rogers' most systematic presentation of theory and applications. In recent years, more books about the PCA have appeared in Britain and elsewhere that testify to the continuing evolution of person-centred theory and practice. The final chapter of this book lists and discusses some of the work that has appeared during the last ten years, and directs you to some websites and organisations that are useful for further inquiry into the PCA.

Many books on counselling are good at describing a particular theory, and often give case-studies and examples of how counselling works in real life. However, it is hard to find books that help develop the attitudes, values and qualities that effective person-centred counsellors need. *Exercises in Helping Skills* (Egan, 1990) operates from a different theoretical base from the PCA and the same is true of *The Theory and Practice of Counselling* (Nelson-Jones, 1995). *First Steps in Counselling, Third Edition* (Sanders, 2002) takes a broader view than I do here, identifying common themes, skills and qualities for counselling generally, though its main inspiration is clearly person-centred. The present book concentrates more or less exclusively on person-centred counselling, but it is not an instruction manual for counsellors who have no other training or experience in counselling. In other words, I do not pretend that reading this book (or any book) will turn you into a counsellor.

About Carl Rogers

Person-centred counselling was developed by Carl Rogers, an American psychologist and counsellor, who died in 1987, aged 85. He was one of the founders of humanistic psychology, and his influence and ideas have now spread around the world.

Carl Rogers is such an important figure in the development of counselling, that it will help to know a little more about him because his life and work were so tied together. More discussion can be found in Brian Thorne's biography of Rogers (Thorne, 1992), and the new book *Carl Rogers the Quiet Revolutionary* (Rogers and Russell, 2002), so only a brief sketch is given here.

Born in 1902 in Oak Park, near Chicago, Rogers first started working as a psychologist in New York, with the Society for the Prevention of Cruelty to Children. After a while, he became disenchanted with mainstream psychology, with its emphasis on testing and treatment, and began to develop his own theories and ways of working with clients. He disliked the way psychology, at that time, seemed to treat people as objects for study rather than as individuals deserving of understanding and respect.

Rogers' own emphasis and distinctive 'non-directive counselling' became visible with the publication of his book, *Counseling and Psychotherapy: Newer Concepts in Practice* (Rogers, 1942) after receiving his Doctorate at Columbia University. By the early 1950s, non-directive counselling became known as 'client-centred therapy', particularly after the publication of *Client-Centered Therapy: Its Current Practice, Implications and Theory* (Rogers, 1951).

Later, the term 'Person-Centred Approach' was adopted when it was shown that the theory and philosophy of counselling could be transferred to other settings where people's growth and development were of central importance — in education, for example (Rogers, 1983; Merry, 1995; Barrett-Lennard, 1998).

In the 1940s and 1950s Rogers revolutionised the study of counselling and psychotherapy by making sound recordings of counselling interviews (not easy in those days), and trying to identify the significant factors contributing to successful outcomes. His book, *Counseling and Psychotherapy: Newer Concepts in Practice* (1942), contained the first ever transcript of a full therapy session. From these and other observations, he developed a theory of counselling and personal change that could be tested through further research and clinical experience.

Rogers devoted the last few years of his life mainly to writing and to peace work, for which he was nominated for the Nobel Peace Prize in 1987. He also ran workshops, gave demonstrations, and contributed to seminars in countries all round the world, including Poland, Hungary, England, South Africa, Ireland, South America and the then Soviet Union.

Cain (1990) has provided a summary of seven ways in which Rogers and his colleagues influenced the development of counselling and psychotherapy:

- Emphasising the central role and importance of the counselling relationship itself as a significant factor in promoting change.
- Describing 'the person' as resourceful and tending towards actualisation of potential.
- Emphasising and developing the central role of listening and empathy in counselling and other relationships.
- Using the term 'client' rather than 'patient' to signify respect for the person coming for help and to acknowledge his or her dignity.
- Making sound recordings of counselling interviews for the first time and using them to learn about the counselling process.
- Engaging in scientific research and encouraging others to do so.
- Making the counselling process more democratic and encouraging non-psychologists and non-medical people to become counsellors.

Rogers was not alone in his development of the person-centred approach: many people contributed to its formation and evolution, and others made significant contributions in the years following the pioneering work of Rogers and his students and colleagues. Though there are arguments about the extent to which some other workers have departed from Rogers' original philosophy, Gendlin's work on 'focusing' (e.g. Gendlin, 1981, 1984) is worthy of mention here, as is Natalie Rogers and her colleagues' development of Person-Centred Expressive Therapy, where clients are encouraged to express themselves through dance, music, painting, writing and drawing, etc. (see, for example, N. Rogers, 1993; Merry, 1997).

Julius Seeman's work on personality integration (Seeman, 1983) spanned several decades and provided much empirical research support for some of the central concepts in the PCA, and John Shlien's discussion, *A Countertheory of Transference* (Shlien, 1984, reprinted in Cain, 2002) demonstrates the novel and revolutionary nature of the PCA. Barrett-Lennard's 1998 book documents the many influential theorists who contributed to the evolution of the PCA in America and elsewhere from the pre-war era to the present day, and the book itself carries this evolution further. Garry Prouty's development of 'Pre-Therapy' is a particularly important application of the principles of the PCA to working with seriously disturbed and uncommunicative clients. (See, for example, Prouty, 1994, and my brief discussion in chapter 5.) Recently, Ned Gaylin has shown how the principles of the PCA can be employed in family therapy (Gaylin, 2001) and Margaret Warner (2000, 2001), in the USA, has been developing her approach to working with very seriously disturbed clients. Marlis Pörtner (2000) has described how the PCA can be used in caring for people with special needs, Leslie McCulloch (2002) has discussed the PCA in relation to work with 'antisocial personality disorder', and Elisabeth Zinschitz has shown how the PCA can be used with people with learning disabilities (e.g. Zinschitz, 2002).

David Mearns and Brian Thorne (e.g. 2000), both separately and together, have made enormous contributions to the development of person-centred counselling in the UK, as have others too numerous to mention here. While I am aware that the approach to person-centred counselling discussed in this book is of the fairly traditional kind, I have incorporated some recent developments in both theory and practice. Not to do so would run the risk of presenting the PCA as if it had somehow reached its final evolutionary stage on the day of Carl Rogers' death. This is very far from the case, even though it is Rogers and his work that provide the main inspiration for this book. The important developments that have emerged in person-centred theory and practice during the last decades find their place within the pages of this book. I hope that readers will appreciate the liveliness and creativity inherent within the PCA, and understand how it has kept abreast of, and in many ways anticipated, developments and new directions within the counselling field.

Counselling and the Person-Centred Approach

Person-centred counselling is also known as client-centred counselling, and more generally as the Person-Centred Approach, and this can lead to some confusion. I take the term Person-Centred Approach (PCA) to refer to a particular set of attitudes and values, and a philosophy that can be applied to any setting where people's personal growth and development is of concern.

An 'approach' is not a formal theory or a method, or a hypothesis to test in research. An approach, in this case, is a *way of being* in situations that is based on certain attitudes and values. The application of person-centred values and attitudes to counselling is generally known as 'client-centred' or 'person-centred' counselling, which does have a theory of personality and change and has been subject to a good deal of research. It is the application of a set of values and attitudes known as the PCA to a specific situation (counselling) that this book is all about.

In this book I present person-centred counselling in its traditional or mainstream form, which means I believe person-centred counselling to be, of itself, an effective means of promoting personal change, and one which has a specific theoretical base and discipline of its own. I have also included some of the most influential of the new developments in theory and practice that have emerged during the last decade or so.

Is it counselling or psychotherapy?

There are many points of view about the differences, if any, between psychotherapy and counselling. I use the term 'person-centred counselling' or 'client-centred counselling', but I could just as easily have used 'person-centred therapy'. Rogers did not distinguish between counselling and psychotherapy and the distinction between them, if there is one, is very difficult to make with any real precision.

At one time, counselling was thought of as short term, and psychotherapy as long term, but now there is increasing interest in brief psychotherapy, and counsellors often work with clients for 50 or 60 sessions or more, so the distinction is becoming increasingly blurred.

Another distinction is that counselling is believed to be concerned with identifiable problems, and psychotherapy with more profound psychological disturbance. But more and more counsellors are finding that they cannot confine themselves to working only with identifiable problems, which may represent only the surface layers of much more deep-seated issues.

Finally, it is thought by some that counsellors and psychotherapists have different training requirements. Psychotherapists have long periods of intensive training, which usually includes their own therapy or analysis. Counsellors, on the other hand, have much shorter training, and are not necessarily required to undergo their own counselling.

There was some truth in this, but the picture has changed a lot in recent years. Most training institutes in person-centred counselling offer training periods of three or four years of part-time study. If they do not actually require their students to be in personal counselling as part of the training process, they do advise them to enter personal counselling before starting to see clients themselves. The British Association for Counselling and Psychotherapy (BACP) requires people to have had experience of being in the client role in ways that are appropriate to their model of counselling, when they apply for Accreditation.

The term 'counselling' or 'psychotherapy' is often determined by the work context, rather than by any inherent difference between the two. What is important is that person-centred relationships with clients require the deepest commitment to understanding the unique individuality of the people with whom we work. This holds true whether we call what we do counselling or psychotherapy.

The social context of counselling

There are two areas I consider briefly here. The first is concerned with the current professional context of counselling, and the second, broader area is concerned with the wider political and cultural context in which counselling takes place.

The professional context

Counselling has evolved, during the last thirty years or so, into an identifiable profession with its own organisations, academic journals and codes of conduct and ethical practice. In Britain, the BACP has developed an ethical framework for good practice in counselling and psychotherapy and an accreditation procedure through which people may apply for professional recognition of their training, experience and competence. To be accredited, people have to show they have had appropriate training and experience of working with clients under supervision, and they also must agree to abide by the BACP statement of ethics for counselling and psychotherapy.

At present, accreditation is voluntary, and accredited counsellors need to maintain their commitment to ongoing personal and professional development, and are expected to have an appropriate level of clinical supervision of their work. Accredited counsellors can apply to join the United Kingdom Register of Counsellors as Registered Independent Counsellors, again a voluntary scheme, though some form of statutory registration is likely in the future.

The BACP also has an accreditation procedure for courses in counselling. To be accredited, a course has to be substantial in terms of time and content, and must meet a number of exacting criteria. If you have successfully completed a BACP Accredited course, it is assumed that the training requirement for individual accreditation has been met, but you would still have to complete 450 hours of supervised practice over three years before accreditation could be given.

There is now a separate body — the UK Council for Psychotherapy, whose aim is to establish professional standards for training and qualifications in psychotherapy. Membership of this council includes representatives from the majority of training organisations in psychotherapy, and representatives of allied professions like the Royal College of Psychiatry, the British Psychological Society, and the British Association of Social Workers.

Recent developments among person-centred practitioners towards greater organisation include the formation of the British Association for the Person-Centred Approach (BAPCA) in 1989, which now has over 1000 members. Moves towards the foundation of an international association for the PCA are complete, and a new international journal will be published by December 2002. In the USA, the major organisation is the Association for the Development of the Person-Centered Approach (ADPCA), and both ADPCA and BAPCA have developed their own journals. You will find more information about both these organisations and others in the Resources section of this book.

The increasingly organised and regulated manner of the counselling profession brings with it some advantages, but also serious concerns for some practitioners. Arguments for increased regulation and control are usually couched in terms of protection for the public against bad, incompetent or exploitative practice. Agreed standards and criteria for training, for example, are designed to ensure that all counsellors achieve a basic level of competency, and are thus less likely, wittingly or otherwise, to do damage to people who are already vulnerable. The requirements of accrediting organisations include the demand that practising counsellors receive continuing clinical supervision. Codes of ethics and practice serve to reassure the public that the profession is monitored and bad behaviour sanctioned.

Sceptics of 'professionalisation', however, argue that regulation is a covert but outwardly respectable means of self-promotion, and limits the opportunities for many unqualified but otherwise competent people to offer psychological help to people in distress. They argue that there is a difference between professionalisation (which is about the protection of interest groups and the exclusion of 'outsiders'), and professionalism (which is about skill, integrity and good practice). The case against currently proposed forms of registration for psychotherapists was made persuasively by, for example, Richard Mowbray in 1995 (see also Mowbray, 1997).

Regulations for accreditation of individual practitioners emphasise the establishment of baseline standards, but they bring with them increased bureaucracy and expense that do nothing to promote good practice. The current mood for cost-effectiveness, evidence-based practice and standardisation of treatments is leading to the setting of spurious objectives and the mechanisation of counselling into a series of skills that can be objectively evaluated. Creativity, inventiveness and experimentation become less likely in an atmosphere dogged by a complaints culture, in which professional organisations are keen to be seen as protecting the assumed public interest, rather than encouraging the active development of counselling, which is not a risk-free undertaking. This is not, however, an argument for the irresponsible experimentation by maverick practitioners at the expense of vulnerable or anxious clients. It is questionable in any case how much real protection is afforded to the public by the increasing regulation of practice. Other, older professions such as medicine and law have been subject to stringent control and regulation for many years, but incompetence and exploitation continue to exist.

Andy Rogers (2001), questions the promotion of counselling as a profession akin to the medical profession and argues that this 'medicalisation' '. . . does my work a *disservice* because it fails to acknowledge the uncertain, unscientific and existential dimensions of the encounter and the particular demands of indwelling in such territory. Paradoxically, it also *talks-up* counselling, dishonestly downplaying its imprecision, fallibility, and "might-work-sometimes-with-some-people" reality, and thereby misrepresenting it to clients' (p. 76).

The standardisation of counsellor training courses (in the UK largely under the influence of the BACP since the Courses Recognition Scheme, as it was called then, was launched in 1988), also brings advantages and disadvantages. Without much doubt, the scheme forced training providers to think carefully about what they were doing, raise standards of delivery, and provide value for money for their students. Sceptics, however, pointed to the extra cost (passed on to students) that entering into the scheme incurred, the insistence on the teaching of a core model (not a universally admired principle — see, for example, Feltham, 1997b), and the mechanistic way that courses and their students were forced into counting up hours and minutes spent in theory sessions and skills training workshops in order to satisfy the BACP's stringent criteria. Some perfectly adequate courses which, for good reasons did not want to enter the scheme, suffered in reputation and popularity without any real justification. Other courses were tempted to fulfil BACP criteria, not because they were persuaded of their value, but because not to do so would make them uncompetitive in a very competitive market place.

To be fair, the BACP scheme is by peer evaluation, and evaluators are drawn widely from across the membership. This allows for great variety (though not infinite variety) in the interpretation of the criteria, and the BACP is keen to allow the various theoretical approaches to counselling to be represented in the material that is taught on courses and the way in which it is delivered.

Current preoccupations of the counselling field, at least as represented in the counselling literature, are with contracts and boundaries. On the surface, the issue of contracting seems sensible and uncontroversial. There is everything to be gained from ensuring that both client and counsellor are as fully aware as possible of, for example, time commitments, venues and financial arrangements. Problems occur, however, if counsellors become so afraid of being called to account at a later date for unethical or unprofessional behaviour, that they defensively place the apparent need for agreeing a contract above the need to meet a distressed, vulnerable or anxious client with a warm, open and inviting attitude from the outset.

Issues of boundaries seem to create much concern, confusion and defensiveness, particularly among training or newly trained counsellors. It is right that counsellors should have a deep appreciation for the protected nature of the counselling encounter. Very rarely is it appropriate for counsellors to become participants in the lives of clients, over and above the profound commitment they make to accompanying their clients on their unpredictable journeys into 'self' during the counselling hour. However, the formalisation of boundaries into a set of injunctions that prevent spontaneous acts of human kindness, understanding and love can only serve to place barriers between a hurting human being and one who is setting out to offer the opportunity for healing through a person-to-person encounter.

Those counsellors whose personal, moral framework is shaky or underdeveloped, or who have psychological needs for intimacy or sexual contact, of which they are largely or even wholly unaware, will continue to exist whether or not they have signed up to a stringent code of ethics. This does not, of course, imply that the counselling profession should abandon its commitment to moral and ethical practice. The general tone of the new BACP Statement of Ethics for Counselling and Psychotherapy does recognise the uncertainties and risks that are inherent characteristics of the profession, and is to be welcomed for that. Boundary issues are likely to continue to exercise the minds of practitioners, but the new Statement offers more understanding of the complexities of the counselling encounter than did its predecessor.

The cultural and political context

Counsellors do not work in isolation from the rest of the society and culture in which they live. Our society is rich in cultural differences, and is also one in which some people enjoy more power and privilege than others. Counselling can be criticised for being available more to the relatively well and economically advantaged than to the very disturbed, poor or otherwise disadvantaged.

Seeing a counsellor often involves paying fees — there is some counselling and psychotherapy available through the National Health Service, and through Employee Assistance Programmes, but it is limited — so this fact alone means that some people who need it cannot afford to pay for it. This is not an argument against counselling, but it is a reminder to would-be counsellors that they may find it difficult to work with some clients whose need may be great, but whose capacity to pay is limited or non-existent.

The social context also includes groups who have particular needs, different from those of the majority. Such groups include members of cultural or ethnic groups whose attitudes to therapy, and what they need from it, may be very different from those of the majority. It is also likely that many such groups (if not all) will have experienced prejudice or some form of discrimination, and may therefore be justifiably suspicious of what counselling has to offer if it remains a largely white, middle-class activity, (see, for example, Patel and Fatimilehin, 1999).

Although counselling certainly is not politics, it does have a political dimension that therapists need to acknowledge and, more importantly, do something about. At the very least, counsellors should be aware of the social and cultural values they hold, and be prepared to confront the racism, sexism and other 'isms' they have unwittingly absorbed, in an effort to free themselves of unhelpful attitudes towards people who have very different experiences and expectations from themselves.

Counsellors will be more effective if they are aware of the social backgrounds and contexts of their clients, and knowledgeable enough to see how different people bring different experiences and expectations with them into counselling sessions. Being understanding of individuals includes being sensitive to the cultural norms and values that influence different people to see things in very different ways.

However, simply knowing about different cultural characteristics does not necessarily lead to more effective counselling practice. The idea that the culturally sensitive or culturally aware counsellor needs to develop techniques appropriate to different cultural groups is problematic. Descriptions of various groups tend to describe the average person, something that can unwittingly lead to the development of stereotypes, and assumptions about the characteristics of particular groups can lead to a self-fulfilling prophecy. If clients from certain groups are believed to share certain patterns of behaviour, preferences and values, it is likely that 'they will be treated as if these things were true and they will respond to confirm the counsellor's beliefs' (Patterson, 1996).

There is a limit to the extent that any counsellor of whatever approach can change his or her behaviour to take into account the presumed preferences of people from different cultural groups without seriously compromising the theoretical basis of their counselling. This holds true whether we are talking about race and ethnicity, sexual orientation, class or gender, etc. The problem, then, is one of balancing the need to know and understand factors affecting discrimination and oppression with the need to remain consistent with one's theory and philosophy of counselling.

There are two levels to be considered here. Firstly, there is a need to know and understand something about the social, economic and political construction of the society in which we live and work. This includes some knowledge of the cultural groups and sub-groups from which our clients are drawn so that their concerns can be appreciated in terms of their cultural norms and values. In relation to this is a need for counsellors to understand the nature of prejudice and how discrimination, both overt and covert, is an everyday experience for some people.

The second level is the personal level in which counsellors themselves confront the nature of their own prejudice and stereotyping. I argue, along with Bernard and Goodyear (1992), that the starting point for this is with an examination of our own cultural norms and expectations as a first step to understanding others. Later in this book I explore some ways of developing greater awareness at both these levels.

Finally, there is a broader political dimension to the PCA that includes, but goes beyond, its application to the field of counselling and psychotherapy. The PCA encompasses not only a theory of counselling and human relationships, but also provides a radical critique of the theories and assumptions contained within modern discourse about human relationships, in the broadest sense of that term. For example, the rejection, by the PCA, of contemporary attitudes towards the assessment, diagnosis and labelling of people represents a radical departure from traditional forms of psychological treatment. The metaphor of therapist/counsellor as a companion on a journey into another's person's inner world, directly challenges the model of the therapist/counsellor as an expert diagnostician. The expertise of the person-centred practitioner is dedicated to gaining a deep understanding of a client's unique experience and the meanings derived from that experience. The essentially non-directive attitude of the person-centred counsellor is built on a trust in the individual's capacity (and inherent tendency) to move further towards more constructive, pro-social and self- and other-enhancing behaviour, values and attitudes, in an environment that facilitates growth and development from within the person.

The PCA, then, is not simply an alternative model or theory of counselling. It represents a fundamentally humanistic attitude towards persons as being essentially creative in outlook and pro-social in attitude. Its 'politics' reside in the redefining of helping relationships away from the conventional medical model towards a more collaborative one where power is redistributed and clients are able to reclaim their capacity for their own psychological determination.

Ethical issues in counselling

People who enter counselling can be in a vulnerable and anxious state. They may recently, or in the more distant past, have had experiences that resulted in immense despair for them. In such states, people are more open to being exploited than when they are at peace with themselves, and it can be easier for them to fall prey to unscrupulous and unethical practices. These range from keeping clients dependent for longer than necessary in order to keep collecting fees, through to sexual exploitation. A counsellor can be a powerful figure in the lives of lonely or vulnerable people, and clients can develop strong feelings towards a counsellor who appears wise, and is giving them time, care and attention.

If a counsellor or therapist is a member of a professional body, he or she will be bound by a code of professional ethics, or, in the case of the BACP, the ethical framework referred to above. This framework, published in April 2002, is far more flexible than the Code of Ethics it replaced, and is indicative of how the BACP's thinking has evolved over the years. It replaces the former rather prescriptive list of 'do's and don'ts' with an altogether more thoughtful discussion of values, principles and moral qualities; it recognises that choices are often not clear-cut, and that sometimes difficult decisions need to be made that, even when taken in good faith, may have unpredictable and unwanted outcomes. The new spirit embodied in this framework is far more representative of the fluid, constantly changing dynamics of counselling relationships than the original Codes of Ethics and Practice. It openly confronts the reality that knowing the right course of action to take in a particular circumstance cannot be codified into a book of rules and regulations, but instead is guided by a set of principles and values that underlie the commitment counsellors make to provide relationships with clients based on a deep sense of personal integrity.

What person-centred counselling is not ...

This book contains a lot of information about the theory, philosophy and practice of person-centred counselling, and it discusses some of the issues that face counsellors in their work, like supervision and ethics, for example.

It also contains some suggestions about how you can explore person-centred counselling for yourself, either alone or as part of a training group. What this book is not, as I have said before, is a manual or a set of instructions as to how to do person-centred counselling. Person-centred counselling is not a set of skills or techniques, nor is it synonymous with 'reflection of feelings'; it is not a group of communication skills, and it does not offer a range of strategies thought to be appropriate for different groups of clients.

Person-centred counselling is only partly about feelings; it would be more accurate to say that person-centred counselling concerns itself with clients as persons, and that includes feelings, but also thoughts, experience, ideas, fantasies and other sensations.

... and what it is

Person-centred counselling is a way of being with people based on a particular theory of helping relationships which, in turn, rests on a deep respect for and trust in the individual's capacity for growth, development and creativity. It has a set of theoretical ideas aimed at exploring the processes of human growth and development, and it has a sophisticated and developing theory of personality. Of most interest to readers of this book is its theory of counselling relationships based on the presence of a counsellor with certain personal qualities, attitudes and values. It has a firm foundation of careful research into the factors that promote change, and is one of the most influential models of counselling currently in use in Britain.

It is a democratic, non-authoritarian and non-directive approach to people that emphasises constructive human relationships as the key to the change process. The PCA, perhaps more than any other approach, requires the enduring commitment to encounter clients in a direct, person-to-person manner without providing a set of rules or an armoury of techniques and strategies that control the process. This can be a daunting task for the beginning counsellor as well as for the more experienced. In the modern, technological age there is a high premium placed on the abilities of expert practitioners of any profession to identify problems quickly and apply known, effective techniques for their speedy solution. The drift towards 'evidence-based practice', time-limited counselling and solution-focused therapy, finds the person-centred counsellor swimming against an increasingly powerful tide.

If person-centred counsellors do not offer techniques, strategies and interventions, what, then, do they offer? Though this is a question that I explore in the remainder of this book, it would be churlish in the extreme not to attempt some answer near the beginning. (To avoid clumsy constructions like 'he or she', 'he' here refers to people of both genders):

The counsellor attends to the whole person of his client, listening to and responding empathically to the client's experiencing process as it is lived in the therapeutic hour. He has no goals for his client, only for himself.

He sensitively and progressively becomes familiar with his client's frame of reference with its changing and fluid content, process and nuance. He becomes progressively more sensitive to and responsive to his client's ongoing, idiosyncratic struggle to allow more experience into his awareness with decreasing distortion or denial, to gain meaning from that experience, to change old, outmoded meanings, and to construct, for himself, a contemporary, more realistic picture of himself both as he now is and what he may become. The counsellor, in some measure, achieves this through his active engagement with the lived and experienced world of his client, without judgement but with respect and authenticity. The counsellor extends himself towards his client as a person, and allows his client to affect him, each making a difference to the other. He neither absorbs the client's experiencing into himself, taking ownership of it for himself, nor does he direct it. Rather, he participates in it without losing his own sense of himself as both a separate person and as someone who, however temporarily, shares in this existential moment, this hour of cooperative living. He is an alert companion and, simultaneously, an empathic and non-judgmental observer. (Adapted from Merry, 2002.)

I am aware that this answer begs a lot of questions. How does the counsellor respond empathically, and what does empathy really mean in this context? How does the counsellor achieve active engagement, and what does it mean to 'share in this existential moment, this hour of cooperative living'? What is the process through which a client goes for it to be possible to 'allow more experience into his awareness', and how does this promote lasting psychological change? I hope that some answers to these and other questions appear in the pages that follow.

The evolution of person-centred counselling

It is possible to identify three phases in the development of person-centred counselling, with one phase melding into the next rather than representing a sudden change of emphasis. Raskin (1996) describes twenty historical steps in the development of the person-centred approach, but here I offer a very general evolutionary process beginning in the 1940s:

- The first phase, from about 1940 to the early 1950s, could be called the 'non-directive' phase. It emphasised acceptance of the client and the establishment of a non-judgmental atmosphere in which the accent was on the skills of the counsellor to promote the counselling process.

  The essential non-directivity of the counselling process remains in place today, but there is more emphasis on the counsellor being present as a whole person, expressing him or herself more openly than was the case during the early development of this approach.

- The second phase, from about 1950 to the early 1960s, can be thought of as the 'client-centred phase'. Here the emphasis was placed on counsellor attitudes rather than skills, and on reflecting the client's feelings. Theoretical ideas of resolving discrepancies between the client's 'real' and 'ideal' self became incorporated, and the idea of the counsellor as a person involved subjectively in the counselling relationship began to take shape.

• The third phase, from the 1960s to the present, is the 'person-centred phase', which emphasises counsellor attitudes and values and relationship qualities. The counsellor's role is seen even less as skilled performance and more as an expression of the counsellor being responsively engaged with the client.

The evolution of the PCA continues, and I suspect that it may now be entering a fourth stage. Pete Sanders (2002, private communication) has labelled this as the 'client-centred and experiential counselling/ psychotherapy stage'. This is based on his observation that there is now a genuine exploration of theoretical origins, commonalities and differences emerging among various therapeutic approaches that share many of the fundamental philosophical concepts that are characteristic of the PCA. These approaches, loosely called 'experiential approaches', have developed new ideas of their own that, in various degrees, depart from traditional person-centred counselling, but still share many of its philosophical roots. In a challenging article, Sanders (2000) suggests ways in which approaches that have emerged over the last thirty years or so could be included under a general person-centred umbrella so that differences and commonalities can be recognised and clarified.

About the exercises and checklists in this book

I hope you will find this book useful as part of a training programme, or as a means of helping you discover ways in which you can become more effective in your own professional and personal relationships. The exercises and checklists are designed to help you experience what I am describing, rather than just reading about them.

The best way to approach them is to get together with a small group and work your way through them. There should always be time at the end of each exercise for general discussion and sharing of the things you have learned. Most of them can also be done on your own as a way to check what you are reading and learning about counselling.

Before you go on to the next chapter, you may like to explore what you know and think you know about person-centred counselling at the moment by working through the checklist that follows. It may be that you have heard some things about person-centred counselling, and some of them might be accurate and some not. Every form of counselling gives rise to myths, legends and misunderstandings about itself. When you have finished the book and tried some of the exercises, come back to this checklist and see if your ideas about person-centred counselling have changed.

Checklist: True or false?

Person-centred counsellors think
that people are basically good.   Agree / Don't know / Disagree

Person-centred counselling is OK for
relatively well people, but no good for
very disturbed people.   Agree / Don't know / Disagree

Person-centred counselling is where
you repeat what the client has said.   Agree / Don't know / Disagree

Person-centred counsellors do what-
ever they feel like doing.   Agree / Don't know / Disagree

Person-centred counselling does not
have a theory of personality.   Agree / Don't know / Disagree

Person-centred counselling cannot
cope with evil or destructive people.   Agree / Don't know / Disagree

Person-centred counselling is good for
establishing rapport with clients, but
then you need other techniques to
treat them.   Agree / Don't know / Disagree

Person-centred counselling cannot
help people with problems like fear of
confined spaces, or obsessions etc.   Agree / Don't know / Disagree

Person-centred counselling is too slow,
and does not go 'deep enough' really
to help people much.   Agree / Don't know / Disagree

Person-centred counselling is best
used with a mixture of other tech-
niques and methods.   Agree / Don't know / Disagree

Human nature, actualisation and the emerging self   2

Every approach to counselling that has a theory of the change process and a theory of human development has an implicit or explicit model of human nature. There is an underlying 'philosophy of the person' that establishes a set of assumptions or ideas to explain, at least in some measure, what makes people the way they are, what motivates them and what their inherent characteristics might be. This chapter sets out to explore the assumptions about human nature contained within the person-centred approach, and to help you clarify your own ideas. This an important process because the ideas you hold are likely to affect the approach to counselling you prefer and with which you can be comfortable. As Rogers remarked (1957b), 'One cannot engage in psychotherapy without giving operational evidence of an underlying value orientation and view of human nature. It is definitely preferable, in my estimation, that such underlying views be open and explicit, rather than covert and implicit' (p. 199).

Before you go any further, you may like to spend a little time thinking about the assumptions you presently hold about human nature. To help you, try the exercise on the next page.

A humanistic psychology approach to human nature

In the 1960s a number of psychologists emerged who shared the concern that psychology was not adequately addressing some important aspects of social behaviour or individual experience. The term 'third wave' or 'third force' began to be used to describe a psychology that '. . . supplemented the behaviouristic and psychoanalytic approaches to the study of psychological processes' (Wrightsman, 1992, p. 17). Later known as 'humanistic psychology', this approach reflected '. . . a growing belief that the assumptions about human nature required by a strictly "scientific" approach to human behaviour communicate an image of humankind that is mechanistic, passive, and — most important — incomplete' (ibid. p.17).

The person-centred approach falls into the group of psychological theories that became known as 'humanistic psychology'. Carl Rogers, along

Exercise: Your own philosophy of human nature

Aims of the exercise. To explore and describe your currently held philosophy of what it means to be a person.

What to do. Describe your own philosophy of human nature by responding to the statements that follow. If you are doing this in a small group, take about thirty minutes to do the exercise on your own, then compare your ideas with the others in the group. The point is not to anticipate what person-centred philosophy is, but to identify and share your own attitudes and ideas. Write down how close to or different from the statements your own ideas are.

• *People are basically self-centred and concerned about their own welfare more than that of others.*
• *Society needs firm rules and laws to control people who would otherwise exploit the people around them, because this is only human nature.*
• *People who become psychologically disturbed are in need of firm but kind help and direction from properly trained experts.*
• *We are all social, each of us has needs that cannot be met by remaining isolated from the rest of humanity.*
• *God created humankind to hold a privileged position in the world, superior to all else in creation.*
• *Everything about people is determined by the material conditions existing around them.*
• *The kind of person you are is determined by the kind of society in which you are brought up.*
• *Every mental event has a cause. Nothing is ever completely haphazard or accidental.*
• *Our consciousness is controlled and shaped by internal forces of which we are not aware.*
• *Experiences and events in early childhood create our character which soon becomes fixed and more-or-less unchangeable.*
• *Humans were not created for any particular purpose. We just are, and we have to decide what to do about it.*
• *There is no limit to personal freedom.*
• *Every aspect of our mental lives is intentional, and our sole responsibility. We choose who we are, and how to be.*
• *People behave in ways that are determined entirely by their environmental conditions.*
• *Our behaviour is subject to the same natural laws that apply to animals.*
• *People are basically constructive and social. Destructive behaviour is learned behaviour and results from destructive experiences in childhood.*
• *People have the capacity to decide for themselves how they want to change and develop.*
• *There's not much you can do to change the way you are once you become an adult. The best thing is to learn to live with it.*
• *Normal people never need counselling.*
• *Psychological disturbance is like an illness that can be cured with the proper treatment once the cause is known.*
• *People are basically good. They do bad things because they have been corrupted by society.*

with Abraham Maslow and others, was among the first to describe a philosophy that stood in sharp contrast to those of the psychoanalytic and behaviouristic approaches that dominated psychology throughout the twentieth century.

The most important aspects of the philosophy underlying humanistic psychology can be summarised as follows:

- Humanistic psychology takes a *phenomenological* approach to the person. This means that we behave in the world in response to our personally experienced reality. The way we experience the world, and therefore the way we respond to it, results from the sense and meaning we each derive from our unique mixture of needs, history and expectations. Each of us, then, lives in our own subjective world, which cannot be fully and completely understood by anyone else.
- A humanistic approach to understanding human nature is to appreciate people's personal worlds from within their own frames of reference, that is, from their own subjective points of view. Humanistic psychologists are interested to discover how people make sense from their experience, how they arrive at conclusions about themselves and others, and how it feels to be them.
- Humanistic psychology takes an *existential* view of life and the process of living. It emphasises the potential for individual freedom and for individuals' ability to take personal responsibility for their experience. It stresses the importance of free will, and while there are many obstacles and limitations to our freedom, we can make worthwhile efforts to overcome them. There is a rejection of the concept of humans as under the control either of external forces or unconscious instincts. Humankind is responsible for whatever it has become (and can become) because people can choose, to a significant degree, 'how to be'.
- Humanistic psychology views the person as always in process, always developing, and never static or fixed. Although the process of 'becoming' can be damaged or corrupted, the potential for growth and enhancement is always present. People are not seen as 'deficiency motivated', that is only motivated to act when they experience some lack or deficiency in their environment, but are also motivated by the need for enhancement, for growth and for continuing development.

It would be inaccurate to suggest that humanistic psychology has a definition or description of human nature with which all humanistic psychologists could agree on every detail. For example, two influential figures in humanistic psychology, Rollo May and Carl Rogers, differ from each other somewhat in their assumptions about human nature. Rollo May views people as 'an organised bundle of potentialities', and has coined the term *daimonic*, which refers to the urge in every being to affirm, assert and perpetuate itself (May, 1969). May believes that it is the integration into the personality of this daimonic urge that is the purpose of counselling. Failure to integrate this urge can lead to the daimonic taking over the whole personality, as it does in times of collective paranoia, war or oppressive behaviour towards individuals or groups (May, 1982).

In the PCA, the model of human nature is an optimistic one. Humans are viewed as social, creative and constructive. Rogers described his ideas partly in terms of observations of what humans are *not*, as well as what they *are*:

> *I do not discover man to be well characterized in his basic nature by such terms as* fundamentally hostile, antisocial, destructive, evil.
>
> *I do not discover man to be, in his basic nature, completely without a nature, a tabula rasa on which* anything *may be written, nor malleable putty, which can be shaped into* any form.
>
> *I do not discover man to be essentially a perfect being, sadly warped and corrupted by society.*
>
> *In my experience I have discovered man to have characteristics which seem inherent in his species, and the terms which have at different times seemed to me to be descriptive of these characteristics are such terms* as positive, forward-moving, constructive, realistic, trustworthy (1957b, p. 201, emphasis in original).

Elsewhere, Rogers (1957c) described his trust in human nature in the following terms: ' . . . the basic nature of the human being, when functioning freely, is constructive and trustworthy . . . When we are able to free the individual from defensiveness, so that he is open to the wide range of his own needs, as well as the wide range of environmental and social demands, his reactions may be trusted to be positive, forward moving, constructive . . . his total behavior . . . as he moves toward being open to all his experience, will be more balanced and realistic, behavior which is appropriate to the survival and enhancement of a highly social animal' (p. 202).

Rogers has been criticised for taking such an optimistic stance on the question of human nature, and has been described in various ways as being overly idealistic or naive. This criticism rests, in part, on the mistaken belief that Rogers described humans as 'basically good'. This misinterpretation of Rogers may stem from his use of the term 'the good life', which he described as involving, ' . . . a wider range, a greater richness, than the constricted living in which most of us find ourselves. To be a part of this process means that one is involved in the frequently frightening and frequently satisfying experience of a more sensitive living, with greater range, greater variety, greater richness' (1957c, p. 196). Rogers viewed human beings as always in process, always moving towards the actualisation of potential to the extent that social and environmental circumstances would allow. He did not deny or avoid the human capacity for destructive, anti-social acts, thoughts or impulses, but at the same time did not see these potentials as indicators of an inherently destructive nature.

There are a number of characteristics of human beings that distinguishes us as 'highly social animals' from the rest of the animal kingdom. We can, for example, think about ourselves, reflect on our experience and deliberately plan for the future. Language enables us to symbolise our experience and communicate it to others. A sophisticated means of communication makes human psychological growth and development in a social environment possible. The creation of complex social organisations of the kind typical of humankind would be impossible without a highly advanced means of communication between individuals and groups. Our inherent capacity for language is a defining characteristic of our nature, and it enables us to share with others something of our own private, inner worlds.

It is to this latter theme, the communication of our private, inner worlds to each other, that Kenan Malik (2001) turns his attention in his excellent book, *Man, Beast and Zombie: What Science Can and Cannot Tell us about Human Nature*. Malik, in discussing how we know that our private worlds share things in common with others makes the following points:

> *This can only be if my inner feelings are not truly private, if I become conscious of my inner world in the same way as you—in other words, through a public process. The contents of my inner world means something to me, in some part at least, in so far as they mean something to others. I can make sense of myself only insofar as I live in, and relate to, a community of thinking, feeling, talking beings. Language provides the means to bridge the gap between our private worlds, because language is itself a social activity. A language that only one person understands is not a language, but a private code. Language necessarily has to be social. Paradoxically, then, our inner feelings are not located entirely inside our heads. They are also the products of our existence as social beings* (p. 219).

The idea that actualisation of human potential takes place in a social, organised environment, and is to some extent constrained by that environment, is a point I turn to next in this chapter. Here, I want to emphasise that, whatever our model of human nature, however partial or incomplete it may be, it is necessary for counsellors whose job is to enter into the subjective worlds of others, to acknowledge their assumptions about what it is to be human. This requires a searching examination of our own inner, private worlds and to question what we find there. It also requires an acknowledgement that our 'self' is shaped by our unique histories, genetic predispositions and the inescapable fact that we live in societies that place demands and constraints upon us. Living in a social world gives us both rights and responsibilities, and provides us with opportunities for self-expression, creativity, and relationships with others.

Actualisation

In person-centred theory, the *actualising tendency* refers to the tendency in all forms of organic life towards more complex organisation, the fulfilment of potential, and, in human beings, the actualisation of the whole person, including the person's 'self'.

Actualisation is a theory about the processes of growth and development that attempts to explain what we can observe about those processes. In other words, a plant or an animal will develop from a relatively simple form (an egg or a seed, for example) into a much more complex form as it matures towards adulthood. This process will carry on unhindered provided the environment in which the organism lives is suitable for it. The extent to which the environment is unsuitable, or even hostile in some form, will determine the extent to which the organism is able to become all it is capable of becoming. This process does not depend on the organism being consciously aware of it, because it is an inherent and universal property of life itself. In Rogers' words, the human being 'has one basic tendency and striving — to actualize, maintain and enhance the experiencing organism' (Rogers, 1951, p. 487).

In the PCA, the actualising tendency is considered to be the sole motivation for human development and behaviour. Constraints on the actualising tendency arise from the environment in which a person lives. The organism as a whole exhibits this tendency, but aspects of it, particularly those concerning the perception of 'self', can distort the whole organism's actualising tendency. Actualisation is not restricted to need or tension-reduction, but includes the urge towards creativity, learning, and the enhancement of the person.

The term 'actualisation' refers to the person as a whole — the physical, psychological, cognitive and emotional interrelated parts that together make up the whole person. Actualisation, then, is an abstract concept — it articulates a general process that we can observe happening around us. A biological organism, including a human being, tends to grow and develop as a unified whole towards greater maturity and higher levels of functioning. In other words, it tends to develop in a way that makes best use of all its potential. This directional growth is not haphazard or chaotic or a matter of chance — it is a property of the growing organism (or person) itself. Whatever it is that makes up a human being, from our DNA to our cells and organs, from our brain and problem-solving abilities to our capacity for deep feeling and creativity, is intricately organised and adapted to live in a complex environment. The fundamental processes of growth and development are not consciously directed activities; they are, in a sense, taken care of for us by our biological nature, and we do not need to be aware of them for them to work for us. In an ideal environment (which, for human beings, includes the relationships we have with others) there is no reason why any organism (including a human being) should not grow towards a state in which it actualises all of its creative potentials. Given such an environment, potential for destructive or violent behaviour, for example, would not be actualised.

The trouble is that the environment is never (or very rarely) ideal or perfect. Environmental factors may act to constrain a person's capacity for growth towards the theoretical ideal of being fully functioning. These factors may, at times, be so overwhelming that the actualising tendency becomes seriously inhibited. Each individual, then, interacts with its environment, including those aspects of the environment that tend to inhibit growth, and seeks the best way it can to become all it is capable of becoming under less than ideal circumstances. Some growth inhibitors are obvious, some less so. For example, the lack of clean water, or adequate food, or the presence of disease, can inhibit or destroy the organism's tendency towards ideal physical growth. If the developing person experiences relationships with others that are hostile, intimidating or aggressive in some way, then the person's need for care, love, nurturing and emotional warmth will be frustrated. This is likely to have an inhibiting effect on the individual's emotional or psychological development, and these effects are likely to manifest themselves in some way throughout the individual's life. Nevertheless, the actualising tendency is still present, no matter how unsuitable the environment in which the individual person finds herself. The only way to destroy the actualising tendency completely is to destroy the organism itself.

Actualisation is a *holistic* concept. The human person is a complex, organised whole in which the development (or lack of it) of one aspect affects the development of other aspects. The human being is active, aware of her surroundings and constantly interacting with them. Relationships with others are vital components of the environment, and such relationships coexist with personal autonomy, independence and self-esteem. The theory of actualisation is, then, a natural science theory, not a moral theory. There are no values like 'good' or 'bad' that can be ascribed to the process of actualisation. Humans have the capacity for both constructive and destructive thoughts and actions, and they have a tendency towards pro-social behaviour, values and attitudes. For example, humans display relationship needs, have empathic abilities and parenting and nurturing capacities. In a conducive environment these pro-social tendencies are more likely to emerge and be expressed than in a hostile environment where the human capacity for destructive, anti-social behaviour can become apparent.

Rogers summed up this theory of actualisation in the following terms:

> *We are, in short, dealing with an organism which is always motivated, is always 'up to something', always seeking. So I would reaffirm, perhaps even more strongly after the passage of a decade, my belief that there is one central source of energy in the human organism; that it is a function of the whole organism rather than of some portion of it; and that it is perhaps best conceptualized as a tendency towards fulfilment, toward actualization, toward the maintenance and enhancement of the organism* (Rogers, 1963).

A contemporary view of actualisation

Humans do not live in isolation from others, and indeed, the continued existence of humankind is dependent on our capacity to create complex and cohesive forms of social organisation. Living co-operatively on a small scale (e.g. in families), and on a much larger scale (e.g. in nations or states) brings both opportunities and constraints. The full expression of what it is to be human depends, at least in part, on the existence of other people with whom we form relationships, on our abilities to describe and share our subjective experiences, and to hear and understand the experiences of others.

However, the very fact that we exist as social beings requires us to be sensitive and responsive to the liberating and constraining forces inherent in any degree of social organisation. We are not free to give expression to all promptings of the actualising tendency in a haphazard or irresponsible manner without running the risk of endangering ourselves or others, or without risking the imposition of sanctions. The actualisation of any individual takes place in a social context in which certain actions and means of expression are positively valued and others negatively so. Though these values may vary from one form of society to another (and from one time to another), it is impossible to imagine a situation where all impulses can be given expression and all are positively valued. As Malik (2001) has remarked, 'The process of the creation of self is the process of socialisation, of a child being inducted into society. It is the process whereby a natural creature is transformed into a social being, an object transformed into a subject, an animal into a person' (p. 367).

As described above, actualisation is not a moral theory, but a biological one which, for humankind, is expressed in social contexts. The tendency towards actualisation means that the individual will make the most constructive use of the environment in which she is located at any one time, but this environment is always likely to limit and constrain the actualisation of some potentials. Mearns and Thorne (2000) suggest, 'There will be times when the pressure of the actualising tendency will inspire a resistance. Such resistance is intimately related both to the actualising tendency and to the person's current existence as a social being. The effect of the resistance serves to maintain a balance which allows for a degree of expression for the actualising tendency while taking care to preserve the viability of the social context within the person's "life space"' (p. 182).

Mearns and Thorne's reformulation of the concept of actualisation takes the mediating effects of social constraints on the individual into account in a way that traditionally the theory of actualisation has not explicitly acknowledged. It no longer views the process of actualisation simply as one in which social constraints act only to corrupt or damage the development of the individual towards becoming a fully functioning person. Instead, it recognises that individuals, in order to live creatively and constructively in a social environment, experience two forces that will, at times, act in opposing directions. In Mearns and Thorne's view, this reconceptualisation results in an 'actualising *process*' (my emphasis) in which a balance is struck between the promptings of the actualising tendency on the one hand, and social mediation on the other. The individual is presented with the need to balance the preservation of her life-space whilst developing and expressing potentials driven by the actualising tendency. 'In some areas of our client's life,' say Mearns and Thorne (p. 184), 'the balance might favour giving more scope to the actualising tendency, while in other areas a different balance of configurations would take care not to be too disruptive to the social environment.'

In Rogers' original theory, the creation of psychological disorder is perceived as a process in which the actualising tendency is subjected to damage or corruption by the imposition of social constraints, or other environmental factors. In Mearns and Thorne's reframing of the theory, disorder is created when the individual is unable to achieve a balance (or homeostasis) between the conflicting demands of actualisation and the need to preserve the life-space. The emphasis of this revised theory is on the process by which this balance is achieved, and the ability of the individual to respond to changes in the social environment. Mearns and Thorne capture this concept in formal language as follows:

> *'Disorder' is caused when the person becomes chronically stuck within his own process such that the homeostastic balance cannot reconfigure to respond to changing circumstances* (p. 184).

This revision to the theory carries with it the implication that the counsellor is urged to consider the promptings of the actualising tendency not as invariably requiring full expression in order to promote the individual's psychological development, without also being aware of the realistic threat this may pose to the person's continuing capacity to live in the real world. Mearns and Thorne remark, 'It is just as much a tyranny always to presume that the feedback from our social world is wrong if it conflicts with our own sense, as to be trapped in the opposite reality where we always favour the social imperative over our own' (p. 186).

Self-actualisation — an expression of the actualising tendency

As infants, our experiencing, sensations and perceptions constitute our unique reality. Gradually, a part of our experiencing becomes differentiated into a 'self' or 'self-concept'. Some of our perceptions, we begin to realise, add up to an 'I', or 'me'. These experiences Rogers termed self-experiences. In Rogers' view this 'self' is fluid and changing — not fixed or established once and for all, though at any one time it has certain consistent characteristics. Thus, the self is a particular part of the person's total experiencing (this total experiencing is sometimes referred to as 'organismic experiencing'). The process of developing a 'self' is a manifestation of the general actualising tendency. In other words, the organism as a whole, as an aspect of its growth, fulfils its potential to differentiate itself as a separate person with a specific identity. The process of *self-actualisation* appears after the development of a self-structure, and it is this process (self-actualisation) that maintains and develops that self-structure.

Self-actualisation does not necessarily result in the most optimal functioning of the person. We are all self-actualising simply because we all have a self to maintain, and this self is likely to be less than ideal because its development has taken place in an environment that is unlikely to have been ideal. In other words, the development of the self takes place through interaction with the environment which includes, perhaps most importantly of all, significant other people with whom we need to form relationships. However, the self should not be thought of as fixed. In Rogers' system the self is fluid, tentative, and open to change through experience.

Mick Cooper (2000) has suggested 'a more logically consistent way of understanding Rogers' fundamental conflict' (p. 89), i.e. that between the general actualising tendency on the one hand, and the self-actualising imperative on the other. In contrast, he suggests 'a conflict between the self-actualising tendency and *non-self actualising sub-systems* of the actualising tendency ... In other words, Rogers' developmental model can be understood as proposing that the organism inhabits a world in which to actualise one potential — it's 'self' — it must inhibit the actualisation of other potentials' (pp. 89–90).

This is a critical point in the exploration of person-centred theory, because it is how the development of a self or self-concept so often results in psychological maladjustment to which we must now turn if we are to understand more fully why it is that person-centred counsellors do what they do in relation to their clients.

Two needs of the developing self: positive regard from others and positive self-regard

As our self develops, we experience the need for love and acceptance from important people in our environment (like parents); in other words, we have a need for positive regard. At the same time, we have a need for positive self-regard — to develop a sense of trust in the accuracy and reliability of our own inner experiencing. After all, it is on this we must depend if we are to become independent from others and able to make good decisions about life and how we are to be in it. However, our need for positive regard from people on whom we depend for our survival is so overwhelming that these important or significant others can have great influence over us by withholding (or threatening to withhold) love and acceptance. Positive self-regard is, therefore, fragile and susceptible to the negative evaluations of others. In order to maintain their positive regard we tend to ignore some aspects of our inner experiencing, or at least not to express them, because to do so might risk the withdrawal of love and protection at a time when we need it the most. Gradually, we learn to view ourselves as others view us, ignoring our inner experiencing whenever we feel it is in conflict with the values of those significant others on whom we depend.

Rogers' term for this was *locus of evaluation*. By this, he meant the tendency of some people to rely on the evaluations of others for their feelings of acceptance and self-esteem — an *external* locus of evaluation. People with an *internal* locus of evaluation are those whose sense of self-esteem is not dependent on outside evaluations, but is generated from within by reference to the person's own value system. The development of positive self-regard is very vulnerable to the evaluations of others, and in the presence of many or powerful negative evaluations we can learn to distrust our own inner experiencing to such an extent that we may abandon it altogether.

Conditions of worth

As infants we begin to acquire *conditions of worth*. We learn from experience that we are only acceptable as long as we think, feel and behave in ways that are positively valued by others. As a result, we tend to seek certain kinds of experiences, and avoid others, according to how far they fit these acquired conditions of worth. Experiences and feelings that match these conditions of worth are perceived accurately and are accepted, but those that are contrary to them are distorted or denied completely. This process can be thought of as the beginnings of psychological maladjustment, when there is a state of *incongruence* existing between 'self' and experience.

To make this process clearer, an example might help. Imagine a young child, a boy aged two or three who experiences a sudden and frightening shock — another, older child snatches a toy from him and pushes him to the ground. His natural reaction is to express what he feels without inhibition. He is frightened and hurt, and he cries, looking for the safety and reassurance of a parent or trusted adult. Instead of finding understanding and protection, the person he turns to shouts at him for crying and mocks him for being afraid. In his vulnerable state, the child becomes bewildered and anxious, and the incident teaches him something. He learns that to respond to his experience in this spontaneous and uninhibited way is negatively judged by someone on whom he depends. He learns that fear is an unacceptable experience and to feel it or express it risks the withdrawal of love and nurturing. If this experience, or similar ones, happen to him a number of times he begins to lose trust in his inner experiencing, and to deny to himself that he feels fear. He is in the process of internalising a condition of worth that says he is not loveable or acceptable should he continue to feel fear in the face of aggression or intimidation, and so he incorporates into his self-concept the notion that he does not experience fear, in order to protect himself from the risk of being regarded as unworthy of love. His actualising tendency prompts him to be open to all of his experiencing and to allow himself to feel it and be guided by it, but his self-actualising process prompts him to deny this part of his experiencing because it has become unacceptable to his self-concept which now includes the condition of worth that to be afraid is to be unlovable.

In technical terms, what is happening is that the child is engaging in what Rogers described as an *organismic valuing process*. He is valuing his experiences in terms of whether or not they maintain and enhance him. If he perceives certain experiences as maintaining or enhancing him, he values them positively. If, on the other hand, he perceives experiences as threatening to his continuing development, he values them negatively. He seeks experiences that maintain and enhance him, and avoids or denies those that threaten him. But the expression of positive regard towards him by someone significant to him becomes more important to him than his own organismic valuing process, and he begins to seek positive regard from others at the expense of any other experience. Most of the time this process continues without him necessarily being aware of it. His actualising tendency prompts him towards being open to all of his experiencing, but his need to maintain positive regard from others leads him to absorb, into his self-concept, values that are in conflict with this process. He is developing a conditioned self, and it is this self that continues to actualise.

Person-centred theory states that if an individual only experienced unconditional positive regard, then no conditions of worth would develop and the needs for positive regard from others and positive self-regard would never come into conflict. The individual would be perfectly psychologically adjusted and would be a fully functioning person — one open to all experiencing who never needed to deny or distort any of it in awareness. Such a situation, though, is thought of as only hypothetically possible, and never occurs in reality. In terms of self-actualisation, he or she would be actualising a 'real' or unconditioned self and the general actualising tendency would continue to prompt towards being fully functioning. His or her actualising tendency and self-actualising process would be in harmony.

This theoretical state of psychological adjustment is similar to the way Seeman (1983) has described psychologically integrated persons:

> *They have a core sense of self which they like, respect and trust. And that makes all the difference, for that one central fact connects with all the rest. Persons who understand and trust their basic organismic self can listen to their own signals. They do not have the same need to screen, shut out, deflect, or distort signals in a way that characterizes more vulnerable persons* (p. 233).

The psychologically adjusted or integrated person (in Rogers' more familiar terms the fully functioning person), has characteristics that enable that person to form positive relationships with others. Seeman (1983) describes the fully functioning person in the following terms:

> *The affirmation of self, the willingness to trust and utilize one's organism, the consequent availability of experiential data, all make for a fully functioning person . . .*
>
> *At the interpersonal level, the acceptance and trust in self permits relationships which are in turn accepting, which are equalitarian rather than status oriented, which make few claims or demands on the other person, and which are positive in valence. Because interpersonal relationships are not fraught with threat or danger, intimacy is more sustainable and enduring relationships are more possible. From the perspective of other persons, the integrated person is readily visible, liked and valued* (pp. 234–5).

The concept of the fully functioning person, or the fully actualised person, should be seen in process terms, and does not indicate an end point in the development of the person. All of Rogers' theories concerned a continuing process of change and movement towards more openness to experience and the concept of self as tentative and dynamic.

The tendency to admit into our awareness only those experiences that are consistent with our self-concept, and to deny those that are not, are psychological defences that serve to maintain our self-concept and protect it from threat. The outcome is the cutting-off of experience from awareness, or the distortion of it in some way so as to fit the existing self-structure.

The process of internalising conditions of worth results in the emergence not of a true or, in Seeman's terminology, *'organismic' self*, but of a false or conditioned self. This conditioned self is the self that operates in the world, and this is the self that continues to actualise. The process of self-actualisation can distort the general actualising tendency, but actualisation will continue in the most constructive direction possible under the prevailing environmental circumstances. Figure 1 gives a simplified scheme of the two possible pathways of development — one where no conditions of worth are internalised, and one where conditions of worth lead to an inauthentic self-concept. The intervention of counselling at a point along the latter pathway can enable the actualising tendency to return the person towards becoming more fully functioning.

To understand the important concept of conditions of worth more completely, it might help to spend some time thinking about and exploring your own conditions of worth. You may be able to identify some of the 'messages' you have internalised from your childhood that still provide the basis for your beliefs and assumptions about yourself. Even though, for the most part, we remain unaware of most of our conditions of worth, you might be able to identify some of them.

The discussion in this chapter has been a review of how the PCA describes what Rogers termed 'the basic nature of the human being', and with the general processes by which the person develops towards becoming 'fully functioning'. The hypothesis, that there exists a tendency

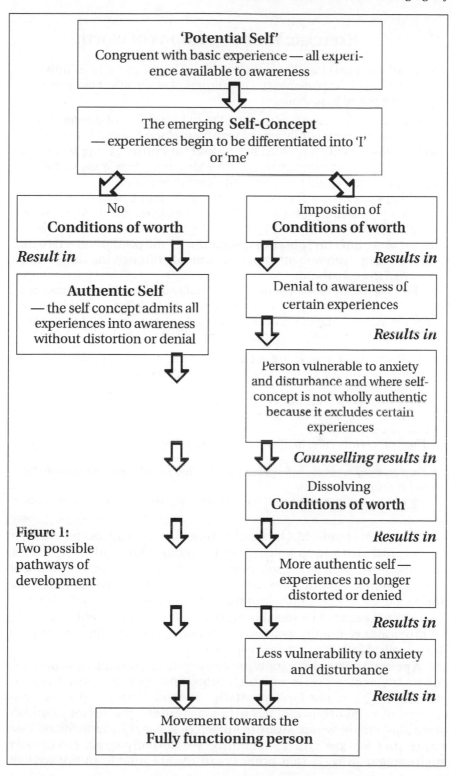

Figure 1:
Two possible pathways of development

'Potential Self'
Congruent with basic experience — all experience available to awareness

The emerging **Self-Concept**
— experiences begin to be differentiated into 'I' or 'me'

No **Conditions of worth**

Result in

Authentic Self
— the self concept admits all experiences into awareness without distortion or denial

Imposition of **Conditions of worth**

Results in

Denial to awareness of certain experiences

Results in

Person vulnerable to anxiety and disturbance and where self-concept is not wholly authentic because it excludes certain experiences

Counselling results in

Dissolving **Conditions of worth**

Results in

More authentic self — experiences no longer distorted or denied

Results in

Less vulnerability to anxiety and disturbance

Results in

Movement towards the **Fully functioning person**

Exercise: Your conditions of worth

Aims of the exercise. To explore and understand early childhood conditioning. To explore how far conditions of worth affect our present-day feelings and behaviour.

What to do. This exercise is designed to help you describe some of the ways in which your conditions of worth developed, and it is best done in the company of an understanding and supportive group. It is not a substitute for your own personal counselling, but it may bring up things for you that you could talk over with a counsellor.

Take plenty of time for every member of the group to share whatever they want to share. Nobody should feel pressured into talking about things if they do not feel they want to. A variation of this exercise is to spend some time on your own responding to the prompts given here, then team up with one other person and talk through the things that occurred to each of you.

First, respond to the prompts that follow and see if you recognise any of them as messages you received as a child. When you think you are familiar with the kinds of issues we are raising here, add to the list those things you think were around when you were a child.

- *Children should be seen and not heard.*
- *Expressing emotions is not OK, especially in company.*
- *Big boys don't cry.*
- *Being emotional is the same as being weak.*
- *Girls are not as important as boys.*
- *It is wrong to be angry.*
- *There are certain rules to life, and if you don't obey them it's because you are bad.*
- *Keep yourself to yourself. It is wrong to let other people know your business.*
- *Other people know best.*
- *There are always people worse off than you. Be grateful for what you've got.*

for all forms of organic life, including humankind, to express potential, is a conceptual platform on which person-centred theory and practice rests. Actualisation is seen as the sole motivating force for the development of more complex organisation, and in human terms this includes the differentiation of experience into the formation of a self or self-concept. This process occurs in a social context, and the environment (including the physical as well as the social environment) both constrains and enables the actualising tendency to find expression.

A person is viewed as a sophisticated organism continually in process, constantly seeking ways in which more and more potential can be expressed. This is not fundamentally different from the process that engages all forms of organic life, but humans are exceptional for a number of reasons. Firstly, we are aware of ourselves as separate individuals, and aware that we are aware. Secondly, we actively engage with our environment in ways that other creatures are unable to do; we can consciously alter our surroundings in order to overcome the constraints they place upon us. Thirdly, our use of language enables us to realise ourselves through our relationships with others and we are able to be active, responsible agents in this process. Fourthly, we have control over our actions and the decisions we take, rather than simply being at the mercy of natural impulses or instincts. Finally, there are those who would include, as part of humankind's basic nature, a capacity to see beyond the material world and develop an appreciation for what many would describe as humankind's transcendent or spiritual nature.

We are, then, active agents in constant interaction with each other and our environment. Mearns and Thorne (2000) have suggested a way of understanding how these interactions in some measure can constrain and, in a sense, shape the persons we become in both positive and negative ways. Our social world, through the interactions we have with others, can be either constraining or facilitative of our development as persons. When the need we have as infants for positive regard from those on whom we depend becomes frustrated, the result is the internalisation of negative conditions of worth, and we actualise a self that reflects this conditioning process. Because the ideas of self and self-concept are so important in person-centred theory and practice, the next chapter takes a closer look at these constructs.

Checklist: Human nature, actualisation and the emerging self

- The Person-Centred Approach is part of a group of similar approaches that together have become known as 'humanistic psychology'.
- Humanistic psychology takes a *phenomenological* approach to the person. It emphasises the person's unique subjective experience as constituting reality for him or her.
- Humanistic psychology takes an *existential* view of life. It values individual freedom and personal responsibility.
- Humanistic psychology regards the person as constantly in *process* — not as fixed or static.
- The *actualising tendency* is regarded as the sole motivator for human behaviour, change and development.
- The actualising tendency prompts the person towards greater differentiation, complexity and the fulfilment of potential.
- Contempoaray views of actualisation account for the tension between the fulfillment of potential and the need to protect the viability of the person's life space.
- The person perceives and responds to the environment as a unified and organised whole, and each from his or her unique *frame of reference*.
- *Self-actualisation* is an expression of the general actualising tendency.
- People differentiate part of their experience as *self-experience* and develop a *self-concept*.
- The human infant has two basic needs; for *positive regard* from significant others and for *positive self-regard*.
- The developing self-concept is vulnerable to the overwhelming need for positive regard from significant others.
- People engage in an *organismic valuing process* which tends positively to value experiences consistent with the self-concept and negatively value those that are in conflict with it.
- *Conditions of worth* become internalised into the self-concept and the person allows only experiences consistent with the self-concept into awareness.

Self and person

3

Rogers was one of the first psychologists to identify the 'self' as an important construct. He described the self as including 'all of the individual perceptions of his organism, of his experience, and of the way in which those perceptions are related to other perceptions and objects in his environment and to the whole exterior world' (Evans, 1975, p. 16). The terms 'self', and 'self-concept' are used interchangeably in Rogers' writing, though the term 'self-concept' is most commonly used to refer to a person's view of him or herself. Rogers viewed the self, whilst showing internal consistency at any one time, as a fluid structure, subject to change and revision, rather than as something fixed at a particular point. This is consistent with Rogers' entire attitude towards the person as being in process throughout life. In other words, the self is not an entity; rather, it is a constellation of perceptions and experiences, together with the values attached to those perceptions and experiences. Since perceptions and values can change, and we can discover new perceptions of old experiences, and since we are continually experiencing ourselves and the world around us, implicit in Rogers' description is the property of the self as fluid, dynamic and open to reorganisation. Contemporary views of the self in person-centred psychology include the idea that there are different 'configurations' of the self available to the individual that emerge at different times to take into account the differing circumstances that an individual confronts in life (Mearns and Thorne, 2000), and that it is possible for the person to develop more than one self-concept (Cooper, 1999). I return to these revised understandings of the self later in this chapter.

Rogers' theory of personality is often described as a 'self theory', that is, it describes in a number of propositions the hypothesised process by which an individual differentiates part of his or her experiencing into a self, or self-concept, and what happens from then on. 'A Theory of Personality and Behaviour' can be found in Rogers (1951, pp. 481–533), where Rogers acknowledges a number of influences including Snygg and Combs, Angyal, Maslow, Lecky and Sullivan.

In his conclusion, Rogers makes the following statement:

This theory is basically phenomenological in character, and relies heavily on the concept of the self as an explanatory construct. It pictures the end-point of personality development as being a basic congruence between the phenomenal field of experience and the conceptual structure of the self — a situation which, if achieved, would represent freedom from internal strain and anxiety, and freedom from potential strain; which would represent the maximum in realistically oriented adaption; which would mean the establishment of an individualized value system having considerable identity with the value system of any other equally well-adjusted member of the human race (p. 532).

Personality theory

The nineteen propositions repay careful reading because together they provide us with an elegant theory of personality which is entirely consistent with Rogers' theory of how and under what circumstances people change, and why certain qualities of relationship promote that change. Interspersed with Rogers' original wording (1951, pp. 483–522) I have added (in italics) some explanations in different and perhaps more familiar terms.

I Every individual exists in a continually changing world of experience of which he is the center.

II The organism reacts to the field as it is experienced and perceived. This perceptual field is, for the individual, 'reality'.
We see ourselves as the centre of our 'reality'; that is, our ever-changing world around us. We experience ourselves as the centre of our world, and we can only 'know' our own perceptions.

III The organism reacts as an organized whole to this phenomenal field.
The whole person works together rather than as separate parts.

IV The organism has one basic tendency and striving — to actualize, maintain, and enhance the experiencing organism.
Human beings have a basic tendency to fulfil their potential, to be positive, forward looking, to grow, improve, and protect their existence.

V Behavior is basically the goal-directed attempt of the organism to satisfy its needs as experienced, in the field as perceived.
The things we do (our behaviour in everyday life), we do in order to satisfy our fundamental needs. If we accept Proposition IV, that all needs are related, then all complex needs are related to all basic needs. Needs are 'as experienced' and the world is 'as perceived'.

VI Emotion accompanies and in general facilitates such goal-directed behavior, the kind of emotion being related to the seeking versus the consummatory aspects of the behavior, and the intensity of the emotion being related to the perceived significance of the behavior for the maintenance and enhancement of the organism.

Feelings are associated with, and help us get, satisfaction and fulfilment. Generally speaking, pleasant feelings arise when we are satisfied, unpleasant feelings when we are not satisfied. The more important the situation, the stronger the feelings.

VII   The best vantage point for understanding behavior is from the internal frame of reference of the individual himself.
To understand the behaviour of a person, we must look at the world from their point of view.

VIII   A portion of the total perceptual field gradually becomes differentiated as the self.
Some of what we recognise as 'reality' we come to call 'me' or 'self'.

IX   As a result of interaction with the environment, and particularly as a result of evaluational interaction with others, the structure of self is formed — an organized, fluid, but consistent conceptual pattern of perceptions of characteristics and relationships of the 'I' or the 'me', together with values attached to these concepts.

X   The values attached to experiences, and the values which are a part of the self-structure, in some instances are values experienced directly by the organism, and in some instances are values introjected or taken over from others, but perceived in distorted fashion, *as if* they had been experienced directly.
As we go about our everyday life, we build up a picture of ourselves, called the self-concept, from relating to and being with others and by interacting with the world around us. Sometimes we believe other people's versions of reality and we incorporate them into our self-concept as though they were our own.

XI   As experiences occur in the life of the individual, they are either (a) symbolized, perceived, and organized into some relationship to the self, (b) ignored because there is no perceived relationship to the self-structure, (c) denied symbolization or given a distorted symbolization because the experience is inconsistent with the structure of the self.
There are several things we can do with our everyday experience: we can see that it is relevant to ourselves or we can ignore it because it is irrelevant; or, if we experience something that doesn't fit with our picture of ourselves we can either pretend it didn't happen or change our picture of it so that it does fit.

XII   Most of the ways of behaving which are adopted by the organism are

those which are consistent with the concept of the self.
Most of the time we do things and live our lives in ways which are in keeping with our picture of ourselves.

XIII Behavior may, in some instances, be brought about by organic experiences and needs which have not been symbolized. Such behavior may be inconsistent with the structure of the self, but in such instances the behavior is not 'owned' by the individual.
Sometimes we do things as a result of experiences from inside us we have denied, or needs we have not acknowledged. This may conflict with the picture we have of ourselves so we refuse to accept it is really us doing it.

XIV Psychological maladjustment exists when the organism denies to awareness significant sensory and visceral experiences, which consequently are not symbolized and organized into the gestalt of the self-structure. When this situation exists, there is a basic or potential psychological tension.
When we experience something that doesn't fit in with our picture of ourselves and we cannot fit it in with that picture, we feel tense, anxious, frightened or confused.

XV Psychological adjustment exists when the concept of the self is such that all the sensory and visceral experiences of the organism are, or may be, assimilated on a symbolic level into a consistent relationship with the concept of self.
We feel relaxed and in control when the things we do and the experiences we have all fit in with the picture we have of ourselves.

XVI Any experience which is inconsistent with the organization or structure of self may be perceived as a threat, and the more of these perceptions there are, the more rigidly the self-structure is organized to maintain itself.
When things happen that don't fit in with the picture we have of ourselves, we feel anxious. The more anxious we feel, the more stubbornly we hang on to the picture we have of ourselves as 'real'.

XVII Under certain conditions, involving primarily complete absence of any threat to the self-structure, experiences which are inconsistent with it may be perceived, and examined, and the structure of self revised to assimilate and include such experiences.
When we are in a relationship where we feel safe, understood and accepted for who we are, we can look at some of the things that don't fit in with our picture of ourselves and, if necessary, change our picture to fit our experience more accurately. Or we can accept the occasional differences between our pictures of ourselves and our experience without becoming anxious.

XVIII When the individual perceives and accepts into one consistent and integrated system all his sensory and visceral experiences, then he is necessarily more understanding of others and is more accepting of others as separate individuals.
When we see ourselves more clearly and accept ourselves more for what we are rather than as how others would like us to be, we can understand that others are equal to us, sharing basic human qualities, yet distinct as individuals.

XIX As the individual perceives and accepts into his self-structure more of his organic experiences, he finds that he is replacing his present value *system* — based so largely upon introjections which have been distortedly symbolized — with a continuing organismic valuing process.
We stop applying rigid rules to govern our values and use a more flexible way of valuing based on our own experience, not on the values we have taken in from others.

A reading of the nineteen propositions gives a clear sense of how person-centred personality theory reflects a view of the person continually in *process*. The person is able, or potentially able, to become free of conditioning and to move away from its debilitating effects towards becoming more integrated and fully functioning. In other words, Rogers viewed the negative effects of early relationships imposing conditions of worth as being largely responsible for the development of emotional or psychological disturbance; the other side of this coin is the person-centred idea that whilst some relationships can be damaging, others can be positively growth promoting.

Contemporary views of the 'self' in person-centred psychology

Throughout the nineteen propositions and, indeed, all of Rogers' publications, the self is presented as a single configuration of perceptions, e.g., 'The self concept [or self structure] is an organized configuration of perceptions of the self which are admissible to awareness' (Rogers, 1951, p. 501). Like a single-celled organism, the self is viewed as being contained within a single 'cell wall'. This imaginary cell wall is the boundary of the self and it contains 'perceptions of one's characteristics and abilities; the precepts and concepts of the self in relation to others and to the environment; the value qualities which are perceived as associated with experiences and objects; and the goals and ideals which are perceived as having positive or negative valence. It is, then, the organized picture, existing in awareness either as figure or ground, of the self and the self-in-relationship, together with the positive or negative values which are associated with those qualities and relationships, as they are perceived as existing in the past, present, or future' (p. 501).

The phrase 'the organized picture' (above) clearly imparts Rogers' view that the self is conceptualised as a single, though complex, phenomenon. The self may contain numerous perceptions, values, precepts and concepts, but it is not, in Rogers' formulation, divided in any sense into 'parts' — it is not multi-cellular. Furthermore, contained within the self's 'cell wall' are only those phenomena that are available to awareness or admissible to awareness. Rogers was careful not to associate the self with unconscious material, or material out of the person's awareness, and not admissible into it. Experiences that, for some reason, have been denied to awareness are not present within the self as shadowy objects, exerting an influence on the self without the person being aware of such influence.

Mearns and Thorne (2000) have suggested a revision of the self in person-centred psychology that does allow for something akin to a 'multi-cellular' organisation. Coining the term 'configurations of self', they propose the self as consisting of any number of configurations which themselves are composed of 'elements which form a coherent pattern generally reflective of a dimension of existence within the Self' (p. 102). Mearns and Thorne recognise a number of influences on their thinking, among them Mick Cooper, who suggests a plurality of distinctive self-concepts, any one of which could become 'figure' (as opposed to 'ground') in response to environmental circumstances (Cooper, 1999).

Our metaphor of the multi-celled organism may still be too rigid accurately to capture the concept of configurations, unless we imagine the internal boundaries around each configuration contained within the main cell wall as being permeable and soluble. New configurations can emerge from existing elements of the self in response to the changing needs of the person, or in response to the admission into awareness of hitherto denied material. In other words, Mearns and Thorne do not conceptualise configurations as existing as separate, dissociated entities within the self. They clearly identify configurations as each being known by their owner as a different dimension of his or her self.

A further aspect of Mearns and Thorne's revised theory of the self is their idea that the self is most accurately defined as consisting of the self-concept and 'edge of awareness' material (p. 175). This does contrast with Rogers' view that the self can consist only of those things of which the person is aware. The term 'edge of awareness' carries the implication that emotional material located there is not in the person's awareness, and so not a functional component of the self in Rogers' terms, but in Mearns and Thorne's view edge of awareness material does at least influence the self and theoretically becomes a component of the self.

Cooper (1999) offers further ideas about the development of the self-concept. He argues that while Rogers was right to suggest that the self-concept can develop as a consequence of the need for positive (self) regard, there are, almost certainly, other ways in which a person can develop a concept of who they are. Cooper's position is very compatible with the Mearns and Thorne position described above. He suggests two ways in which Rogers' model could be revised to allow for the development of multiple self-concepts. Firstly, Cooper acknowledges the possibility that significant others in the person's life could offer positive regard for different self-experiences. It follows from this that the individual might develop a plurality of self-concepts, each one in response to a specific social context. Secondly, Cooper accepts the basic Rogers position that an individual maintains self-consistency by denying or distorting certain threatening experiences in awareness, but suggests that the person could also maintain self-consistency by identifying with the denied or distorted self-experiences, thereby developing an alternative self-concept.

Further implications for the practice of person-centred counselling of both the configurations concept and revisioning of the self as consisting also of edge of awareness material are left to a later chapter. For a complete discussion of these concepts, and a number of other creative and original developments of person-centred theory and practice, I suggest you consult Mearns and Thorne's book, *Person-Centred Therapy Today: New Frontiers in Theory and Practice*, published by Sage in 2000.

From the 'conditioned self' to becoming a person

Whether we maintain allegiance to Rogers' original formulation of the self as it is described in the nineteen propositions, or if we accept the new formulations offered by Mearns and Thorne and Cooper, we are left with the position that the self, and the structure of the personality, are not regarded as fixed. Change is not only possible, it is inevitable, and in person-centred terms is a continuing process. The idea that the person is able to move away from a way of being limited by conditioning towards one that enables more complete expression of potential, raises two important questions.

The first of these is, 'Under what conditions is a person likely to become more fully functioning?' In other words, if it is negative aspects of interpersonal relationships that distort the process of actualisation, what kinds of relationships might serve to correct the effects of negative conditioning? This question I explore in later chapters with a detailed exploration of the person-centred counselling relationship. A second question is, 'What are the characteristics of a person who has overcome the effects of negative conditioning?' Can we, in other words, describe with some measure of confidence the qualities that a person might exhibit whose conditions of worth have been significantly dissolved and whose locus of evaluation is moving towards the internal and away from the external?

In attempting some answers to this second group of questions, Rogers offered a re-statement of his ideas on personality and interpersonal relationships in his 1959 paper, which stands as the most comprehensive and distilled expression of his theory. He hypothesised that a person moving towards a more integrated state, who experienced decreasing need to distort or deny experience into awareness, would show a number of characteristics. The person would be:

- More congruent, more open to experience and less defended.
- More realistic and better at overcoming personal problems.
- More psychologically adjusted and less vulnerable to threat.
- More realistic in his or her perception of an ideal self; and the actual self and ideal self would be more congruent.
- Less liable to tension and anxiety.
- More able to experience positive self-regard.
- More confident, self-directing and trusting of his or her own values.
- More realistic in his or her perceptions of others.
- More acceptant of others.
- More acceptant of him or herself.
- More socialised and mature.
- More creative, adaptable and self-expressive.

A development from these ideas of the direction of changes in personality and behaviour was Rogers' further description of the optimal or 'fully functioning person'. In other words, if the process of actualisation was able to continue unhindered, or if a person could return to a state where the negative effects of conditioning were reversed, what might the qualities of such a person be? Again, Rogers (1959) attempted to identify those characteristics of the actualised person that are implied in his personality theory and theory of change, though I stress that they are conceptualised in process terms rather than end-points. They can be summarised as follows:

The fully functioning person would:
- Be open to experience.
- Exhibit no defensiveness.
- Be able to interpret experience accurately.
- Have a flexible rather than static self-concept open to change through experience.
- Trust in his or her own experiencing process and develop values in accordance with that experience.
- Have no conditions of worth and experience unconditional self-regard.
- Be able to respond to new experiences openly.
- Be guided by his or her own valuing process through being fully aware of all experience, without the need for denial or distortion of any of it.
- Be open to feedback from his or her environment and make realistic changes resulting from that feedback.
- Live in harmony with others and experience the rewards of mutual positive regard.

Barrett-Lennard stresses that the 'mature' person is unpredictable in the sense of not responding to experience as if programmed in some manner, but is also consistent in terms of, 'a distinct inner direction results, but not in the form of "directive" control by a part (the conscious self, for example) over the whole. Instead, the direction emerges from free interplay and combined action of all processes and levels activated in the individual's whole being' (1962, p. 101). In a later formulation, Barrett-Lennard (1998) distinguishes seven primary qualities of well or optimally functioning persons offered from a person-centred perspective. These include, for example, a model of the person as complex, open to experience, self-accepting, self-trusting, active and responsible, curious, exploratory, adaptable and creative (pp. 180–1).

The question arises about how such a theoretical fully functioning person might be able to translate the qualities summarised above into everyday life. The change process is always in motion, but in general if conditions are favourable, then change tends to show certain characteristics. Individuals who suffer no conditions of worth are open to experience, have an internal locus of evaluation and therefore possess a trust in their own valuing processes as a guide to behaviour, and are optimally adapted to living in whatever society they find themselves. In some circumstances, 'adaptation' might be expressed through opposition to, or escape from, some norms and values of the society. Because the theory predicts no specific behaviour, it is possible to describe some universal qualities of the fully functioning person that are not culture-specific. For example, some cultures do not value the individual as highly or in the same way as does Western culture in general. In such cultures, a more appropriate characteristic of the fully functioning person might be the tendency to value the welfare and continued survival of the group more highly than valuing oneself.

Rogers offered a general set of values and ways of being which he saw as both enabling individual expression, and valuing social organisation and co-operation. The 'ways of being' that resulted in optimal satisfaction of the need for positive regard from others and positive self-regard, would spring from each person's cultural context. That individuals are always in the process of 'becoming' and are not entirely rigid or fixed at some stage of development from which it is impossible to develop and move beyond is thought to be a universal human characteristic.

It is possible to observe or determine whether or not a person is becoming more fully functioning; certain qualities can be observed and described as indicators of this process. In other words, their presence tends to show that a person is developing and growing, and their absence tends to show that a person has become stuck, though the experience of being stuck need not be a permanent one.

The characteristics described in the next exercise tend to exist in people with a high degree of personal congruence, but they are not comprehensive, and they are not intended to act as a kind of diagnosis of what is wrong with us. We might experience these things as being true of us, but not all the time and not in every circumstance. Change is often a very fluid process; at times we move towards being more fully functioning, and at others we move away from it, but once set in motion the change process tends, in general, to show a direction towards the maximisation of potential.

Counselling is often experienced in this way, with two steps forward and one step back, but over time the general direction will be a movement towards positive outcomes, with some gains being made more easily than others.

Exercise: Your ideas about the fully functioning person

Aims of the exercise
To explore the characteristics of a person moving towards fully functioning.

What to do
STEP 1: Before you read through the rest of this chapter, stop for a moment, and take some time to think about what you consider to be the fully functioning person. You can do this on your own, but another way is to brainstorm some ideas in a small group.

STEP 2: Think of people you know or have known who seem to you to use more of their personal resources (and have more of them) than most other people. They do not have to be successful people in the conventional sense of being in important or influential positions, though this may also be true of many of the people you can think of.

STEP 3: Make a list of what you come up with, and compare it with the characteristics of the fully functioning person described here.

• *Acceptance of oneself*
Movement towards the ability to recognise introjected values (those adopted from outside oneself), and conditions of worth, and the ability to develop values that are more consistent with the basic organismic valuing system.

• *Living more fully in the present*
Movement towards freedom from control by past events and fear of the future. More energy and attention available for the present moment, and a more complete engagement in what is happening right now.

Unresolved issues from the past can lead to self-doubt, confusion and repression of feelings. A common experience is for people to know that there is something inside, from the past, that still controls them. They often know it has to be dealt with somehow, but they are either too afraid to, or do not know how.

At times, many people feel that they have to pretend to themselves that they are OK. This means that life, at least in part, has an unreal quality to it, but many find it increasingly difficult to acknowledge their feelings to themselves, or express them openly to others.

The process of becoming fully functioning includes being increasingly

---

in touch with feelings, and an increasing trust in them as useful guides to our values and behaviour. Because we are not so afraid of feelings, we have less need to deny them, and this means that more of our attention is available to living in the present moment.

• Valuing all of oneself
Our culture tends to encourage us to think of ourselves as divided into different aspects, as if they are only vaguely connected to each other. For example, we think of the intellectual, the physical, emotional and spiritual as distinctly different, almost independent aspects of ourselves.

Becoming more fully functioning includes an integration of these aspects into a unified whole, so that all are available to be expressed equally and appropriately according to our needs.
Many times people are uneasy with the emotional part of themselves, particularly emotions that are negatively valued such as fear and anger. They may also be afraid to acknowledge and express feelings of love, or tenderness. They feel that such emotions are in control of them, or could take them over in some way, and they want to be in control of their feelings.

Our ideal, fully functioning person is aware that emotions are present for good and valid reasons, and that they play an important part in life. Emotions are indications that something either positive or negative (or sometimes a mixture of these) is taking place. If they are acknowledged and valued they can help us move on. Of course the acknowledgement of some feelings can itself be a painful process.

Recognition of the important role of emotions in our functioning often has a releasing effect on other aspects of human experience, and enhances the quality of living. This is especially true for those of us who were taught to squash feelings, or mistrust them in some way.

• Experiencing life as a process
Movement towards an openness to experience, and a willingness to accept responsibility for one's role in that experience, are strong characteristics of the process. There is a discovery that trusting in oneself and acting on that trust brings positive benefits.

Fully functioning people are just as able to suffer hurt and pain as anyone else, but they have the resources to deal more effectively with them. They are also able fully to experience, appreciate and enjoy the more positive aspects of life.

None of us knows what the future holds, but if we can act on our own basic beliefs, then the consequences of our actions can be integrated into our own developing meaning systems; we can learn something definite from our experiences. If we act on how we believe we ought to act, determined by the pressures of others, then it is more difficult to develop our own points of view, or to grow, because it is more difficult to integrate our experiences.

The process does not involve fixed goals or end-points for oneself or one's relationships, and often there is a scepticism of conventional measures of success. A basic trust in oneself, and a strong desire to have meaningful, purposeful and authentic lives, are much more important.

• *Purpose and meaning in life*
The process tends to move towards experiencing a high level of self-esteem; seeing oneself as of high value as a person, but not in a competitive sense or at the expense of others. As social beings, there is a tendency towards making contributions to the benefit of society as a whole, without being dependent on others for approval.

• *Healthy scepticism of society*
There tends to be movement towards a strong desire for authenticity; in society as well as in oneself. Anything that indicates hypocrisy, deceit, secrecy and double standards tends to be rejected. Bureaucratic institutions that can de-personalise human beings tend to be avoided.

• *Relationships with others*
There is an awareness of the need for their total 'humanness' to be given attention and to find expression. Authenticity in relationships tends to be valued.

Deep, trusting relationships in which people can be themselves without barriers to communication, tend to become very important. In all relationships, there tends to be a concern with the nurturing aspects of relationships, and intimacy is enjoyed.

Open communication with others with whom people feel close tends to develop and non-possessive love and caring can be given and received.

• *Creativity*
Personal creativity tends to develop. This does not necessarily mean in the conventional sense of art, music or literature, but in all aspects of people's lives. There is a willingness to taking risks, and to finding new and creative 'ways of being', which can be brought to personal and professional relationships.

There is movement towards being innovative and experimental, and change is seen as both necessary and desirable.

Implications for interpersonal relationships

The features of the fully functioning person described above are fairly general characteristics of those able to live in the world in ways that satisfy fundamental individual needs. But because the need for unconditional positive regard is best met through relationships with others of varying degrees of intimacy, the theory of the fully functioning person has clear implications for the mutuality and reciprocity of relationships if they are to be experienced as satisfying.

According to Barrett-Lennard (1998), 'Rogers' theoretical view of the process of 'deteriorating relationships' pivots on a process set in train by personal incongruence. The opposite conditions and process are conceived to occur in an improving relationship' (p. 181). Rogers viewed counselling as a particular example of an interpersonal relationship in which movement towards personal congruence was likely to be promoted. Other relationships, provided they contained some or all of the same characteristics of an effective counselling relationship, could also promote the personal development of the participants. The 1959 paper referred to above contained a description of the processes of relationships that are likely to be experienced as satisfying the needs of both people concerned for positive regard and positive self-regard. Comparison of this process and the process of counselling given in the next chapter reveals many similarities, and we can summarise Rogers' view of an improving relationship as follows:

- There is a matching or congruence between experience, awareness and communication.
- This congruence is experienced as clear communication, and responses also show congruence between experience and awareness.
- Responses are perceived accurately and empathy for the other's internal frame of reference is experienced.
- Being empathically understood results in some satisfaction of the need for positive regard.
- Empathically understanding the frame of reference of another person results in the experience of having made a positive difference to the other person, and there is an increase in the feeling of unconditional positive regard for the other person.
- A person experiences him or herself in relationship with someone who, in the area of communication, is congruent, is empathically understanding of their internal frame of reference and who shows them unconditional positive regard.
- It follows that there is less need of defense and less need for the distortion of perception.
- It further follows that communication is perceived with more accuracy.
- Communication in both directions is increasingly congruent, perceived more accurately and offers more reciprocal positive regard.

Finally, Barrett-Lennard (1998) outlines a number of qualities or characteristics of a 'well-functioning relationship' (pp. 182–3), summarised as follows:

- Communication is open, expressive and clear.
- There is a climate of trust in which participants are free of fear and can express acceptance of each other.

- There is mutual interest and positive expectations of each other.
- Self-trust leads to interdependence, with each person discovering their own meaning from the experience, interest in the other's meaning and appreciation of both joint and self-discovered meaning.
- The relationship is open, self-regulating, growthful and welcoming of feedback from within the relationship and from the external environment.
- The presence of well-functioning relationships within a wider community contributes to, and benefits from, the health of the wider community.

This review of the main theoretical and philosophical components of the person-centred approach gives us a sense of both the simplicity and complexity of Rogers' profound understanding of the person. People are viewed as fluid, ever-changing and seeking satisfaction through interpersonal relationships of various kinds. The theory and philosophy of the person is clearly reflected in Rogers' attitude towards the counselling process, depending as it does on the formation of a client/counsellor relationship characterised by certain qualities and attitudes. It is this special kind of interpersonal relationship to which I turn in the next chapter, but before doing so I suggest you check your understanding of person-centred theory and philosophy by working through the following checklist.

Checklist: Self and person

- Rogers' personality theory is a '*self-theory*' and is organised into *nineteen propositions.*
- Contemporary views of the self suggest that different configurations of the self emerge in reponse to different experiences.
- People tend to *deny* or *distort* experiences that threaten the self-concept when the self-concept has internalised conditions of worth.
- *Incongruence* results when there is conflict between the actualising tendency and the need to actualise the conditioned self.
- The internalisation of conditions of worth can result in a person depending on an *external* rather than an *internal locus of evaluation.*
- The theory of the fully functioning person is a process theory that describes the hypothetical state of a person free of conditions of worth and open to all experiences without distortion or denial.
- The theory of the fully functioning person is reflected in the theory of 'well-functioning' relationships characterised by personal congruence, clarity of communication, empathic understanding of each person's subjective frame of reference and reciprocal positive regard.

Towards a theory of person-centred counselling 4

Rogers recounted three incidents from his early career that provide some insight into the process by which person-centred counselling began to take shape (Rogers, 1961). The first involved his work with a 'youthful pyromaniac'. Rogers believed he had discovered that this youth's desire to start fires was traceable to a sexual impulse regarding masturbation (p. 10). Unfortunately, this 'insight' had no effect on the youth's behaviour, who continued to start fires when placed on probation. Rogers gradually came to realise that the insight that existed in the counsellor's mind was not the same as self-understanding and acceptance that occurred within the client, and that intellectual insight did not carry with it the power for personal transformation.

Much of Rogers' work was with the parents of 'problem' children, and a second turning point was the realisation that what he at first regarded as good practice was actually:

> . . . *a clever legalistic type of questioning by the interviewer which convicted this parent of her unconscious motives, and wrung from her an admission of guilt . . . It made me realise that I was moving away from any approach which was coercive or pushing in clinical relationships, not for philosophical reasons, but because such approaches were never more than superficially effective* (p. 11).

The third concerns his work with the mother of an intelligent but difficult boy. Rogers believed the boy's problems stemmed from the mother's early rejection of him, but he failed to convince her of the significance of this theory and he gave up working with her in this manner. When the mother asked for help for herself, 'She came to the chair she had left, and began to pour out her despair about her marriage, her troubled relationship with her husband, her sense of failure and confusion, all very different from the sterile "case history" she had given before. Real therapy began then, and ultimately it was very successful.'

Rogers remarked:

> *This incident was one of a number which helped me to*

experience the fact — only fully realized later — that it is the client who knows what hurts, what directions to go, what problems are crucial, what experiences have been deeply buried. It began to occur to me that unless I had need to demonstrate my own cleverness and learning, I would do better to rely upon the client for the direction of movement in the process (pp. 11–12).

Whilst it is beyond the scope of this book to trace the history and development of person-centred counselling in any detail, I might add a fourth experience as significant in that process. In the 1930s Rogers had developed a method of assessing a child's situation he called the Component Factor Method. Based on eight factors, ratings were designed to indicate whether any factor was either destructive of the child's welfare or contributed to healthy adjustment and behaviour. The eight factors were: quality of family life and influence; the health history or constitution of the child; economic and cultural background and influence; intellectual development; social experience; hereditary factors; education; and the degree of the child's self-understanding, self-insight and acceptance of self-responsibility.

This method had the advantage of not only assessing the child's current situation, but also suggesting which of the eight factors were changeable. A Masters student at Ohio State University (Bill Kell) found the rating of self-insight to be the most predictive of future behaviour. This result was largely confirmed when the research was later replicated (Rogers, Kell and McNeil, 1948). Rogers now had:

. . . two studies which indicated that the degree of self-understanding, the degree of self-acceptance, the degree to which the child could accept the reality of his or her situation, the degree to which the child was taking responsibility for self — that these factors predicted future behavior (Rogers, cited in Kirschenbaum and Henderson, 1989, p. 208).

Although Rogers was, at first, sceptical of the results of this research, he later began to see the significance of them, especially as the initial results had been largely confirmed by a second study. Without in any way dismissing the influence of the other seven factors, Rogers came to believe that:

Rather than feeling that a person is inevitably doomed by unalterable forces which have shaped him, this study suggests that the most potent influence in his future behavior is one which is certainly alterable to some degree without any change in his physical or social heredity or in his present environment. The most powerful determinant would appear to lie in the attitudes of the person himself (p. 210).

The significance of this research on the development of the person-centred approach is difficult to assess, but in Rogers' words, '... the findings helped to focus my career on the field of psychotherapy' (p. 204). Within it lies some confirmation that the self-concept and issues concerning self-esteem are powerful factors influencing a person's behaviour.

Barrett-Lennard (1998) has provided a comprehensive review of the research and investigation undertaken by Rogers and his many colleagues (including Barrett-Lennard himself) that took place during the years leading up to (and subsequent to) Rogers' publication of his most complete formulation of person-centred counselling theory (Rogers, 1957a). The 1957 paper, when read together with Rogers (1959), provides a clear and detailed account of all the major components of person-centred theory.

What follows is a closer examination of Rogers' 1957 and 1959 papers, and some discussion of their implications. More detailed discussion of how Rogers' theory of counselling is put into practice is left to the next chapter.

The necessary and sufficient conditions for personality change

In 1957 Rogers published his now-famous statement that it was the relationship between client and counsellor that provided 'the necessary and sufficient conditions' for change to happen. It is appropriate at this point briefly to introduce and review that statement, because it helps to understand how Rogers' theory differs so radically from other theories, and where there might be areas of common ground.

Rogers titled his paper 'The necessary and sufficient conditions of therapeutic personality change', and it detailed the hypothesised conditions which if present in a relationship would result in constructive personality change. These conditions are:

1. *Two persons are in psychological contact.*
2. *The first, whom we shall term the client, is in a state of incongruence, being vulnerable or anxious.*
3. *The second person, whom we shall term the counsellor, is congruent or integrated in the relationship.*
4. *The counsellor experiences unconditional positive regard for the client.*
5. *The counsellor experiences an empathic understanding of the client's internal frame of reference and endeavours to communicate this experience to the client.*
6. *The communication to the client of the counsellor's empathic understanding and unconditional positive regard is to a minimal degree achieved.*

No other conditions are necessary. If these six conditions exist, and continue over a period of time, this is sufficient. The process of constructive personality change will follow (Rogers, 1957a).

The publication of this paper prompted some controversy, and a good deal of research. However, much of the research (if not all of it) has not considered the hypothesis with its *six* conditions as a whole, but has concentrated on the provision of conditions 3, 4 and 5, which have become known as 'the core conditions'. These three conditions *alone* are not considered, in Rogers' 1957 hypothesis, as being necessary and sufficient, and some confusion has been created by the misconception that the 1957 hypothesis is concerned only with empathy, congruence and positive regard.

Although attention has concentrated on conditions 3 to 6 (above), some modern developments in person-centred theory have focused on the first condition — that two persons are in psychological contact. Whilst this may seem obvious in counselling (and other) situations, it remains a fact that some clients are unable to form meaningful relationships with their counsellors, or can do so only with considerable difficulty. Examples include some people experiencing psychotic episodes, or those in catatonic states. This phenomenon has been tackled recently by the development of *pre-therapy*, an attempt to establish minimal contact, associated, mainly, with Garry Prouty (e.g. Prouty, 1990, 1994, 2002; Prouty and Cronwal, 1989).

The controversy over whether the core conditions or core qualities described above are both necessary *and* sufficient (in the context of the other three conditions) continues to this day, and may never be finally resolved. Among person-centred practitioners there appears to be two 'camps' emerging — those who believe in the necessary and sufficient argument and those who do not. The former group sees the introduction of any techniques or counsellor-led interventions (i.e. those that do not emerge from within the client's frame of reference) as contravening the basic philosophical assumption of the person-centred approach, namely, that trusting in the client's autonomy and self-determination is undermined by the introduction of techniques drawn from other counselling traditions. The latter group sees it as legitimate to introduce techniques during counselling, and sees them as invitations to clients to explore emotional material in a variety of ways, rather than as instructions or manipulations. Both groups, however, see the core conditions as fundamental to the counselling process.

The position taken by Rogers in his 1957 paper is, however, that the six conditions are necessary and sufficient, though it must be said that this was advanced as a *hypothesis*, rather than as a statement of fact. Whilst most attention has been focused on the meanings of these conditions, Rogers did go on to discuss some implications of this hypothesis that are sometimes overlooked. For example, Rogers did not believe that the conditions were appropriate with one type of client, and other conditions were necessary for different clients with different needs. He did not believe that the six conditions were necessary only for person-centred counselling and that other conditions were necessary for other kinds of counselling. His hypothesis was that the conditions applied to any situation in which positive personality change was a goal, including classical psychoanalysis, behavioural counselling, etc.

Related to this last point is Rogers' hypothesis that the six conditions were not only obtainable in a counselling relationship. He believed, for example, that many good friendships fulfilled the conditions, but that counselling allowed for a heightening of the constructive qualities that existed naturally in some friendships. Rogers also believed that conditions 3, 4 and 5 are qualities of experience, acquired by experiential training and are not intellectual functions.

Rogers was dismissive of psychological diagnosis of clients, and did not believe that it contributed to successful counselling. He felt that making evaluations, diagnoses and assessments of clients may be useful only insofar as they provided counsellors with a sense of security, and thereby enabled them to be more empathic and acceptant of their clients. Rogers proposed that the variety of techniques common to many forms of counselling (dream analysis, interpretation, etc.) are unimportant except where they serve as means of fulfilling one or other of the six conditions. Even the 'technique' most associated with person-centred counselling, *reflection of feelings*, was not considered as essential to successful counselling, except where it acted as a means of the counsellor communicating empathy and unconditional positive regard. Feelings could equally be reflected in ways that communicated a lack of empathy. For example, if a counsellor responded to a client talking about her negative feelings for her mother by saying, '*You really hate her*', this might reflect some part of what she has said, but completely fail to empathise with accompanying feelings of guilt or shame, assuming they were present.[1] In any case, where reflection is employed as a technique it is likely to be experienced as such, rather than as a sharing of genuine empathic understanding. Finally, a major purpose for Rogers in offering his hypothesis was to encourage and assist counsellors to think critically about their own behaviour, attitudes and experience in terms of those that are essential to counselling and those which may be non-essential or even harmful.

Reviewing Rogers' 'necessary and sufficient conditions' in this way illustrates some fundamental differences between person-centred and other approaches. In Rogers' scheme there is no necessity for the diagnosis of mental illness as a precursor to treatment. There is, therefore, no

---

1. Many counselling approaches have included the concept of 'reflection of feelings' into their way of working with clients, but not in the mechanical or contrived way that was once associated with this term. Modern usage of the term among many integrative approaches, for example, has evolved into 'empathic reflection of feeling' and is more consistent with the spirit that Rogers intended, i.e. a close empathic following of the client's experiencing process. The example of a non-empathic reflection given above would be considered bad practice in any form of counselling. In person-centred terms, the example given above runs the risk of being experienced by the client as telling her something about herself, or biasing her in some specific direction. An empathic reflection may be incomplete, but if the counsellor's attitude is one of empathic understanding, it is open to the client to correct the details.

identification of disorders such as neurosis or obsessive-compulsive. All treatment is both generic (in terms of attitudes) and specifically oriented to the individual client, and a diagnosis of a specific disorder is therefore not required. The origins of disturbance are not assumed to reside in the non-completion of developmental sequences in the way described by Freud and others, for example, and, crucially, the phenomenon of 'transference', so central in the psychodynamic model, has little part to play in Rogers' theory or practice (see Shlien, 1984, reprinted in Cain, 2002).

The core conditions

Whilst Rogers itemised six conditions that together were 'necessary and sufficient', most attention has been given to the three that have become known as 'the core conditions': that the therapist is congruent in the relationship, that the therapist is experiencing unconditional positive regard towards the client, and that the therapist experiences an empathic understanding of the client's internal frame of reference.

I explore the meanings of the core conditions in much detail in later chapters, but briefly, empathy refers to the counsellor's capacity to understand the client's internal, subjective world; congruence refers to the counsellor's state of integration, authenticity and 'realness' in the relationship, and unconditional positive regard refers to the counsellor's non-judgemental acceptance of the client as a person. These three conditions describe attitudes or qualities existing within the counsellor. They do not describe strategies or techniques to be applied variably according to client need. However, it will be noted that the core conditions must be perceived by the client, and it follows that the counsellor's experience of them must be expressed. This involves a disciplined behaviour on the part of the counsellor that flows from his or her underlying attitudes, not through a focus on skills. Instead of using terms like 'skill' or 'technique', Rogers more usually spoke of *implementation of the attitudes* of acceptance, warmth and openness to the client's experiencing.

The goals of counselling

The goal of person-centred counselling is not static, and cannot be represented by reference to a fixed end-point. It is best described in *process* terms — movement towards actualisation. Since this is an inherent property or characteristic of all living organisms, it is not a goal that is decided on by either the client or the counsellor.

Another way of putting this is that counselling is concerned to remove obstacles to the organismic valuing process. Patterson (1995) thinks of this process as consisting of 'sub-goals', the development of self-awareness and self-esteem for example. Even so, these sub-goals do not need to be defined in advance with any particular client, as they develop during, and as a result of, the counselling process itself.

Patterson, in describing the ultimate goal of counselling in terms of actualisation, also makes the point that this is a universal human goal, and so person-centred counselling, in not describing specific behavioural goals, forms the basis for a universal system of counselling, i.e. one that is not culture-bound or culture-dependent.

Person-centred counselling, then, aims to help dissolve conditions of worth (see chapter 2), and return the person to a state of congruence — that state in which feelings can be fully felt, accepted and expressed appropriately, combined with a trust and acceptance of the organismic valuing process.

Put another way, person-centred counselling is a sensitive exploration of a person's inner world, a reliving in a safe and caring relationship of those things that hurt and damaged us. It is the release of constructive energy (energy no longer needed to shore up defences and maintain a false self), to enable the experiencing of the joys and sorrows of life more creatively and more authentically.

The idea of an *internal* rather than *external locus of evaluation* is an important one here. People who have internalised many conditions of worth will not have much faith or trust in themselves, and are unlikely to hold themselves in very high regard. They are likely to look outside themselves, to others, for judgements and evaluations, and are likely to have more faith or belief in those judgements than they do in their own. For example, a person may dismiss the idea of applying for promotion at work, even though she is perfectly suitable for it, because she accepts the erroneous judgements of some others that include, 'You can't cope with responsibility'.

A general outcome of successful counselling is a shift away from dependence on the judgements of others, towards a greater trust and belief in the validity of internal judgements. This, of course, is an aspect of the actualisation of a 'self' more and more free of conditions of worth, and more open to experience. A sub-goal of counselling might, then, be expressed in terms of a process that enables people to trust the information obtained from their own senses, to value it, and use it as a reliable guideline for determining personal action.

The counsellor as a person

The core conditions of empathy, congruence and unconditional positive regard are all personal counsellor qualities communicated in different ways to clients. The most directly communicated of these qualities is empathic understanding, and counsellor responses to clients are centred on the counsellor's commitment to understanding the client's inner subjective world and expressing the extent of that understanding. The communication of congruence and unconditional positive regard (which I examine in detail in later chapters) are mostly achieved indirectly, except on those occasions where the counsellor chooses to share something from his or her own world directly with the client. Unconditional positive regard is likely to be perceived through the counsellor's valuing and respecting of the client manifested through the expression of empathic understanding without judgement. How the core conditions can be experienced by clients through the counsellor's behaviour is discussed in a following chapter; here I need to emphasise one further important aspect.

Combs (1989) argues that the belief systems of 'helpers' significantly determines their degree of effectiveness. He identified four general areas that seemed to distinguish between good and poor helpers:

- Effective helpers are 'people oriented' and attend to personal meanings rather than external data. They are sensitive and empathic.
- Effective helpers hold positive beliefs about the people with whom they work. They see them as trustworthy and dependable, etc.
- Effective helpers have positive self-concepts that provide security for counsellor and client alike.
- Effective helpers have broader purposes than ineffective helpers. In counselling contexts these include being less concerned with the solution of an immediate problem and more concerned with the general perspective of actualisation.

Combs suggests that the only theories of any consequence for practice are those held by counsellors in the form of fundamental personal beliefs:

> *Scientific theory may suggest hypotheses for possible inclusion in a belief system . . . Personal belief systems, however, come into being little by little, as counselors discover deeper and deeper meanings, more accurate perceptions, and ever greater consistency of concepts . . . The development of personal theory is a highly individual, private, creative activity* (p. 101).

In person-centred counselling, the counsellor is prepared to engage with clients directly, not mediated through a series of technical interventions or strategies. The core conditions of empathy, unconditional positive regard and congruence imply an open, transparent counsellor with a deep personal belief in the inherently constructive and pro-social nature of people (including him or herself). Implied also is a counsellor with the self-confidence to engage directly in the counselling relationship, rather than as a technician or objective expert. Sustaining the essential non-directive and non-authoritarian stance of person-centred counselling is only possible if the counsellor believes that the process of actualisation is expressed through the client's emerging 'personhood', rather than something to be controlled and directed by the counsellor.

The client as a person

In developing theories of counselling, most attention is given to the causes of psychological disturbance, the process of change, and the approach taken by the counsellor. Less attention is given to the part played by clients in the process, and their ability to make use of the counselling relationship for the purposes of personal change, but Rogers' 1957 theoretical statement includes two conditions relating directly to clients: that they are in psychological contact with the counsellor, and that they are 'in a state of incongruence, being vulnerable or anxious'. (In his 1959 paper, Rogers omitted the word 'psychological' from the first condition.) No other statements are made concerning the ability of the client to become involved with the counselling process, but Patterson (1985) stresses that clients must be able to become engaged in a process of self-exploration, including self-disclosure, for the counselling process to be effective. The 'seven-stage model' discussed later in this chapter does imply some state of readiness or willingness on behalf of clients to engage themselves directly in a process of self-exploration to some degree. Those whose state of incongruence means they are rigid, remote and cut off from their emotions and from other people are most unlikely to commit themselves to a process demanding the recognition of and disclosure of feeling. Prouty's work (e.g. 1990, 1994, 2002) is directly concerned with providing the conditions for people experiencing such remoteness to be able to make psychological contact, thus fulfilling the first of the six conditions.

The level of 'vulnerability' or 'anxiety' (condition 2) varies enormously from client to client and at different stages in the counselling process with the same client. This condition implies that a person is experiencing sufficient psychological discomfort to seek help, and is at some level willing (however tentatively) to begin the process of self-discovery. People whose level of vulnerability or anxiety is not great enough to be experienced as particularly threatening or troublesome, may still enter counselling because they value greater levels of self-discovery and self-awareness, and see this process as leading towards a more satisfying and fulfilling life.

On a more general note, a person is regarded as someone capable of movement away from self-destructive behaviour towards self-enhancing behaviour as an inherent property or characteristic of his or her organism guided by the tendency towards actualisation I discussed earlier. Self- (or other-) destructive behaviour, values and attitudes are regarded, essentially, as learned behaviour, values and attitudes consistent with the person's internalised conditions of worth. It is the client's internal resources for change and development that need to become mobilised within the counselling relationship; in other words, the client's self-resources. If trusting in the actualising tendency is to be more than simply a cliché then it is necessary to recognise, understand and respect each client as a unique person and engage in a collaborative discovery of the person's self-healing resources. Duncan and Moynihan (1994), for example, have pointed out that in reviews of psychotherapy outcome research about 40% of client change in therapy can be accounted for by 'extratherapeutic change variables' (meaning factors that are unique to each client and his or her environment). Another 30% or so is suggested as due to common factors of the client–counsellor relationship, with only about 15% accounted for by therapist technique (similar to the placebo effect).

The importance of the counselling relationship

The source of change is the actualising tendency — the movement towards wholeness and becoming fully functioning. The counsellor tries to provide a relationship with the kind of qualities I have already described to enable the actualising tendency to find expression. If the psychological environment is right, clients will discover for themselves, and in their own ways, the resources they need for change and growth. Just like gardeners do not 'grow' plants — they grow by themselves — counsellors do not 'grow' persons. What both the gardener and the counsellor try to do is create the conditions in which the inherent capacities for growth and development can come to fruition.

As someone once said, 'You have to change by yourself, but you don't have to do it on your own.' This reflects the notion that counselling should never be based on any element of control or authority exercised by counsellors over clients, but that the counsellor is a sensitive and non-judgemental companion to their clients as they explore their experiences.

Holding attitudes towards clients of non-judgemental acceptance and empathic understanding is consistent with the theory of the person and the acquisition of disturbance I explored in the previous chapter, provided that those attitudes are rooted in the counsellor's belief system and not inauthentically adopted as strategies. The theory proposes that certain characteristics of early (and subsequent) significant relationships with others result in the internalisation of conditions of worth, and the over-reliance on an external, rather than an internal, locus of evaluation. Relationships in which the development of positive self-regard is overwhelmed by the need to maintain positive regard from others provide the conditions for the development of disturbance. The introjection of many or powerful conditions of worth results in an inevitable estrangement between the 'real self' and the conditioned self, sometimes to such an extent that a person's defence system is completely unable to maintain itself and the result is a complete breakdown of the self-structure.

An effective counselling relationship needs to provide the client with an experience that is qualitatively different from previous destructive relationships. Primarily, the counselling relationship needs to be one where any perceived threat to the existing self-concept is empathically understood in an environment of unconditional positive regard. In such circumstances the normal defences against threat (distortion and/or denial) can be progressively dissolved, and the self-concept (or certain configurations of the self) can be revised as more experience is admitted into awareness.

The counsellor's attendance to non-judgemental, empathic understanding of the client's world of inner experiencing amounts, for the client, to an experience of unconditional positive regard. The counselling relationship provides, in essence, a corrective experience where the perception of authentic unconditional positive regard leads to an increase in positive self-regard. Admitting into awareness previously denied or distorted experiencing results in a reorganisation of the self-concept, the self-concept becomes increasingly congruent with experience, and the locus of evaluation tends to become internal rather than external. Figure 2 offers a simplified map of this process.

EXPERIENCING

- Self-exploration   feelings at arm's length
                            tentative
                            impersonal

- Exploration of attitudes   may be painful
                             unknown

- Experiencing of new attitudes and the modification of the self-concept

- Trusting in one's own experiencing

RE-ORGANISING

- Discarding of introjected values as a guide to behaviour

DEVELOPING

- Moving towards an internal locus of evaluation

Figure 2: A simple 'map' of the counselling process from the client's point of view. [*Adapted from Seeman (1965).*]

Rogers (1959) provided a concise description of the above process which can be summarised as follows:

If a person experiences a relationship characterised by the six necessary and sufficient conditions, a process is initiated that has a certain generally predictable direction:

- The client is increasingly free to express feelings.
- Feelings increasingly refer to the self.
- The client increasingly discriminates feelings, perceptions, self and experiences and understands their interrelationships.
- Feelings increasingly refer to incongruities between some experiences and the self-concept.
- Such incongruence is experienced as threatening, but the experience of threat is possible because the unconditional positive regard of the counsellor is extended both to incongruence and congruence, to anxiety and to the absence of anxiety.
- The client becomes aware of experiences that have previously been denied or distorted.
- The client's self-concept reorganises to include previously denied or distorted experience.
- The client's reorganised self-structure leads to increasing congruence between the self-concept and experience.
- The client's tendency to distort or deny experience to awareness is diminished since fewer experiences are perceived as threatening.
- The client is increasingly able to experience the counsellor's unconditional positive regard without accompanying threat.
- The client increasingly experiences positive self-regard.
- The client increasingly perceives him/herself as the locus of evaluation.
- The client reacts to experience more in terms of his or her own valuing system, and less in terms of conditions of worth.

The process of change

To complete this brief review of Rogers' theory of counselling, I must make some reference to a further important theoretical development. In 1958, Rogers offered his 'process conception of psychotherapy' (also included as a chapter in Rogers, 1961). This was essentially a description of observable differences in client functioning through the ongoing process of a counselling relationship in which the client experiences the relationship in the way I have already described.

Even though everybody is different, Rogers observed a generally similar process of change taking place each time, whilst recognising that the specifics of each person's behaviour were different. This does not mean that counselling is totally predictable, or that the process is a smooth one, but there does seem to be a series of stages through which clients travel on their journey towards becoming more fully functioning. Barrett-Lennard (1998), drawing from Rogers' own writing, has described this process:

> . . . *significant change in therapy was not a movement from*

> *one kind of fixed but faulty structure to another kind of set but*
> *adequate structure, not a change from one constantly repeating*
> *pattern to a different one. Rather, the essential direction was*
> *from a relatively fixed, closed, self-perpetuating quality, to an*
> *open, flowing, self-transcending quality; from fixity and re-*
> *cycling motion to a formative changingness; briefly, from a*
> *condition of stasis to one of process* (p. 83).

Rogers thought that there were seven of these stages that he could observe, and they enabled him to see whether his clients were making progress in counselling, or whether they seemed to be stuck, for a time unable to move on. Although the process can be erratic, clients do, in general, build on their experiences at one stage before moving on to the next. Only when someone feels accepted and understood do they feel able to take the next step. In other words, wherever a client happens to be on the process scale, the counsellor continues to offer a relationship based on the six necessary and sufficient conditions, and maintains trust in the client's capacity to move in positive directions. There are no direct interventions that can be made or should be made in an attempt to move the client from one stage to the next in an effort to speed up the process.

This *process scale* is quite complex, but here I give a simplified version to show the basic characteristics of each of the seven stages. The descriptions of each stage should be seen as very tentative, and there is a great deal of variation and individual differences in clients' processes.

Stage 1

People in this stage appear to be rigid in personality and rather remote, cut off from their emotions and from other people. Rogers thought it unlikely that such people would see any value in counselling, and therefore unlikely that they would take part in it.

People in Stage 1 are very unwilling to reveal anything about themselves, especially their feelings, with which they are very unfamiliar anyway. They tend to see things in terms of opposites — good or bad, right or wrong, with very little in between. They are governed by rigid rules as to how people should behave, and they are strongly judgemental of others, having a rather pessimistic view of human nature.

They tend to cope with life in ways that divert attention away from themselves and their feelings, and they view a display of emotion as a weakness. Typical of this stage are statements like:

> *'Talking about feelings is a waste of time.'*
> *'Students are all the same.'*
> *'People ought to do as they are told.'*

These kinds of generalised statements indicate a very rigid view of the world where everything has its place, and ambiguity and uncertainty are very difficult to tolerate. The world is seen as an unfriendly, even hostile place, and that is how it is and how it will stay.

Stage 2

Here, there is a slight loosening of rigid constructs, though people find it very difficult to accept any responsibility for themselves, or what happens in their lives. When things go wrong, they tend to blame others, and feel like victims of a hostile world, rather than as participators in it. Generally, people are unlikely to volunteer for counselling at this stage, and if they do they are unlikely to stay.

> *'I'm not responsible when things go wrong, am I?'*
> *'I don't do anything wrong, other people keep creating problems for me.'*
> *'No-one ever sees my good side, they only ever see the bad.'*

There is more of an acceptance that things are not right in their lives, but any fault tends to lie in others, or the world in general.

Stage 3

Most people who enter counselling do so at this stage, and are likely to stay. The loosening of attitudes continues as people are more willing to talk about themselves though they tend to do so in the third person, particularly when it is about feelings:

> *'This is how you feel when someone does something like this to you, isn't it?'*
> *'After all, people do have feelings.'*

People are less comfortable expressing presently experienced feelings, and more comfortable talking about feelings that happened in the past:

> *'When I was a kid, I did a lot of things that made me feel bad. I just couldn't tell anyone about them because of what would have happened if I did.'*

Internal contradictions start to emerge, and the differences between an idealised self and the reality of the situation start to become apparent:

> *'I try so hard to be the perfect husband, but it just doesn't work out. I fail all the time.'*
> *'I feel I'd like to really achieve something in life, but I never get round to doing anything about it.'*
> *'I don't know why I never succeed at the things I try. Maybe that's the way I am. I'm just doomed to failure.'*

In this stage there may be hints that there are different possibilities available, but there is still a tendency to see things in hard and fast terms — if they're not one thing, then they must be the opposite. If not good, then bad, if not a success, then a failure.

Clients who first seek therapy are often at this stage and need to be fully accepted as they present themselves before moving deeper into Stage 4.

Stage 4

In this stage, clients begin to describe deeper feelings, usually those that happened in the past.

'I felt so desperately unhappy when she didn't seem to care. I've never known such deep feelings, it really scared me.'

People have difficulty in understanding and accepting these (negative) feelings and would rather they hadn't existed.

'If this is what falling in love means, then I'd rather not have it.'

Feelings in the present start to emerge, but they are mistrusted and even rejected.

'There's this knot, deep down inside, which stops me from doing things and being myself. I don't know what it is, and that makes me angry. What can I do about it?'

Notice that the client is starting to accept responsibility for what is happening, even though the fearfulness and hopelessness of it are apparent. There may be some recognition of patterns that occur in the experience of life, sometimes accompanied by a wry humour.

'It's crazy, isn't it, the way I keep setting myself up for the same old let-down. Look at me, a man of forty, acting like a kid.'

Also at this stage, clients begin to enter into more direct relationships with their counsellor, but there is often a fearfulness about this.

'I find it difficult to trust people, I even find myself wondering how much I can trust you.'

Explorations of this kind are common in therapy and the loosening up of expression continues into the next stages. These later stages are quite complex, and result in many different ways of expression and viewing of the world.

Stage 5

Clients are never wholly at one stage of the process or another. They may start to move on, then take a step back, rather like dipping a toe into the water and deciding it is too cold (or too hot) to go for a swim.

It is when people feel fully accepted and understood that they feel free to explore deeper feelings. The therapist's role is not to lead them from one stage to the next, but to provide them with opportunities fully to experience each stage in their own process, and in their own unique ways.

By Stage 5, clients feel more confident about expressing presently experienced feelings.

'I experience a lot of rejection in my life, and I wonder — is that how it's going to be with you too, will you end up rejecting me? At the moment I feel quite afraid of this.'

The developing freedom and ability to express current feelings means that they are less likely to be denied. They can start to bubble up inside, and even though they are not fully understood or wholly accepted, clients can find ways of expressing them, however tentatively.

> *'I've just realised something. When I start feeling unsure of myself, I get this strange feeling inside which sort of strangles me, and stops me from being all of myself. It is happening now, but it's gradually fading.'*

There can be a feeling of getting close to something important, but not being able to get into direct contact with it. There is still a reluctance to trust feelings in themselves: they can be talked about but not fully experienced. New insights about life and relationships also start to emerge.

> *'I thought I was bad because I felt angry at my father. Now I realise that I was angry because I was hurt. It's obvious to me now that if I get hurt, it's natural to get angry. It all makes sense now. It doesn't mean that I have to feel love for him all the time, he's not perfect, and neither am I.'*

Here, the client is acknowledging and accepting ambivalent feelings towards another person, and that it is OK to have these contradictory feelings alongside each other.

Stage 6

Rogers described this stage as being very distinctive and often dramatic. It is characterised by feelings, previously suppressed, becoming fully experienced in the present moment. This awareness is acute, clear and full of meaning. The self which hitherto has been experienced as somewhat fragmented is now experienced as an integrated whole — mind, body, emotion and intellect, and clients experience moments of full congruence.

Previously felt ambiguities and uncertainties now start to click into place and become crystal clear. These experiences are irreversible and produce changes in attitude and perception which are quite remarkable. The way the world is viewed is never the same again.

Feelings start to flow freely and reach their full conclusion. Previous fears about the potential destructiveness of negative feelings evaporate, and feelings are seen as enriching experiences, not ones to be avoided.

One of the most striking discoveries made by many people at this stage is the realisation of care, concern and tenderness for oneself.

> *'You know, when I look back and see myself as a three-year-old, and looking at what I had to put up with, I really do feel sorry for myself. And now, when I look at myself, I feel tender and loving towards myself. I know that I need to take care of me, and treat myself kindly and well . . . I never knew it was possible to feel this way . . . it feels really good . . . really warm.'*

Carl Rogers uses the following example (Rogers, 1961, p. 148). The client, a young man, has expressed the wish that his parents would die or disappear:

> CLIENT: *It's kind of like wanting to wish them away, and wishing they had never been . . . And I'm so ashamed of myself because then they*

call me, and off I go — swish! They're somehow still so strong. I don't
know. There's some umbilical — I can almost feel it inside me — swish
(and he gestures, plucking himself away by grasping at his navel).
THERAPIST: *They really do have a hold on your umbilical cord.*
CLIENT: *It's funny how real it feels ... like a burning sensation, kind of,
and when they say something which makes me anxious I can feel it
right here (pointing). I never thought of it quite that way.*
THERAPIST: *As though if there's a disturbance in the relationship between
you, then you do feel it as though it was a strain on your umbilicus.*
CLIENT: *Yeah, kind of like in my gut here. It's so hard to define the feeling
that I feel there.*

Rogers says, of this example, 'Here he is living subjectively in the feeling of
dependence on his parents. Yet it would be most inaccurate to say that he
is perceiving it. He is *in* it, experiencing it as a strain on his umbilical cord.
In this stage, internal communication is free and relatively unblocked.'

Rogers also remarks, 'And, it might be remarked in passing, once an
experience is fully in awareness, fully accepted, then it can be coped with
effectively, like any other clear reality'.

Stage 7
Rogers thought that changes made by clients in Stage 6 tended to be
irreversible, and further change was as likely to occur outside of the
counselling relationship as within it. By this stage people are effecting
change for themselves, and the need for counselling is more or less over.

In the counselling situation itself, client and counsellor are actively
collaborating to explore ways in which new-found confidence can be used
and expressed in the world outside. Clients are open to experience, are
able to trust their own feelings, and have developed a strong internal locus
of evaluation.

There is a fluid, changing quality to life, as people are able to
experience each new event without being bound by interpretations that
belong in the past. There is a strong feeling of living fully in the present, an
ability to relate freely to others, and an awareness that further change and
growth is not only possible, but desirable.

Very few people enter therapy at a particular stage and go on through
to Stage 7. Many leave counselling at an earlier point, and if counselling
has been successful for them, content that real and meaningful change
has happened.

Remember that this *process scale* represents an idealised view of the
counselling process: it indicates the flow of events in a very general way.
Each person will experience counselling differently, will have different
concerns, and will be content to leave counselling at different points. It is
useful as a way of thinking about the process that we go through on the
journey towards becoming fully functioning: it is not a prescription of what
we must do in order to get there.

Phases of the counselling process

It is clear from the process scale (above) that a client's progress through person-centred counselling is predicted to conform to a general process over a period of time, provided the relationship is one where the core conditions are experienced consistently. The specific ways in which the process becomes apparent varies from one individual to the next, but in general, clients tend to move away from being relatively fixed, defensive and rigid, towards a more fluid and open way of being in which experiencing is valued and accepted rather than denied or distorted. Mearns and Thorne (1988) describe three very general phases of counselling in straightforward terms: beginnings, middles and endings, and more recently, Barrett-Lennard (1998) has described five phases which he views as the 'pathway' of person-centred counselling (p. 106).

Barrett-Lennard's five-phase model provides a clear conceptualisation of counselling that is consistent with Rogers' process scale, and provides more concrete examples of client concerns during counselling, again in general terms rather than in specific goal terms. Before I briefly review Barrett-Lennard's model, it is worth emphasising some of his concluding comments:

> *It would be contrary to my own meaning to interpret the 'phases' deciphered here as uniform steps or exact markers. They flow from an attempt to catch the essence of a distinct, unusual quality of association and quest, one which in its specifics is as individual as are the participants in the enterprise. Given the requisite resources and commitment, this enterprise and process builds on itself until it becomes evident that another phase, or level, has been reached. No main level can be entirely skipped, for each is a vital part of the foundation for the next. Thus, also, no phase mode in full expression can simply be switched into at will, or as an instant product of specific technique, for its emergence is a growth process and not just a matter of where or how attention is centred* (p. 121).

Phase A. Beginning: the entry phase
This phase involves the time from the client's first approach to the counsellor and may be concluded at the end of the first interview, or continue for some time beyond it. Implicitly the client is testing the waters, and Barrett-Lennard suggests several signs that show if and when the client is 'launched' into counselling. These include the client accounting for his or her presence partly by acknowledging distress and personal or inner difficulty, expressing immediate feelings (beyond a rehearsed personal story), and experiencing being heard in dialogue with the counsellor.

Phase B. A personal working alliance and the passage from woundedness to hope
Two 'streams' are identified: one is *the development of the client–counsellor*

relationship, the other concerns *client issues and process*. Relationship issues include experiences of the counsellor as being present and helpful, while on the counsellor's side the client begins to be experienced and known as a whole person rather than as a number of feelings and perceptions.

Client issues and process involve a movement from 'woundedness' to hope and belief that change is possible.

Phase C. Trust development, and the quest for self: 'Who am I?' 'How do I want to be?'

Barrett-Lennard characterises this phase by reference to issues such as 'a new intensity and depth of self-exploration', the experience of being empathically understood without judgement, and 'increasing ownership of the self'.

Phase D. Synchronous engagement; and the becoming self in action

Here, there is more development of client congruence and spontaneity, with client and counsellor more 'in tune' with each other, and the client acknowledging personal change and shifting values. There is an increasing sense of freedom from the control of past experience, and an acknowledgement of the importance of close relationships.

Movement towards the termination of counselling (apart from practical considerations) includes an enhanced understanding of 'self', and a greater degree of openness and actualisation.

Phase E. Termination process: ending and entry

This might be quite brief and be seen as a beginning more than an ending; an entry to a new or fuller 'way of being'. Feelings around separation from the counsellor are likely to be expressed, but in context, not as a troubling concern.

Barrett-Lennard clearly sees counselling in process terms involving movement away from restricted experiencing and engagement with life towards more open and authentic engagement springing from an enhanced sense of self and diminished anxiety and defensiveness. Whilst he describes 'phases' of the process, he does not identify either particular skills or strategies for the counsellor or specific behavioural goals for the client at any phase. Counselling is a process involving deeper engagement between client and counsellor as time goes by typified by high levels of trust, authenticity, empathic understanding and non-judgemental regard. The process is facilitated by the counsellor bringing to the relationship the personal values and qualities described by Rogers, including an empathic absorption in the client's inner world of felt experience and meaning. Barrett-Lennard stresses the mutuality and even reciprocity of the counselling relationship. He emphasises how closely tuned understanding is a feature of the relationship between the two people involved with each becoming increasingly sensitive to the other's experiencing and meanings.

Moments of movement

The normal experience for clients in making progress through the stages Rogers described, or the phases identified by Barrett-Lennard, is not one of a smooth transition from one stage or phase to the next. There are often periods of time in which little progress can be observed or felt, and then something happens that moves the process on a little towards another level.

Carl Rogers thought that there were times in counselling during which people took a definite step forward, which he described as *moments of movement* occurring when people have a direct experience of some aspect of themselves without inhibition, that up to that moment had been denied or distorted in some way. This is the first time this experience has been allowed fully into awareness, and it is accompanied by the realisation that it is an acceptable part of the person, not one of which to be ashamed. An example of this, which is taken from a paper Rogers gave to the first meeting of the American Academy of Psychotherapists in 1956, will help to make it clearer:

> CLIENT: *It's just being terribly hurt! . . . And then, of course, I've come to see and to feel that over this . . . see, I've covered it up.*
> [A moment later she puts it slightly differently.]
> CLIENT: *You know, it's almost a physical thing. It's . . . sort of as though I were looking within myself at all kinds of . . . nerve endings and — bits of . . . things that have been sort of mashed (weeping).*
> THERAPIST: *As though some of the most delicate aspects of you — physically almost — have been crushed or hurt.*
> CLIENT: *Yes. And you know, I do get the feeling, oh, you poor thing.*
> THERAPIST: *You just can't help but feel very deeply sorry for the person that is you.*

This experience has the quality of being immediate — it occurs now, and is not just an intellectual insight. Although much of it may have been experienced in different ways before, never so completely, and never with the awareness of it accompanied by such intense physiological reactions. It is accepted as part of the self, and not disowned or denied. Personal integration and congruence are general goals of counselling and this is an example of what integration and congruence mean. The person's feelings flow without inhibition, are accepted and expressed directly.

Rogers suggested that counselling can be described as being made up of moments such as this, in which an increasing number of experiences previously denied or covered up, are experienced directly and integrated into the person's sense of self. The content of these moments varies from one person to the next; the main characteristic is that up until this point it has been thought of as unacceptable to the person involved.

Person-centred counselling is not a mechanical process, in which each step follows smoothly from the one before, but there are general characteristics of the process that are recognisable, and so to this extent predictable. Rogers was concerned to discover ways that the inner, personal power of the client could be mobilised to enable movement towards full congruence.

In Rogers' words:

> *I enter the relationship not as a scientist, not as a physician who can accurately diagnose and cure, but as a person entering into a personal relationship. Insofar as I see him only as an object, the client will tend to become only an object. I risk myself, because if, as the relationship deepens, what develops is a failure, a regression, a repudiation of me and the relationship by the client, then I . . . will lose . . . a part of myself* (Rogers, 1961).

A note on recent research

Barrett-Lennard (1998) has comprehensively discussed and evaluated the significant research that supports and challenges person-centred theory. Recently, some other important research findings have emerged that provide practitioners with more confidence that the PCA is, indeed, an effective way of conducting 'helping relationships'. Unfortunately, much of the reported research tends to label person-centred therapy as either 'non-directive' or even 'Rogerian non-directive' counselling — somewhat outdated terminology. However, Friedli, et al. (1997) showed that 'non-directive therapy' was more effective than routine general practitioner care in the treatment of severe depressive conditions, and Rowland et al. (2000), using studies in which person-centred counselling was the dominant method, established the effectiveness of counselling in primary care for people with depression.

The King et al. (2000) study compared person-centred counselling, cognitive-behavioural therapy and routine practitioner care with people suffering from depression and anxiety. They found that both person-centred counselling and cognitive-behavioural therapy obtained better results than routine general practitioner care, and that there was no difference in effectiveness between person-centred and cognitive-behavioural therapy.

It seems that as more research is done, more evidence emerges that person-centred counselling is able to demonstrate a strong evidence base for its theory which is, in turn, supportive of the clinical experience of person-centred counsellors working in a variety of settings. For example, another recent summary of research by Elliott et al. (in press) is also strongly supportive of the effectiveness of person-centred and experiential therapies.

A summary of person-centred counselling theory

It will be seen from what follows that I give particular prominence to the experience by the client of unconditional positive regard. In doing this I do not mean to suggest a hierarchy of importance in the six conditions. I view them as a *gestalt* or unity operating at the level of counsellor values and attitudes with, generally, the most observable counsellor *behaviour* being empathic following responses. I also make the assumption, following Patterson (1985), that the client has the capacity to engage in the process directly at some level.

Our earlier discussion of the origin of psychological disturbance shows that people, particularly though not exclusively in their early years, are sensitive to the judgements of others and tend to prioritise them over their own, developing an external locus of evaluation in the process. The internalisation of conditions of worth into the emerging self-concept is the origin of psychological disturbance. In addition, according to Mearns and Thorne (2000), a person may experience tension or conflict resulting from the impact of the social environment on the person's tendency towards the actualisation of certain potentials. The central role played by unconditional positive regard, or its absence, in the development of the individual can most easily be appreciated by reference to how Rogers' theory can be applied to family life. In his 1959 paper, Rogers stated that the greater the degree of unconditional positive regard which the parent experiences towards the child:

(a) The fewer the conditions of worth in the child.
(b) The more the child will be able to live in terms of a continuing organismic valuing process.
(c) The higher the level of psychological adjustment of the child.

It is clear, then, that Rogers' theory provides for a process in which the presence of unconditional positive regard and the consequential development of positive self-regard leads to psychological adjustment, and its absence leads to the contrary. Clients experience the counselling process not as one entirely free of threat because the admission of previously distorted or denied experience into awareness is often accompanied by anxiety or threat. Rogers' 1959 paper makes the point that experiencing threat of this kind within the counselling relationship is possible because the counsellor's unconditional positive regard is extended to the totality of the client's experiencing process. In other words, when threat or anxiety arises in the client, the defences of distortion or denial are not aroused with the same strength when the anxiety is responded to empathically and with unconditional positive regard. The gradual weakening and loosening of defences is accompanied by an enhanced willingness and ability to become more open to experience, even of the kind that normally arouses anxiety. Bozarth (1998) argues that:

> *The individual's return to unconditional positive self-regard is the crux of psychological growth in the theory. It is the factor that reunifies the self with the actualizing tendency . . . Rogers hypothesises that one must perceive reception of unconditional positive regard in order to correct the pathological state. The communication of unconditional positive regard by a significant other is one way to achieve the above conditions* (p. 84).

I have suggested that unconditional positive regard exists at the level of counsellor values and attitudes, and that these values and attitudes are communicated to clients through the counsellor attending non-directively and empathically to the client's internal, subjective world. In other words, the client's experience of unconditional positive regard in counselling is achieved in the context of the counsellor communicating his or her empathic understanding of the client's frame of reference. The counsellor's congruence (that is, his or her openness to the experience of the relationship with the client without distortion or denial of any of that experience) provides the internal condition for the counsellor to experience empathic understanding and non-judgmental acceptance of the client's internal world.

The following summary of the main points covered in this chapter states the theory of person-centred counselling using the terms and language defined and discussed in this and previous chapters. This theoretical statement is based on the assumptions that underpin the person-centred approach, in particular that of the hypothesised existence of the actualising tendency, and it incorporates the ideas of Cooper and Mearns and Thorne discussed in chapter 3.

Assumption 1

The actualising tendency is the sole motivation for all activities of the person, operating in a constructive direction towards self-regulation as far as the environment will allow. It is a tendency towards the enhancement, maintenance and full realisation of the potentials of the organism as a whole. Though a universal characteristic of humankind (and all other forms of organic life), individual expression of the actualising tendency is unique to each person.

Assumption 2

It is likely that the tendency towards the full actualisation of potential encounters resistance from factors within the individual's social world and wider environment. Conflict or tension may then arise between the actualising process and the imperatives of preserving the individual's life space. The actualising tendency is vulnerable to hostile or otherwise unfavourable experiences leading to the development of a self-concept in which certain experiences are distorted or denied to awareness, while others are admitted into awareness without distortion. Different configurations of self may develop and emerge in response to the varying demands of the social context.

Assumption 3

The distortion or denial of experience leads to psychological disturbance. Disturbance is a result of (a) conflict between the actualising or formed self with its internalised conditions of worth, and the general actualising tendency of the individual, and/or (b) unresolved tension between the actualising tendency and the mediating effects of the social and wider environment.

If assumptions 1, 2 and 3 are accepted, then:

A. Counselling should provide experiences in which (a) the actualising tendency can dissolve the effects of unfavourable or growth-inhibiting circumstances, including those resulting from significant relationships in which the person experienced a lack of unconditional positive regard, and/or (b) conflict arising from the tension between actualisation and the inhibiting demands of the social and wider environment can be resolved.

B. Counselling should foster the individual's self-healing resources through a relationship in which unconditional positive regard is experienced consistently.

C. Unconditional positive regard is experienced when the client's subjective, internal frame of reference is empathically understood without judgement by a relatively congruent counsellor.

Implications for the counsellor

If the assumptions and the statements which follow from them are accepted, then:

(a) The person-centred counsellor, through his or her behaviour, attitudes and values, proceeds on the basis of the hypothesised actualising tendency of each client.

(b) The counsellor's task is to provide a relationship based on the six necessary and sufficient conditions for positive personality change.

(c) To communicate genuine respect and trust in the client's self-healing resources, the congruent counsellor adopts a non-directive attitude in which non-judgemental, empathic following of the client's emerging process is the primary activity.

Implications for the client

If the client experiences a counselling relationship consistent with a, b and c (above), then:

i.   The client's actualising tendency will (a) correct psychological damage created by the internalisation of conditions of worth into the self-concept (or concepts) with its (their) varying configurations, and the subsequent distortion or denial of certain experiences to awareness, and/or (b) initiate a process of tension resolution or reduction, where it exists, between the actualisation process and the demands of the environment.

ii. A change process will be initiated involving greater openness to experience and the dissolution of the defences of distortion and denial of experience to awareness.

iii. The self-concept(s) including its (their) varying configurations will become increasingly free of conditions of worth, positive self-regard will be restored, and the person will develop towards increasing maximisation of potential.

Our discussion of the theory of person-centred counselling, and the previous chapters outlining the basic theoretical and philosophical assumptions that underpin the PCA, now give us enough background to explore the counselling situation in some detail. The next chapter takes a close look at an example of a counselling interview and uses it to explore how theory is put into practice.

Before moving on to the next chapter, I suggest you review the main points covered here by working through the checklist below.

Checklist: Counselling theory

- There are six conditions hypothesised as both necessary and sufficient for therapeutic personality change.
- Three of the six conditions, empathic understanding, congruence and unconditional positive regard, have become known as the core conditions and are all conditions offered by the counsellor.
- The core conditions describe qualities, values and attitudes of the counsellor, rooted in the counsellor's belief system rather than viewed as counselling techniques or strategies.
- These qualities are best seen as a *gestalt* or unity operating together rather than as separate elements.
- The client is able, at some level, to engage in the counselling process through self-exploration and self-disclosure.
- The experience of unconditional positive regard, made possible by the counsellor's congruence and empathic understanding, enables the client to admit hitherto denied or distorted experiences into awareness.
- Person-centred counselling initiates a generally predictable change process, manifested in specific individual ways for each client.
- Change often occurs in moments of movement that have certain general but definable characteristics.

Person-centred counselling in practice

5

In this chapter, I use an example of a counselling interview to extend our understanding of person-centred theory and practice. This counselling relationship is in its very early stages, and I look closely to see what makes it characteristically person-centred, and what it is that the counsellor is trying to do, and how he (in this case) does it. Following the interview, I revisit the 'six necessary and sufficient conditions', particularly the three 'core conditions' of empathic understanding, congruence and unconditional positive regard.

A person-centred counselling interview

(The scene is the counsellor's office. The client, Jack, has never been to a counsellor before, so he is understandably a little nervous.)

COUNSELLOR: (In a welcoming and warm tone of voice) *Hello, Jack. Do make yourself comfortable. We've got almost an hour, would you like to tell me something about why you have come here today?*

CLIENT: Well, there are so many things. I don't know if you can help with them . . . It just seems that everything gets on top of me so easily these days, much more than they used to. I suppose I have been having a bad time lately. I don't seem to get on with my teenage daughter like I used to . . . I feel very unhappy at work, maybe I've been there too long. My wife and I seem to be at each other's throats . . . I don't know . . . coming to a counsellor seems like a last resort, but I can't keep going like this much longer.

COUNSELLOR: *OK, there's a lot going on for you at the moment, it seems like it's been building up lately and it's getting harder to cope with . . .*

CLIENT: Yes, too many things, and all at once. Maybe I'm getting older . . . it feels like I'm losing my way or something. Life doesn't have the same happiness I used to feel. It makes me feel I'm just whingeing when I try and talk about it to anyone. Really there's nothing definite I can put my finger on, but sometimes I just want to chuck it all in . . . but really I'm just so unhappy . . .

COUNSELLOR: (Manner is tentative, exploratory) *So it's a feeling of just drifting, is it? Life seems to have lost its purpose or something like that? No one thing, no crisis or anything, but you just feel so much sadness, and maybe a bit alone with it?*

CLIENT: I do feel a bit on my own. In fact I feel alone a lot of the time. Because there isn't anything specific, I can't really talk much about it. My wife says I'm moody and closed off . . . but how do you talk about something and nothing? It all seems a bit futile.

COUNSELLOR: (Slightly rewords the client's question) *How can you open up when you don't really know what it is yourself . . . ? But you do feel the loneliness, and (with warmth) I do hear the sadness in your voice.*

CLIENT: I just feel like I'm complaining when I have no real right to. I've got everything I need . . . why do I feel so, so unhappy?

COUNSELLOR: (Reflects, is tentative) *It feels so unreasonable to complain, make a fuss, when there doesn't seem to be a real reason?*

CLIENT: Yes, I've always believed you should be happy with what you've got, there are so many worse off . . . I mean I'm not starving or in the middle of a war or anything. It's so hard to talk about this . . . it would almost be better if I did have some big issue that I could point to and say, this is what's making you unhappy, but there isn't anything . . . it all feels a bit phoney, making a mountain out of a molehill.

COUNSELLOR: *It doesn't seem right just to say, 'Look, I'm unhappy and I don't know why.'*

CLIENT: No, it doesn't. I usually just keep these things to myself. Most people would never suspect I feel this way. I know my wife knows I'm unhappy. I think she's a bit scared of it, as if it's something to do with her. I want to tell her it isn't, but if we do start to talk about it we end up rowing, or I deny there's anything wrong.

COUNSELLOR: (Summarises) *It's like you're used to sitting on your feelings, not letting them out, as if it's not quite right to do that. And if you do start to talk a bit, it all goes wrong, something like that ?*

CLIENT: Yes, and that makes it worse . . . It just seems to make things worse. Like I want to tell her it's not her, but I think sometimes I do end up blaming her, or at least she feels like I am. I mean, I know that it's me, something in me that isn't happy being who I am, doing what I do, (sighs, shakes head slowly) . . . but how do you change that when you don't really know what it is?

(Pause)

CLIENT: When I think about that, about what I just said, it does feel like there's another person in me, or perhaps it's another bit of me, (sighs) . . . who has kept quiet for a long time, and not really been happy with what's going on. I mean, the main bit of me is successful and all that, but . . . I need to think about this more . . .

(Quite a long pause, looks at counsellor, shakes head and shrugs.)

COUNSELLOR: (Warm tone, quiet voice, hesitant) *As if there's part of you that has been ignored for a long time, not taken into account or something?*

CLIENT: *(A little more animated)* It seems weird, but it does feel a bit like that. Like someone got left behind in the rush to get on with things. But now it's beginning to feel like that part is saying, 'what about me?' That scares me a bit, that thought . . .

This dialogue is a fairly accurate reconstruction of a real interview that went quite well, and is quite typical of the early stages of person-centred counselling. The problem with the written word is that it doesn't capture the warm tone of the counsellor's voice, or the slightly despairing and weary voice of the client, though the 'stage directions' in brackets help a little.

Clients, not patients

The first thing to notice is that Jack is referred to as a *client* and not as a *patient*. At first, this might seem trivial, but really it is quite significant. Carl Rogers took the view that the people who came to him for help were *not* sick, and dependent for a 'cure' on the interventions of an expert physician. He believed that the resources for change lie within the person him or herself, and that these resources become available within a helping relationship of particular qualities.

Calling Jack a 'client' implies that his distress is a temporary state, *and that he has an active part to play in the process of alleviating that distress.* The person-centred counsellor has the skills and qualities to be a *companion* to Jack as he explores his own world in his own way, and does not see clients as dependent and powerless.

This means that one of the first concerns of the person-centred counsellor is to act consistently with the belief that the power for change resides in clients themselves, and not within counsellors or their techniques. The implications of this apparently uncontentious attitude are highly significant, as will be seen further on in this chapter in the discussion on 'non-directivity'. This central idea is so important in person-centred counselling, that it needs to be attended to right from the start of the counselling relationship. The ways in which counsellors greet their clients, discuss fees with them, set out their counselling rooms and so on, all contribute to establishing a situation in which clients are respected, valued and trusted to make decisions for themselves.

The way the counsellor introduces himself immediately indicates both the collaborative and non-directive nature of the counselling relationship. Whilst it is true that the counsellor is there to listen to and try to understand Jack and not the other way round, the counsellor does not want to establish the relationship as one in which the counsellor 'does' something to Jack. Both counsellor and client, in different ways, play active parts in the relationship.

Professional and ethical issues

This is the second meeting between the counsellor and his client, though the first counselling session. In the previous meeting, they discussed fees and how to pay them, times and regularity of meetings, what the counsellor would prefer Jack to do if he were unable to make an appointment and the number of sessions they would meet for in the first instance. They agreed to meet six times, and then to review the situation so that Jack would know what he was committing himself to. Whether or not they would continue to meet after the end of the sixth session was left open for decision closer to the time. The counsellor took details of Jack's address and telephone number and informed him what notes of sessions he would keep, where and how he would keep them and who would have access to them. They discussed issues of confidentiality, and the extreme circumstances in which it might become necessary to break confidentiality. The counsellor also talked to Jack about the need for counsellors to be in supervision, and what that meant in terms of him talking in supervision about his relationship with Jack.

This first meeting is sometimes called a 'contract setting session'. Its purpose is to ensure that all arrangements are clear to both people, and it also gives Jack an opportunity to decide whether or not he wishes to continue working with this counsellor. The counsellor also has this opportunity, but in person-centred counselling the first meeting does not usually take the form of a psychological assessment of Jack or his problems. The counsellor needs to determine whether or not he thinks it possible to form a good working relationship with his client, or even if the client's problems could more easily be dealt with elsewhere. For example, if Jack simply wants advice about changing his job, the counsellor might think it more appropriate for Jack to see a careers counsellor.

It is, however, very important that the client's needs are not overridden by the counsellor's need to collect information about the client or to complete a formal or semi-formal 'contracting session'. In this first meeting, the counsellor's concern is directed towards listening to and empathically understanding his client as far as possible. Clients often take time to get used to the counselling situation and a counsellor who is over-concerned with information about the client is in danger of missing more subtle or tentative expression of client needs. The key is patient, active and attentive listening combined with a genuine willingness to respond to the client's needs as the client experiences and expresses them.

Assessment and diagnosis

Issues concerning psychological assessment and 'diagnosis' are complex, but the person-centred approach tends to view these activities as unnecessary and even harmful to the development of a counselling relationship. The theory of person-centred counselling postulates that emotional and psychological maladjustment result from conflicts arising between the general actualising tendency, and the actualisation of a false or conditioned self, and Bozarth (1998) has argued persuasively that this makes the diagnosis of specific forms of dysfunction redundant. He goes further in denouncing the notion that there should be specific treatments for specific disorders as a 'fundamental fiction' (p. 163). Bozarth's review of the relevant research in this area leads him to the conclusion that 'there is not a research foundation for the underlying assumption of our mental health care system; that is, that there are specific treatments for specific dysfunctions' (p. 172).

In most counselling systems, assessment is the beginning of a process of developing a particular treatment plan thought to be appropriate for clients with particular psychological problems. In other words, 'assessment' can vary according to the counsellor's perception of the client's needs. But, in person-centred counselling, according to Shlien (1989/2002), there is only one 'treatment' — the development of a counselling relationship based on the necessary and sufficient conditions hypothesis.

Bayne et al. (1999), offer ten criticisms of 'psychodiagnosis', which I briefly summarise below:

- Diagnostic labels are often meaningless and poorly defined.
- Labels can become self-fulfilling prophecies.
- Clients diagnosed with particular disorders can be treated in stereotyped ways by practitioners and others (including clients themselves) long after the disorder has disappeared.
- Practitioners can become preoccupied with a client's history, and neglect current attitudes and behaviour.
- Counsellors can become preoccupied with pathology and underestimate a client's strengths.
- There is a risk of gender role-socialisation influencing diagnosis. For example, women socialised into being emotionally expressive may be vulnerable to being diagnosed in particular ways, as histrionic or dependent, for instance. Similarly, men socialised into being more distant may be seen as paranoid or antisocial. Diagnosis might reflect the potential for seeing as pathological those aspects of behaviour that are normative for men or women who have been well socialised.
- Emphasising diagnosis can lead to clients becoming dependent on experts.
- Practitioners need to be well trained to use the various systems of diagnosis which still have relatively low reliability and validity.
- Diagnostic labels can have the surface appearance of being scientific and objective, thus heightening the mystique of professionalism and investing practitioners with authority.

Making contact — the first of the six conditions

The first of the six necessary and sufficient conditions (see chapter 4) is that 'Two persons are in psychological contact', and this seems so obvious that until recently it was largely ignored or taken as read (see Wyatt and

Sanders, 2002, for an up-to-date review). In his original 1957 paper, Rogers regarded this first condition as a simple one, and that it should, perhaps, be termed an assumption or precondition.

In the extract given above, it is clear that the two people involved are making contact with each other. Each is making a difference to the other, and an exchange is taking place that clearly indicates this. There are, however, situations in which the establishment of contact is not so easy to determine, and it is here that the work of Garry Prouty should be acknowledged. Prouty works with people who have been labelled as retarded, schizophrenic or demented, and with those who are psychologically withdrawn and presenting with autistic features, i.e. 'contact impaired' clients.

Prouty's development of 'Pre-Therapy' (e.g. Prouty 1994, 2000, 2002) evolved from his work with psychotic and retarded clients for whom any form of contact seemed deeply and chronically impaired. He describes a number of ways in which 'contact' can be established and maintained with such clients that are derived from, 'the understanding that [such] incoherence and disorganized experiencing is potentially capable of transforming into a meaningful form' (Prouty, 2001, p. 158). In other words, Prouty has developed ways in which a counsellor can gradually make contact with those whose degree of psychological impairment seems to make such contact appear, at first, to be an impossibility. 'Pre-Therapy' is not, strictly speaking, 'person-centred counselling', but it is a major development of the principles of the PCA and their application to this group of clients. It depends on the counsellor's ability to make empathic contact with an apparently disorganised, chaotic or non-communicative client, and Prouty describes a number of methods of initiating that process (e.g. Prouty, op. cit.).

The core conditions in close-up

The hypothesis that Rogers formulated in 1957, and restated in a slightly different form in 1959, identified six conditions as necessary and sufficient. Three of them, the 'core conditions', are widely known throughout the counselling world, but not always understood in the way Rogers meant them. Next, I offer some detailed discussion of these core conditions as they have traditionally been understood in the PCA, and then briefly consider some more contemporary perspectives on them.

Listening, and communicating — the importance of empathic understanding

The most obvious counsellor attitude in the extract given above is the counsellor's concentration on trying to *understand* his client — what he is saying, how he is feeling, or more accurately what he is experiencing and how he is experiencing it. He attends to all of the client's communication; not just the words, but also the tone of voice and other non-verbal clues.

The counsellor is continually checking the extent to which he has accurately understood his client. For example, when he responds with,

'It's like you're used to sitting on your feelings, not letting them out, as if it's not quite right to do that. And if you do start to talk a bit, it all goes wrong, something like that?' But understanding, of itself, is of no value unless Jack knows he is being understood, so the counsellor is also trying to communicate his understanding as clearly and sensitively as he can.

The kind of understanding that tries to see what life is like for another person, without judging it or evaluating it, is known as *empathy*. A good example of empathy occurs when the counsellor says: *'So it's a feeling of just drifting, is it? Life seems to have lost its purpose, or something like that? No one thing, no crisis or anything, but you just feel so much sadness, and maybe a bit alone with it?'*

Here, the counsellor is quite *tentative* in his communication. He is not trying to tell Jack what he is feeling, but is *exploring* how far he has accurately understood what Jack is trying to express.

The next thing is that the counsellor is quite *economical* in his responses. He does not make any big speeches, or drift off into speculations. He tries to summarise what Jack is saying and to *reflect* both the content and the emotional meaning of his words. For example, *'It feels so unreasonable to complain, make a fuss, when there doesn't seem to be a real reason?'*

Finally, the counsellor goes just a little further than the client's spoken words, *'. . . and maybe a bit alone with it?'* The counsellor thinks he has sensed something that Jack didn't quite say. From Jack's tone of voice or other non-verbal clues, he noticed a feeling of aloneness, and he tried to reflect that sensing back to Jack, again in a tentative, exploratory way. It can be seen from Jack's next statement that the counsellor was right in his sensing: *'I do feel a bit on my own. In fact I feel alone a lot of the time. Because there isn't anything specific, I can't really talk much about it. My wife says I'm moody and closed off . . .but how do you talk about something and nothing? It all seems a bit futile.'*

Although I use the word 'reflect' here, it does not imply a passive activity, and definitely not one that involves simply repeating clients' words back to them. *Reflection of feelings* is one of the processes that help us to check out our listening, and keep us on the right track. Carl Rogers preferred terms like 'testing understanding', and this implies a much more active process. Empathic understanding arises within the counsellor as he or she attends closely and without judgement to the client's experiencing. In essence, empathic understanding is an attitude or inner experience, not a skill.

Deep empathic understanding is all too rare in most people's daily lives, and is one of the qualities that makes the therapeutic relationship different from usual relationships. Being deeply understood helps dissolve feelings of isolation and gives us the courage to risk expressing more of our thoughts and feelings. Although empathic understanding is particularly highly valued in person-centred counselling, it is a core quality of many counselling systems.

In 1986, Carl Rogers underlined the importance of empathy as he saw it:

> *To my mind, empathy is in itself a healing agent. It is one of the most potent aspects of therapy, because it releases, it confirms, it brings even the most frightened client into the human race. If a person is understood, he or she belongs* (p. 376).

Empathy is usefully thought of as a process and a quality rather than simply as a skill. It is a process because it develops as time goes by: it arises out of the relationship between client and counsellor, but it is not left to chance. It is more likely to develop if therapists attend to and nurture their ability to see the world in the ways their clients see it. This is sometimes known as 'entering into the frame of reference of another person'.

In our example, even though it is very early in the relationship, there is a sense that the two people are *mutually* engaged in exploring meanings and working towards understanding. In successful counselling relationships, mutuality can develop into an intimate and close sharing of thoughts, emotions and experiences.

Barrett-Lennard (1993) describes empathy as having an 'aroused, active, reaching-out nature'. To Rogers, empathy meant:

> ... *entering into the private perceptual world of the other and becoming thoroughly at home with it. It involves being sensitive, moment by moment, to the changing felt meanings which flow in this other person, to the fear or rage or tenderness or confusion or whatever that he or she is experiencing ... It includes communicating your sensings of the person's world as you look with fresh and unfrightened eyes at elements of which he or she is fearful ... You are a confident companion to the person in his or her inner world* (Rogers, 1980, p. 142).

Rogers' concern with his clients' inner, subjective experiencing meant that it was most important for him to achieve as complete an understanding of a client's personal world as possible. Almost without exception, counsellors from any school of thought would agree that empathy is an important characteristic of effective counselling, although they mean different things by it. However, Rogers went further by observing the therapeutic benefits of listening and understanding, and concluding that this form of listening, when communicated to the client in the form of empathic understanding, was helpful in its own right, not as a preparation for other counselling techniques.

In the person-centred approach, empathic understanding involves a process of 'being with' another person, that is, attempting to 'step into the other person's shoes' and 'see the world through the other person's eyes', laying aside one's own perceptions, values, meanings and perspectives as far as possible. This makes it essential to understand the difference between the development of empathic understanding as an *experience* on the one hand, and empathy as an identifiable set of measurable behaviours or skills on the other. To view empathy only as a skill or set of skills can lead to some rather facile attempts to teach 'empathic reflections' or 'empathic responses' in the misguided hope that mastering such skills is the same as 'entering into the private perceptual world of the other and becoming thoroughly at home with it' (op. cit.).

Two other aspects of empathy deserve to be emphasised here. The first is the *as if* quality of empathic understanding. This refers to the idea that one can enter the frame of reference of another person to the extent that events, feelings etc. can be experienced, to some extent, *as if* those events etc. were one's own — but without losing the *as if* quality. In other words, empathically understanding someone does not imply getting lost in their world. The empathic person maintains his or her separate identity, and does not become overwhelmed by what may be strong or frightening feelings.

The second aspect for emphasis is that empathic understanding needs to be experienced by the client for therapeutic benefit to accrue, so the counsellor needs to express it if the client is to become aware of being understood. This communication is usually, though not exclusively, verbal — the holding of someone's hand, or even crying along with someone, may be as empathic as anything said, if this is a spontaneous expression of deep understanding. It is the necessity to communicate empathic understanding that has sometimes been responsible for the mechanical learning of 'empathic responding' referred to above. Most descriptions of empathic understanding suffer from the tendency to stress the observable behaviour of the empathic person, and to concentrate on describing verbal responses. If we are to regard empathic understanding as a developing process and an experience which becomes deeper and more accurate as time goes by, it is essential to understand the relationship between the people involved, the way it has developed, and the existential meaning it has for them.

Warmth, respect and unconditional positive regard

Other characteristics of the above extract are the *warmth* and the *respect* shown to the client. The counsellor is relating to Jack as a person struggling to come to terms with new and vaguely frightening feelings. Carl Rogers called this counsellor attitude *unconditional positive regard*. It means that the counsellor is listening attentively and caring for his client. He *prizes* Jack as a unique, worthwhile and valued human being. A good example of this comes when the counsellor says: '. . . *But you do feel the loneliness, and I do hear the sadness in your voice.*'

Of course, warmth cannot be turned on and off like a tap. I use the word 'warmth' here to indicate a welcoming, open approach by the counsellor. Expressing warmth that you do not really feel would be seen through straight away by most people. Warmth, in the sense of affection or liking, is something that either develops naturally, or does not happen at all. The expression 'to warm to somebody' indicates that a process is under way.

I do not use the word 'warmth' to mean the same thing as affection, although as counsellors we often develop feelings of liking and affection for our clients. In this context, the opposite of warmth would be 'distance' or being 'over-objective' or 'aloof'.

Excessive warmth, or being over-friendly, especially early on in counselling, might make it hard for clients to express angry, hostile or destructive feelings. Being warm does not mean being protective, overly sympathetic or just plain nice. These qualities may make it very difficult, if not impossible, for clients to express anger, or disappointment or other strong feelings towards their counsellors.

Unconditional positive regard does not mean that counsellors have to approve of everything their clients do, especially as people often do very hurtful and destructive things to themselves and others. It means that the counsellor understands and accepts people, as non-judgementally as possible, as imperfect beings trying to change how they feel and behave. Unconditional positive regard is aimed at the basic humanness present in us all, even though that humanness may have become very damaged.

Look also at the *rapport* the counsellor is establishing with Jack. The two people present seem to be meshing quite smoothly. If you were able to see and hear this interaction, you would probably notice that the counsellor's voice is calm and unhurried, and that this is more than just a conversation. There is a sense of purpose about it, one in which client and counsellor are engaged in a process in which layers of meaning, experience and feeling are gradually being uncovered and talked about. In other counselling systems, this is often referred to as the *therapeutic* or *working alliance*, and it indicates that counsellor and client are working closely together to explore the client's world.

Unconditional positive regard implies a consistent acceptance of each aspect of a person's experience. An essential aspect is the lack of *conditions* of acceptance, i.e. no sense of 'I feel positive towards you on condition that your behaviour conforms to certain standards'. It involves feelings of acceptance for both 'positive' and 'negative' aspects of a person, and can also be expressed as non-possessive caring for a person as a separate individual. Rogers (1957a) thought that the term itself might be a little unfortunate as it had an absolute, 'all-or-nothing' ring to it. Unconditional positive regard, like empathy and congruence, cannot be considered as a skill or part of a counsellor's repertoire of techniques. It is part of a person's system of values and is an integrated aspect of that person, not something that can be adopted temporarily in order to fulfil the core conditions.

Ideally, clients should experience unconditional positive regard as a quality exhibited by their counsellor that makes it possible for clients to express any part of themselves and their experience, without the fear that they will be judged as persons. Whilst it is not helpful to pick out one of the three core conditions as being the most important, there is a view among some person-centred practitioners that the empathy and congruence experienced by counsellors may be the 'ways of being' that enable them to develop attitudes of unconditional positive regard, and this perspective is included in the statement of theory at the end of chapter 4.

Congruence, being real, being yourself

There is another, very important, characteristic of this extract that is difficult to notice from the written word. It is sometimes termed counsellor *congruence*. Congruence, or authenticity or realness, means that the counsellor is willing to be who he is, meeting his client, Jack, face to face, respecting him as a person in his own right, and entering into a relationship with him as an equal. He is not trying to be a magician or an expert technician or anything other than who he is.

In the context of counselling, congruence includes counsellors being aware of the feelings that arise in them during the relationships they develop with their clients. Sometimes it is appropriate for counsellors to share these feelings with their clients, particularly, but not only, when such feelings begin to interfere with the ability to listen attentively.

This is most likely to happen after counselling has been going on for a few sessions, when counsellor and client have learned something about each other, and the counsellor is beginning to get more of a picture of the client's experience and concerns. For example, a counsellor may notice that whenever a particular client talks about the death of his mother, he tends to do so in a very matter-of-fact and seemingly unemotional way. Each time this happens, the counsellor feels disturbed; this is not the way this client usually talks about things. It is as if this client becomes some other person at these times, and the counsellor feels he loses contact with him, finding it more and more difficult to understand how the client really feels about the loss of his mother.

This persistent, disturbed feeling makes it difficult for the counsellor to listen properly, and he begins to lose touch even more with his client. The counsellor decides to express this feeling and says:

Whenever you talk about your mother's death, I feel as if I can't get near you. I feel like I'm being held at arm's length, as if you're saying, 'don't get too close to me with this.' It feels uncomfortable to me, and I'm torn between wanting to help you explore your feelings, and respecting your need not to let me get too close to them.

This is an example of congruent communication, characterised by an honest and accurate attention to inner symbolisation (what the counsellor is thinking and feeling). In general, the disclosure of feelings by the counsellor should be approached with care and sensitivity. Sometimes, especially when difficult feelings like anger, for example, or fear or boredom, are involved, it is better for counsellors to talk their feelings through with a supervisor or experienced colleague first.

In other words, congruent communication in the form of honest self-disclosure does not mean expressing feelings in an undisciplined or haphazard way. Sharing feelings with clients appropriately is one thing, taking over the counselling session and talking about yourself is something else.

In the psychodynamic approach, feelings that develop within the counsellor that become directed towards clients are thought to be examples of *counter-transference*. In the above example, this might indicate that the counsellor is experiencing his own mixed feelings concerning loss and bereavement, and unconsciously *projecting* them inappropriately onto his client. In person-centred counselling, feelings like these can become a useful part of the process, provided counsellors are aware of them and are willing to explore them to see if they have any meaning for their clients.

Congruence is defined in several different ways by Rogers. For example, the Rogers (1959) definition includes:

> *. . . when self-experiences are accurately symbolized (in awareness), and are included in the self-concept in this accurately symbolized form, then the state is one of congruence of self and experience . . . terms which are synonymous . . . [are] integrated, whole, genuine* (p. 206).

As Brodley (1995, private communication) points out, this definition is couched in terms of Rogers' distinction between self and experience, not in terms of counsellor's behaviour. This emphasis is consistent with Rogers' (1957a) definition where, in discussing the six necessary and sufficient conditions for therapeutic personality change, Rogers defined congruence in the following terms (p. 97):

> *. . . the counsellor should be, within the confines of this relationship, a congruent, genuine, integrated person. It means that within the relationship he is freely and deeply himself, with his actual experience accurately represented by his awareness of himself . . . It should be clear that this includes being himself even in ways which are not regarded as ideal for psychotherapy. His experience may be, 'I am afraid of this client', or, 'My attention is so focused on my own problems that I can scarcely listen to him'. If the counsellor is not denying these feelings to awareness, but is able freely to be them (as well as being other feelings), then the condition (congruence) we have stated is met.*

In counselling, congruence is a condition in the sense that it must be:

> *. . . a state or condition within the therapist. This state permits the therapist to succeed in his intentions to experience unconditional positive regard and empathic understanding. It does so by permitting the therapist to experience an unconflicted and undistracted dedication to acceptant empathy . . . The therapist's integrated authentic appearance facilitates the client's clear perception of the therapist's attitudes of unconditional positive regard and empathic understanding* (Brodley, 1995, private communication).

In ideal terms, the core-conditions (all subjective states or attitudes existing within the counsellor) need to be fully present together, but in practice it is rarely possible for a counsellor to be so consistent:

> *The theory predicts that to the extent the therapist experiences*
> *these three therapeutic attitudes while with the client, and if*
> *the client perceives the unconditional positive regard and the*
> *empathic understanding, to that extent the client will*
> *experience therapeutic change. The therapeutic attitudes are*
> *experienced only to some degree, not absolutely, in any*
> *relationship* (Brodley, 1995, ibid).

Because the therapeutic attitudes are seen as existing together rather than separately, it is not usually helpful to ascribe more importance to one or other of them, but Rogers did believe that counsellor congruence sometimes takes priority (Rogers, 1959, p. 215). In other words, at those times when counsellors are unable to experience empathic understanding, or are unable to be unconditionally accepting, then counsellors should be aware of those experiences, attend to them and allow them accurately into awareness. Most certainly, counsellors should not attempt to deny such experiences or distort them in awareness, because to do so would result in counsellors becoming unintegrated and thus incongruent in the relationship.

The question often arises about the degree to which it is necessary for counsellors directly to communicate their feelings and thoughts to their clients in pursuance of congruence. In his 1957 paper, Rogers did not refer to any necessity directly (or otherwise) to communicate congruence. He did, however, make the following comment:

> *It would take us too far afield to consider the puzzling matter*
> *as to the degree to which the therapist overtly communicates*
> *this reality [referring to a therapist who is afraid of a client, or*
> *unable to listen to the client] in himself to the client. Certainly*
> *the aim is not for the therapist to express or talk out his own*
> *feelings, but primarily that he should not be deceiving the client*
> *as to himself* (pp. 97–8).

Later (Rogers, 1959), the wording of the necessary and sufficient conditions changed slightly: 'The therapist is congruent (or genuine or real) in the relationship, his picture of himself and *the way he communicates* matches his immediate experiencing' (my italics). However, Rogers, in this instance, is still referring to the way a counsellor communicates, not what a counsellor communicates, and there is still no component of the condition that a counsellor *should* communicate thoughts and feelings that arise from within the counsellor's frame of reference.

In a 1980 article (Rogers and Sanford, 1980), the question of the communication of counsellor's thoughts and feelings was taken up again in the section on 'Genuineness or Congruence'. Here, Rogers and Sanford went into some detail:

> *Being real involves being thoroughly acquainted with the flow*
> *of experiencing going on within, a complex and continuing*

> *flow. It means being willing to express the attitudes that come*
> *persistently to the fore, especially perhaps the negative*
> *attitudes, inasmuch as the positive ones can rather easily be*
> *inferred from behavior and tone. If the therapist is bored with*
> *the client, it is only real to express this feeling ...* (p. 1381).

Rogers and Sanford gave a number of examples of therapists experiencing
and expressing negative feelings, including boredom and anger, but:

> *Note that in each instance the therapist is voicing a feeling*
> *within herself, not a fact or judgement about the client. To say,*
> *'I feel bored at the moment', does not pass any judgement on*
> *the client as a boring person. It merely puts into the relationship*
> *the basic data of the therapist's own feelings. As this boredom*
> *and sense of remoteness are shared, the therapist's feelings*
> *change; certainly she is not bored when trying to communicate*
> *self in this way. The therapist who expressed anger could then*
> *more clearly hear the client, and the client caught a glimpse of*
> *his own behavior, which seemed to have been hidden from him.*
> *The therapist is, in fact, quite sensitively eager to hear the*
> *client's response. Empathic responses begin again to be*
> *experienced. To be real is to reduce barriers* (p. 1382).

Rogers and Sanford realised that this concept could create difficulties and
was open to misinterpretation:

> *It certainly does not mean that the therapist burdens the client*
> *with all her problems or feelings. It does not mean that the*
> *therapist blurts out impulsively any attitude that comes to*
> *mind. It does mean, however, that the therapist does not deny*
> *to herself the feelings being experienced and that the therapist*
> *is willing to express, and to be, any persistent feelings that exist*
> *in the relationship* (p. 1382).

Key phrases here are 'the therapist does not deny to herself the feelings
being experienced', and 'the therapist is willing to express and to be any
persistent feelings that exist' (my italics). In other words, the critical issues
are the counsellor's ability to remain open to her experiencing without
the need to distort or deny that experiencing, and the existence of *persistent*
feelings, i.e. those that have remained for some time and are interfering
with the counsellor's experiencing of empathic understanding and
unconditional positive regard.

Finally, Mearns and Thorne (1988, p. 81), point out that congruent
communication is not the same as self-disclosure, and that being
congruent does not imply that a counsellor has to be open about herself
and her life:

> *When the counsellor is being congruent she is giving her*
> *genuinely felt response to the client's experience at that time.*
> *Only rarely would this response disclose elements of the*

counsellor's life, and even then the focus of attention would remain on the client rather than the counsellor (p. 82).

Some contemporary perspectives on the core conditions

Empathy

Bozarth has long warned against equating 'empathy' with 'reflection of feelings' (e.g. 1984/2001). He has suggested that, although a reflection can be empathic, it may also undermine the principles of the PCA if it places the locus of control and authority in the counsellor rather than in the client. His concern is that if 'reflection of feelings' becomes merely a verbal clarification technique, and is assumed to be the major (if not only) means of communicating empathic understanding, then other empathic modes become ignored. He argues that close, intuitive attention to the subjective world of the client allows for quite idiosyncratic forms of empathic communication to emerge. (See chapter 6 for further discussion of 'idiosyncratic empathy'.) Bozarth develops his argument in a later publication (Bozarth, 2001b), where he more explicitly links empathy with unconditional positive regard, and underlines his view that empathy is most accurately conceptualised as an 'attitude' rather than as any particular way of responding to a client.

Shlien (1997/2001) takes the view that empathy is not difficult to achieve, but the problem lies in 'how to use it wisely and well' (2001, p. 41). 'Empathy', he remarks,

> *has been taken as both a means and an end; it has become an easy substitute for the real motive, and the real work, in therapy — sympathy and understanding. Sympathy — 'feeling for' — is a type of commitment. Empathy is not. Is it perhaps time to call sympathy 'an unappreciated way of being'? In my view, it works at a higher stage of moral development than empathy . . . The difficult task is to understand. Empathy alone, without sympathy, and even more, without understanding, may be harmful* (2001, p. 41).

The significance of empathy has recently been explored in relation to work with severely disturbed clients (Binder and Binder, 2001), work with clients with cognitive disabilities (Zinschitz, 2001), and those experiencing what Warner (e.g. 2001) describes as 'fragile' and 'dissociated process'. It has been suggested that empathy is an evolved characteristic without which social organisation could not exist (Baughan and Merry, 2001), and Cooper (2001), in describing 'embodied empathy', argues that empathy can include a knowledge of how clients feel at a bodily level, in other words 'resonating with [the client] at a somatic — as well as a cognitive and affective — level' (p. 218).

Finally, Zimring (2000/2001), has proposed a new theory of change, in which he stresses the concept of 'self' as an ' involved, acting self involved in a transaction that is central . . . The person is not a separate object or entity, but rather is part of an interacting system' (Zimring, 2001, p. 88). Following from this, Zimring suggests three 'targets' for empathic understanding: the speaker's self-sense and self-reactions; the speaker's intentions within the transactions in which he or she is engaged, and the nature of the representations that are the context in which these intentional transactions are occurring (p. 93–4). In other words, he suggests that the person-centred counsellor responds to the client's intentions, i.e. to what the client is trying to convey about what is happening to him, not just to 'feelings'.

Zimring's belief is that, in responding empathically to intentions and transactions, the counsellor is demonstrating a belief in the validity of the person's intentions and inner world, and this leads to clients responding from an internal, rather than external frame of reference.

Congruence

In a review of the research literature published during the last few decades, Grafanaki (2001, p. 32) remarked that research has not adequately examined the concept of 'congruence', and its meaning and significance, and that it '. . . remains too general and abstract in theory and research literature, and its impact on therapy interaction and communication is still quite vague'.

Many writers point out that the 'Rogerian hypothesis' has never been properly tested by thorough research (e.g. Watson, 1984; Lockhart, 1984). In other words, Rogers' hypothesis was that there were six conditions that needed to be present in a relationship for it to be regarded as potentially therapeutic in client-centred terms, and no methodologically reliable research has been published that tests this hypothesis adequately. However, Orlinsky and Howard (1978) found that of 20 studies on therapist genuineness or congruence they reviewed, two thirds of them showed a significant relationship between genuineness and outcome. The picture from research studies is, then, somewhat unclear, though Patterson (1984) concluded, from his review of the research up to 1984, that 'the evidence for the necessity, if not the sufficiency of the therapist conditions of accurate empathy, respect or warmth and therapeutic genuineness is incontrovertible' (p. 437).

Seeman (2002) defines and discusses congruence in much broader 'human system model' terms, and describes it in a number of ways, including as involving, '. . . a directness and harmony, a free flow of communication, within our whole being at all levels of functioning, from biochemical processes up through interpersonal relationships' (p. 211). He regards congruence as being both a 'within-person process' and a 'between-person process' (p. 211) depending on the context at the time.

Ellingham (1999/2001) views the concept of 'congruence' with some major misgivings, and argues that Rogers' definition of congruence belongs to an obsolete Cartesian-Newtonian scientific paradigm. He calls for a reappraisal of the concept from a modern, holistic paradigm, more in keeping with the general thrust of Rogers work that is couched in process-oriented terms and concepts.

Finally, Barrett-Lennard (2002) has suggested five ways in which congruence contributes to effective interpersonal relationships, including counselling relationships. For example, he thinks that congruence facilitates trust, self-expression, self- and interpersonal exploration, perhaps in that order, and that congruence on the part of the listener enables the other person to be more open. In addition, Barrett-Lennard sees a kind of 'modelling' role where a congruent and communicative person encourages similar behaviour in others, and that while some factors of modern society tend to produce guardedness and incongruence, others give people more opportunities to be responsive to their own nature. Finally Barrett-Lennard suggests that a counsellor's faith and confidence in the importance of congruence increases its effectiveness as a therapeutic condition (p. 46).

Unconditional positive regard

Bozarth (2001) views unconditional positive regard, 'as the curative factor for the pathological development of personality', and asserts that 'This has to be true given Rogers' conceptualisation of personal dysfunctions being predicated upon the introjection of conditional positive regard by significant others and by society. Conditional regard is countered by the unconditional positive regard of the therapist' (p. 16). This position is echoed in the summary of person-centred theory given in chapter 4 of this book, and similarly by Wilkins (2001) whose view is that, 'if any condition is more important than another, it is the communication of unconditional positive regard' (p. 46). Wilkins believes it necessary for person-centred counsellors to accept that their ability to offer unconditional positive regard is limited, and then to try to address and expand those limits (p. 46).

Prouty (2001), in the context of 'Pre-Therapy' (see the brief discussion earlier in this chapter), has identified a number of possible 'components' of unconditional positive regard — non-sexual love, care, compassion, non-judgementalism, acceptance, nurturance, valuing, prizing and, finally, respect. In a similar vein, Lietaer (2001) views unconditional positive regard as having, 'aspects of dedication, confirmation and non-possessive warmth' (p. 105). He suggests that research has shown these dimensions of unconditional positive regard,

> *create[s] a high level of safety which helps unfreeze blocked areas of experience and to allow painful emotions in a climate of 'holding'; it functions as a medium for interpersonal corrective experiences through which self-acceptance, self-empathy and self-love are fostered; it helps the client to become more inner-directed, more trusting his organismic experience as a compass for living and hence to become a better 'therapist for himself'* (p. 105).

Freire (2001) echoes Bozarth in her estimation of the central importance of unconditional positive regard, and believes it to be 'the revolutionary feature of the person-centred approach' (p. 152), which has not been integrated into other counselling models. She views the unconditional acceptance of the client's experience as the counsellor's sole aim in person-centred therapy, and believes this to spring from the counsellor's trust in the client's actualising tendency. Finally, Friere makes explicit the need for counsellors to experience unconditional self-regard, as it is the extent of this experience that Friere believes determines the capacity of the counsellor to experience unconditional positive regard towards clients.

The 'core conditions' have, from time to time, been treated as a somewhat simplistic and inadequate formulation of what is both necessary and sufficient in the counselling context by those whose understanding of the PCA is itself limited and inadequate. As noted earlier, the core conditions are not, in themselves, regarded as sufficient, given that Rogers identified six conditions that needed to be present before a relationship could become a therapeutic one in a counselling context. A closer examination of the core conditions reveals them to be anything but simple, and their complexity is best appreciated by those who attempt to 'live them' in relation to others, whether clients in counselling or not. It is, perhaps, best to view the core conditions together as a set of attitudes which are most likely to be experienced by another person as facilitative and encouraging of personal risk-taking. They are *embodied* by the counsellor as a person whose genuine aim is to offer non-judgemental understanding, rather than *adopted* instrumentally as 'techniques' or 'strategies' aimed at producing particular, pre-determined effects or outcomes.

The counsellor as a person

In many of the helping professions, people are taught that getting too involved with clients is something to avoid. They are advised to retain a professional distance, to remain objective, and outside of the client's world.

On the face of it, this is good advice. To over-identify with clients in distress and to worry about their welfare excessively might lead us to become so bound up in their worlds that we find it increasingly difficult to return to our own. On the other hand, taking an objective, distant and uninvolved stance will have the effect that people see us as only having a professional interest in them, that we are not really concerned about them as individuals with unique life stories.

Person-centred counsellors try to engage with their clients in ways that go beyond simply taking a professional interest. They are prepared to be moved by their clients, to respond to them as one person to another, and to show genuine concern and care. Person-centred counselling sees it as most important that counsellors are aware of themselves in their relationships with clients, aware of all their thoughts, feelings and emotions. At first sight, this seems a difficult if not impossible task. On the one hand, counsellors are expected to attend closely to their client's frame of reference, and to put aside their own value judgements. On the other hand, counsellors are asked to remain aware of their own internal process, at least to some significant extent. The resolution of this paradox resides within the counsellor's intention to dedicate him or herself to a process of becoming familiar with the world as it is experienced by another person (the client). This process involves an active attention to the client's frame of reference, but it does not imply a loss of the counsellor's sense of self. Indeed, the way we feel about our clients, our own experiences of fear, or boredom, or love towards our clients at different times, are all important factors in the development of a genuine relationship in which each makes a difference to the other.

Trust

Counsellors who are able empathically to understand their clients, and who are non-judgemental and congruent, are likely to be regarded by clients as genuinely trustworthy. Trust is an important element in all relationships — its presence enables us to be more open and less defensive with each other.

In counselling, trust is something that is earned as clients realise that their counsellors are not concerned with manipulating them, and that acceptance is not conditional on behaving in ways that will win approval. One understandable concern that clients have is, 'How far can I trust my counsellor to accept parts of me that I can scarcely accept myself?' If clients can begin to see us as genuinely concerned for them, that our unconditional positive regard is not just something we put on or use as a technique, then they can begin to see us as reliable and safe.

The client is in charge: the non-directive attitude

At one time, person-centred counselling was known as 'non-directive counselling'. This term fell out of use when the terms 'client-centred' and then 'person-centred' were adopted. However, the non-directive nature of person-centred counselling remains just as important, even though the name has changed. The meaning of 'non-directive' has often been misunderstood, and I need here to be clear what I mean by it.

Firstly, the term 'non-directive' does not mean 'being passive', or 'doing nothing'. It refers to an underlying attitude that contributes to the quality of the relationship between client and counsellor. The client is regarded as the 'expert' in his or her life, and the counsellor is intent only on creating the kind of relationship in which this expertise can be expressed. There is an absence, on the counsellor's part, of controlling or directing the course of the counselling. The counsellor does not choose the 'agenda' for the client, or attempt to control or determine the processes that occur within the client.

A non-directive relationship enables clients to experience the freedom to choose for themselves the directions they gradually discover are important to them. It demonstrates a trust in them and their tendency to actualise in positive and creative ways in an environment that facilitates the exploration of all aspects of 'self', both positive and negative.

Non-directiveness, then, refers to a general non-authoritarian attitude maintained by a counsellor whose intention is empathically to understand a client's subjective experience. It refers also to the theory that the actualising tendency can be fostered in a relationship of particular qualities, and that whilst the general direction of that tendency is regarded as constructive and creative, its particular characteristics in any one person cannot be predicted, and should not be controlled or directed. This attitude is reflected in the behaviour of the counsellor through his or her trust in the capacity of clients to discover their own internal resources for change. Because of this, the person-centred counsellor does not value giving directions, making interpretations or suggestions, or behaving in any way that is likely to distract the client from focusing on his or her own experiencing, feelings and meanings.

However, it is probably not possible to avoid influencing people to some extent in any relationship, and often that influencing will be unintentional. For example, what we choose to respond to, even if the response itself is empathic, might influence the direction of counselling if we have chosen to respond to one thing at the expense of another. Similarly, our own world-views, prejudices and moral values are likely to affect how we respond and what we respond to. The point here is not to deny that unintended influence and direction might result from the ways in which we respond to our clients, but to acknowledge the intention to maintain an attitude as free as possible of the desire to control or direct people towards particular predetermined goals.

Finally, it is important to recognise that counselling is a process involving influence — if this were not the case there would be little point in establishing a counselling relationship in the first place. In an unpublished paper, C. H. Patterson remarks that, 'The goal of this influence is to free and foster the process of self-actualisation in the client. This is a goal not chosen by either the therapist or the client — it is given by the nature of the client as a living organism.'

In a recent article, Merry and Brodley (2002) remark:

> *The process of change in client-centered therapy is predictable only in very general terms. It is idiosyncratic and, in detail, unpredictable for each individual. It is this unpredictability, and the person-specific unique processes that it represents, that makes therapist attempts to direct the process both unnecessary and countertherapeutic. Directivity implies foreknowledge both of the destination and of the most efficient way of arriving there. Because each client's 'journey' is personal and idiosyncratic, direction needs to emerge from within the client, supported by the understanding relationship, rather than imposed by the therapist (p. 72).*

The question of power

The non-directive attitude in person-centred counselling acts to minimise the possibility that the counsellor behaves, either knowingly or not, in ways that diminish the client's autonomy. In this regard, Grant (1990/2002) distinguishes between 'instrumental' and 'principled' non-directiveness. 'Instrumental' non-directiveness he regards as akin to a technique, in that it is an attitude adopted by the counsellor because the counsellor regards it as helpful to the client. 'Principled' non-directiveness, on the other hand, Grant regards as more akin to a moral choice, i.e. to respect clients as autonomous individuals. Principled non-directiveness is an expression both of respect for the client's own self-resources, and of the determination on the counsellor's part not to control the course of the counselling, but to follow the client's individual process as it unfolds.

The person-centred counselling relationship explicitly challenges the traditionally accepted role of the counsellor as expert, and replaces it with a more collaborative and egalitarian one, which Natiello (2001) has described as being 'in radical conflict with the prevailing paradigm of authoritarian power' (p. 11). Proctor (2002) has characterised the non-directive attitude as one that 'certainly challenges the fundamental inequality in the roles of therapist and client in its emphasis on the person-to-person relationship and its focus on the "*power-from-within*" or "*personal power*" of each person' (p. 103).

The possibilities for the abuse of power within the counselling relationship are ever present, but person-centred counselling confronts these possibilities and overcomes them in a number of ways. Firstly, as already mentioned, the non-directive attitude is an important buffer against the misuse of power. Secondly, the guiding principle of the PCA — the existence of the actualising tendency — means that attempts to direct the process of counselling in any instrumental way is considered countertherapeutic. Thirdly, the metaphor of the person-centred counsellor as an 'empathic companion', with its overtones of mutuality, rather than as a 'guide' or 'expert', places the source of directivity where it belongs, i.e. with the client. Finally, the acknowledgement that counselling is a means of accessing the internal, self-healing resources of clients, frees the counsellor from having to make 'interventions' and enables her to focus attention on the creation of a facilitative relationship as the context within which self-healing can occur.

Values, qualities and attitudes are not a prescription

It is important to emphasise that nothing I have said about the core conditions, or any of the qualities, values and attitudes characteristic of person-centred counselling, amount to a prescription of how to do person-centred counselling. Exactly how each one of us puts these qualities and so on into practice with clients will be determined by our own preferences and ways of communicating. Person-centred counselling is not about how to do something correctly; it is about discovering your own capacity to empathise with others, and your own 'way of being' with people. This book can offer some perspectives on the theory and philosophy of this approach, and it can encourage you to experiment with your relationships with others (and with yourself) so that you find a way of being with people that is authentic for you, and which conveys your intent to understand them and their worlds. We can all become more skilled at conveying what we mean, we can all develop higher levels of empathy and we can all work towards becoming more congruent and more open to experience.

The counselling relationship ...
The core conditions and the generally non-directive stance of the counsellor can readily be thought of as attitudes or personal qualities displayed by the counsellor; they do not describe techniques, and this is the most obvious difference between person-centred counselling and many other forms of counselling. In other words, person-centred counselling is built on the relationship between client and counsellor, rather than on techniques that can be learned. In Rogers' words, it is a *way of being* with people, rather than a way of doing something to them. (This is not to say that there are no *skills* involved in person-centred counselling. I shall be looking more closely at skills later.)

... not technique
It is partly because of this lack of emphasis on technique that person-centred counselling has been misunderstood in the past. Carl Rogers sometimes despaired at the way person-centred counselling was misrepresented (say what the client last said, say 'Hm', ask open questions etc.). While these things, and others, may be useful, they are not the essence of person-centred counselling. Rogers, as I have said before, even had difficulty with the term 'reflection of feelings'. For him, this was too passive. What he was doing was checking how well he had understood his clients' words and feelings. He was not passively 'reflecting' in the way that a mirror reflects, but actively striving to understand his clients' ways of being ever more deeply.

Staying with the client

Everything I have said so far points in one direction — the counsellor aims to stay as closely attuned as possible to the client's subjective experiencing. The counsellor tries to put aside his or her own ideas about what the client should do, or needs to do, and instead is concerned to follow the direction taken by the client. The counsellor is a genuine, non-judgemental, empathic and non-directive companion dedicated to providing the conditions in which the client can feel accepted and respected. Once again I stress that this is a process, not something that is necessarily established at the beginning, but one that is worked towards.

Staying with the client — in the client's frame of reference — doesn't always happen naturally. It often seems, especially at first, as if this somehow is not enough, that something else should be done to further the client's progress towards becoming more fulfilled and less defensive. Nevertheless, the idea of being an empathic companion is so central to person-centred counselling that it will help if we take a closer look at its implications. One way to do that is to take some examples of counselling that stray outside the client's frame of reference, and think through what might be some of the effects of that on the counselling process. This next exercise focuses on some counsellor responses, and compares them with responses that are more closely attuned to the client's experiencing.

Exercise: Staying with the client

Aims of the exercise
To show how we can unwittingly move away from the client's frame of reference. To practise ways of responding which stay closer to the client's experiencing.
What to do
Read each client/counsellor interaction, and discuss with your group, or think on your own, about how you might have responded. Remember, there is no perfect counselling response, but some are more likely to help clients move forward than others, and some might serve to put a complete stop on the proceedings.

1. Imposing values
CLIENT: I've got myself into so much trouble. My parents don't know I've been sleeping with my boyfriend for some time . . . we do love each other . . . but now I'm pregnant. I just don't know what to do for the best . . . I want to go to college soon, but I couldn't with a baby. I don't know how to tell my Mum, or even if I should.
COUNSELLOR: *Well, you really ought to tell your Mum and Dad, I'm sure they'll understand, parents usually do. You could put off going to college for a while, you're still young enough.*

2. Telling the client what the problem is
CLIENT: My partner and I just don't talk much any more about anything. We used to talk a lot about things, make decisions together, but these days we just sit in silence most of the time. We don't do much together either. If I don't suggest something, nothing happens. I don't know what's wrong, or how we got like this.
COUNSELLOR: *You've drifted apart, lost touch with each other. This often happens after a few years of living together. You've probably got different interests and ideas now.*

3. Telling clients how they are feeling

CLIENT: I don't sleep much these days, and I worry about things all the time. I don't seem to have much energy and I don't do half the things I used to. I get bad-tempered if anyone tries to get me to do anything. The house is a mess, but I can't bring myself to clean it up. This morning I couldn't even be bothered to take the dog for a walk.

COUNSELLOR: *You're over-anxious and depressed — this often happens when people are under some kind of stress.*

4. Giving advice

CLIENT: My boss is always complaining about me these days. My work isn't any different from anyone else's, but as far as he's concerned I can't do anything right. He picks on me all the time, and it's so unfair. It all seemed to start when he made a pass at me a couple of months ago, and I turned him down.

COUNSELLOR: *You should speak to your Union Officer about it, or think about leaving.*

5. Asking closed or leading questions

CLIENT: I feel lonely most of the time, even though we have a big family, there are seven of us kids. The others seem to be OK, but I feel out of things most of the time, and do most things on my own. Nobody seems to take much notice of me, and I find myself going my own way most of the time. I'd like to feel more a part of things, but I just don't.

COUNSELLOR: *When did you first notice you were feeling this way?*

6. Asking for more information

CLIENT: Since my mother died, I haven't really felt well in myself. I get nervous about going out, and I don't like meeting new people. I spend most of my time at home, sometimes I don't even answer the phone, not that it rings that much. At weekends I sometimes don't go out of the house at all, and on Monday mornings I feel sick when I have to go to work.

COUNSELLOR: *How long ago did your mother die? Do you have any other family?*

7. Identifying with the client

CLIENT: Since my marriage broke up I haven't had any interest in any new relationships. I don't go to places where I might meet anyone, I just don't like doing that, and I don't want to do it. My friends say I'm becoming a recluse, that I should get out and meet people, but I can't be bothered.

COUNSELLOR: *I know what you mean. It took me three years to get over*

my divorce, but like you, I enjoyed being on my own for a while.
CLIENT: No, I don't like being on my own, but I don't want to take the risk of being hurt again, or getting into a sexual thing that I can't control.
COUNSELLOR: *Yes, I know. Many people go off sex for a while, I know I did.*
CLIENT: Well, sex is the one thing I miss most.

8. Being over-reassuring

CLIENT: I feel like I must be getting ill with something serious. I keep seeing things, and getting dizzy spells. I'm really afraid of dying. My father died of cancer, and I'm terrified it might be hereditary or something. I keep getting these headaches, and I really feel in a panic.
COUNSELLOR: *I'm sure there's nothing much wrong with you. A lot of people get dizzy spells, and I'm sure cancer isn't passed on.*

9. Being uncomfortable with silence

CLIENT: I feel very close to some kind of crisis. Maybe it won't be a bad thing, but it feels like some big change is about to happen for me. It scares me quite a bit, it's like I'm anticipating something, but I don't know what it is. I need to spend some time thinking about it, or just being with it, there's not much I can actually say about it.
(Very short pause)
COUNSELLOR: *Do you have any idea what it is?*

10. Blocking emotions

CLIENT: I feel really angry with my ex-husband. He's started phoning me up all day and all night. I try to tell him how angry I am about it, but he just won't listen at all. I can feel the anger coming up just talking about him . . . the way he treated us . . . and now he wants things from me . . . Jesus . . . sometimes I feel I could kill him if he does it any more. I'd like to break his neck. If he walked in here now I'd murder him.
COUNSELLOR: *Try and relax, and tell me how all this started.*

11. Talking about others

CLIENT: Every time I see my father, we end up having a big row. Give us two minutes and we're at each other's throats. He's just so closed minded about everything, and stuck in his ways. I feel like kicking him whenever I see him. It didn't used to be like that, we used to be quite good friends, but I just can't stand the sight of him now. He finds fault in everything I do.
COUNSELLOR: *Maybe your father is as upset by all these rows as you seem to be.*

12. Being analytical

CLIENT: I just don't seem to be able to find anyone I really like enough to want to be with them other than as a friend. I'd like to find someone special, but I'm very suspicious of most of the men I meet. I mean, they seem all right at first, then it all starts going wrong. I'm afraid I'll end up with someone like my father, always running off and getting drunk. He used to be quite violent sometimes when he drank too much.

COUNSELLOR: *You probably still have unresolved feelings towards your father, and this is why you're still so afraid of men — because they remind you of him in some way.*

Commentary on the exercise

I hope the exercise helped you to frame responses that were more open and understanding than the ones given above. In all of the above examples the counsellor is trying to be helpful, and the counsellor's intention is clearly to help the client go further, or think things through further. The trouble with most of them is that they do not really respect the client's ability to come to his or her own conclusions, and they often serve to close down exploration rather than open it up. What follows is a more detailed analysis of how the counsellor moves outside of the client's experiencing.

1. This response is an obvious imposition of a set of values which may be miles away from those of the client. In any case, it is not the counsellor's job to be providing value judgements at all. Much better would have been to reflect the various dilemmas this client faces, and help her explore ways in which she might deal with the situation herself.

2. This is a diagnosis of this person's problem. The counsellor cannot possibly know what the situation is, or whether these two people have developed other interests or not. The response comes from within the counsellor's frame of reference: it does not try to get into the client's shoes at all.

3. This is another diagnosis. According to the counsellor the client is stressed, and this explains the problem. There might very well be some stress here, but a much better response would have been one that showed some understanding of the different feelings the client is having, and not an attempt to generalise the problem.

4. In different circumstances, this might be very good advice. But again, it is not the counsellor's job to advise clients about how to solve their problems. Better would have been to understand the client's feelings

about her boss's unwelcome advance and its consequences, and to help the client explore her own strategies for dealing with them, if that is what she chose to do.

5. In training groups I encourage people to try not asking any questions at all, particularly not closed questions like this. Sometimes questions, if they are open and exploratory, or which reflect a counsellor's genuine need for information in order to understand the client better, are helpful in enabling counsellors to deepen their empathic understanding, but closed questions are hardly ever of any use at all.

    Again, it would have been better to try to understand the client's loneliness, and to offer some understanding of it. This would have had the beneficial effect of the client feeling heard.

6. Asking for more information often brings with it the feeling that the information given so far is somehow not enough, or not valuable enough, or that it is the counsellor who knows what information is most valuable. Also, such questions have the effect of leading and directing the client's narrative. There is plenty of feeling in this client's statement so far to be able to understand something of how life is for her at the moment. Better to respond to this with empathy than ask for something else.

    One question I would like all counsellors to strike from their list would be, 'How did that make you feel?' Usually this question comes in response to a statement from the client that was bursting with emotion — but the counsellor just did not hear it!

7. This speaks for itself. This counsellor identified with the client, and thought he knew how the client must feel. He was wrong twice.

8. This client's fear of death is real and understandable, particularly as she witnessed her own father's death. The counsellor simply ignores this very real fear, and offers something not very helpful at all. To go on now and explore feelings about death and illness would be very difficult for this client: after all, she's been practically told she's making it all up!

    It would be a good idea, however, to check out with this client, at some appropriate point, whether she had sought some medical advice.

9. Being able to stay with silences and be comfortable with them can be very difficult for some people. But in counselling, silences are often very important. Clients need the space and time to feel things and let them develop. This counsellor jumps in with a question, but the client has already said how hard it is to talk about what he feels.

    Clients often work very hard during silences. They will share their feelings with you when they are ready to, and when you have shown yourself to be trustworthy.

10. Counselling being what it is, clients often need to express very strongly felt emotions. These might be, for example, despair, feeling suicidal, feeling violently angry or feeling great love and affection. Whatever they are, it is essential that counsellors are not afraid of emotions, can be comfortable with their expression, and not feel the need to dampen them down.

This counsellor appears to be afraid of anger and its open expression.

11. One of the commonest mistakes I see with counsellors in training is the way they latch on inappropriately to people other than the client. This client's father is not in the room, and it's very doubtful if the client knows how his father feels anyway. Besides, the counsellor is there to help the client make sense of *his* world and *his* feelings.

Getting the client to talk about someone else in this way is likely to take him away from his present feelings. The counsellor should try to stay within the client's frame of reference as much as possible, but in this example, the counsellor has diverted attention away from the client's direct experience.

12. This is a home-spun version of Freudianism, which is dangerous because it is the counsellor's own theory and shows ignorance and insecurity. It might very well be true that this client has unresolved feelings about her violent father, but is it helpful to point this out in this way? I think probably not. Much better would be to stay with this client and her feelings, and help her explore her past feelings when she is ready to do so, and in her own way.

In general

Most of the above are examples of counsellors trying too hard to 'do counselling', rather than form acceptant, understanding relationships with their clients. In person-centred terms, counselling is not something that one person does to another. Change happens when two people experience a relationship that is understanding, non-judgemental and authentic *in the way that Rogers defined and understood those terms.*

In person-centred counselling, clients are offered relationships that they discover to be trustworthy, where their innermost feelings can be expressed without fear, and where they are respected and valued as people in a process of change. This is why the basic attitudes and values of the counsellor are so important. Technique cannot hide a lack of understanding, or a judgemental attitude, neither can it make up for a counsellor who hides behind a role or facade and is unable or unwilling to meet clients person to person.

Checklist: Counsellor attitudes

Carl Rogers offered a series of questions he asked himself about his ability to form creative therapeutic relationships with his clients. We give an abbreviated form here — it is useful as a kind of checklist that can certainly be used in training, but ought to be returned to periodically throughout one's professional life.

Before you read through these ideas, you may like to take some time now to stop and think through what kinds of questions you have about yourself and your abilities to form good relationships with clients. Then compare your questions with the ones offered by Carl Rogers:

- *Can I be, in some way which will be perceived by the other person as trustworthy, as dependable or consistent in some deep sense?*
- *Can I be expressive enough as a person to communicate unambiguously what I am?*
- *Can I let myself experience positive attitudes towards this other person — attitudes of warmth, caring, liking, interest, respect?*
- *Can I be strong enough as a person to be separate from the other? Can I be a sturdy respecter of my own feelings, my own needs as well as his?*
- *Am I secure enough within myself to permit him his separateness? Can I permit him to be what he is — honest or deceitful, infantile or adult, despairing or over-confident? Can I give him the freedom to be? Or do I feel that he should follow my advice, or remain somewhat dependent on me, or mould himself after me?*
- *Can I let myself enter fully into the world of his feelings and personal meaning and see these as he does? Can I step into his private world so completely that I lose all desire to evaluate or judge it?*
- *Can I receive him as he is? Can I communicate this attitude? Or can I only receive him conditionally, acceptant of some aspects of his feelings and silently or openly disapproving of other aspects?*
- *Can I act with sufficient sensitivity in the relationship for my behaviour not to be perceived as a threat?*
- *Can I free him from the threat of external evaluation? In almost every phase of our lives — at home, at school, at work — we find ourselves under the rewards and punishments of external judgements.*
- *Can I meet this person as a person who is in the process of becoming or will I not be open enough to the many possibilities for change both in him and in myself?*

Working at 'relational depth': the kid with the chips

6

The term 'relational depth' is a useful one coined by David Mearns, who succinctly describes its meaning in the following way:

> *Only when they [the core conditions] are all present in high degree do they unite into their mutually enhancing integration and offer the client something really special. They offer a relationship of incredible safety and vitality in which even the most feared dimensions of existence can be faced. This is what is meant by offering the client a meeting at 'relational depth'. Here, we are not interested in a 'partial' representation of the therapeutic relationship where the counsellor is fairly empathic, quite accepting and moderately congruent — that is offering nothing more than a tolerable 'therapeutic alliance'* (Mearns and Thorne, 2000, p. 87; see also Mearns, 1996, 1997).

The extract with which I started the previous chapter is from a first counselling session. Although it is true that, to some extent, the counsellor is experiencing the core conditions, the relationship is very new and, unsurprisingly, little work is yet being done that would qualify as 'relational depth'. The session represents a useful and constructive beginning in which a relationship is initiated, and some real progress made. Some counselling relationships become established very quickly, and incredibly deep material can be worked on very early in the relationship, but this is not often the case in my experience. It seems to me that clients need time to establish their trust in the counsellor and in the relationship as one of consistent safety. As far as the counsellor is concerned, this process is not one simply of doing and saying the 'right' things in a somewhat mechanical fashion in an attempt to appear to the client as trustworthy. The level of trust that is required to operate at relational depth can only be found in a counsellor who has deeply and authentically integrated the core conditions into him or herself. If that process is well advanced, he or she will be experienced by clients as 'living' the core conditions, rather than making 'empathic responses' that may accurately reflect surface issues but fail to resonate with the deeper and perhaps most defended aspects of the client's sense of self. This is the most crucial aspect of person-centred counselling that is so often overlooked by those who regard it as no more than a strategy to establish 'rapport' with clients, before moving on to a more technique-led approach. It is crucial because it highlights the very real differences that exist between person-centred counselling and other approaches, including those from the humanistic school.

Person-centred counselling requires what Rogers termed 'a way of being' with people, and others have described as particular qualities of 'presence'. These concepts are scientifically imprecise, and do not lend themselves easily to objective measurement, if at all. They refer, at least in part, to the intention of the counsellor to engage directly and openly with clients in a process that requires transforming the concept of the core conditions from 'technical expertise' to a genuine existential encounter.

My use of the term 'existential encounter' deserves some explanation here. I mean the term to express a meeting of two persons that goes beyond the commonplace, the everyday meetings that are characteristic of much of our daily lives. The 'everyday self' is the defended, public self that keeps our internal, private and subjective world from being deeply known by others. It is often necessary for us to present ourselves to the world in this defended manner, because not to do so makes us vulnerable to the judgements and critical evaluations of others. Until we do share our most inner, subjective self, we do not, however, feel met and understood at any real depth. The therapeutic 'existential encounter' to which I refer goes far beyond the ritualised meetings familiar to us all, so that aspects of self that are usually held in reserve emerge without the usual layers of defensiveness.

I'd like to stress that achieving relational depth is a matter of 'process'. It is not something that is always achieved with every client, and some clients do not welcome it, nor do they feel a need to work at depth. It is not my intention to imply that work on more 'surface' issues is somehow wasted or not 'proper counselling' — far from it. In short-term work, for example, there may simply not be enough time to achieve a relationship of consistently deep trust. Clients are the arbiters of 'depth', and will work in a way that is comfortable for them, or just on the edge of comfort. A counsellor who is too keen to achieve relational depth is in danger of forcing the pace, or setting goals for clients, and this is likely to compromise the non-directive essence of person-centred counselling.

On the other hand, counsellors who never, or very rarely, achieve what they consider to be relational depth, even with long-term clients, should, perhaps, examine the extent to which they are experiencing and offering the core conditions consistently. This may be something to be explored in supervision.

The brief extracts presented below are not fictitious, but not entirely factual either in order to protect anonymity and confidentiality[1]. Details have been changed, but the essence remains true to the original and is an

---

1. Client material used with permission.

accurate representation of it. The words in italics are my thoughts and feelings that reflect my internal process as the sessions proceed.

From the 7th session:

GEORGE: Often it all seems pointless, what's the point of trying to get somewhere. There's nowhere to go anyway . . . Nothing works, nothing takes away this terrible feeling that I'll always be alone . . . except the alcohol sometimes, but then there's a price to pay later . . . It's like I have no . . . life.

TONY: It just feels so hopeless to you . . . there doesn't seem to be a place for you anywhere . . . kind of drained of life?

I feel for him. I can sense something of his desperation, the pointlessness of it all. Fleetingly, I feel I need a drink myself. I imagine what it might be like to feel so alone, and that this feeling will never leave me. I don't like the feeling, it almost makes me shudder.

GEORGE: Yes . . . empty . . . except for this terrible lonely feeling . . . that's all there is. It's why I drink so much . . . for a time I feel nothing at all.

TONY: It seems better to feel nothing than to feel this awful thing of being so alone.

The power of his words, especially the word 'empty' impresses me, though they are spoken softly. I feel inadequate for a moment or two. I want to reach out to him, and offer him some friendship, but this is an impulse and quickly passes, though the sentiment behind it stays with me. I want, just for this hour perhaps, to be genuinely by his side, but I don't know how much companionship he wants, or could tolerate. I certainly don't want to force myself on him.

From the 11th session:

GEORGE: I feel very close to the end . . . I don't mean I want to kill myself, but it is as if I'm dying slowly . . . I'm killing myself with drink. But the drink is my only real friend . . . my friend is killing me . . . it's just slower, that's all. I'm on the edge of a cliff, looking down, but I can't see anything, anyone.

TONY: It feels, kind of step by step, little by little, slowly getting near some final point. It's like the brief comfort you get from the drink is also a destroyer, and you just can't see anyone or anything, it's all kind of empty . . .

This is the 'pit' that George has described before, empty, without soul. He feels alone in it. I wish I could find a way in, but I just want to stand by, be there, even if he doesn't really notice me. Part of me wants to wave to him. I know I must respect his right to stand at his cliff-edge, but I want him to notice me if he can. It's also OK by me if he doesn't want me there. When I reach into myself, I recognise something of the emptiness of which he speaks, but it is his empty space, not mine.

GEORGE: Yes, each step a bit closer . . . I don't feel I'm in charge of it . . .it seems inevitable . . . sort of drifting . . .
TONY: Kind of unable to stop it, you just feel it . . . 'I'm going to fall, and there's nothing I can do'.

I'm experiencing a deep empathy for George at this moment. There doesn't seem to be any barriers between us, at least I don't feel as if I'm preventing myself from really meeting him. (I shouldn't assume it is the same for him, though. I guess it probably isn't.) For a time it has felt as if he just hasn't the energy or the will to keep me at a distance, and my feeling of closeness to him may simply be my imagination. I'm not sure if he really senses my presence at all. But I certainly am aware of his presence. Paradoxically, it is a powerful presence.

GEORGE: I don't know why I'm coming here every week . . . it feels like a waste of time . . . I feel close to a kind of death . . . I can't stop it, yet here I am again . . . just a waste of time, for both of us.
TONY: You kind of feel, 'No-one can help me, this doesn't help. I'm going to fall, whatever happens'. To be so alone, so lonely . . . It feels desperate to me George, and I want to say, I'm here, and this really isn't a waste of time for me. I want to be here with you right now.

At first, I was surprised, but then I realised how consistent this was with everything he had said before. And I feel recognised by him; he feels it's a waste of time for both of us, not just him. My impulse to reach out to him is not just 'rescuing'. I really do feel I am here for him and with him. I want to be direct about it. He moves me, I feel touched by him.

GEORGE: [He begins to cry softly, silently] I've always known this would happen . . . that I'd never be able . . . to . . . live.
TONY: It goes back such a long way . . . 'I'll never be able to be truly alive in this world.'

I realise I've been speaking in the first person, but I know he isn't confused by that. It seems natural to me. I am deeply struck by the magnitude of his despair. Though I can feel some of that despair in myself, for him and for myself, I am not intimidated or overwhelmed by it. It's as if his despair awakens some life in me that I'd forgotten about. My spoken words seem inadequate to me.

GEORGE: Yes, it seems crazy to come from such a big family and yet feel so alone . . . not part of anything, not part of life, somehow.
TONY: So many people around, but no-one for you, kind of?
GEORGE: Yes, no-one for me, and I was and am no-one for anybody.

I hadn't really appreciated this last part — that he had no-one for himself, but also that he felt he was no-one to anybody else, and still feels that way. His need for contact and intimacy was frustrated at every turn. He never received it, and he never gave it. Yet, again paradoxically, I feel an intimacy with him right now and, strangely, a sense that he is offering me that intimacy. I am glad to accept it.

GEORGE: What was wrong with me . . . that others seemed to have so much of something, but I didn't?

TONY: You think, maybe it was in you, maybe there was something wrong in you, that nobody came to you, or asked for you?

GEORGE: Yes, and . . . and . . . I'm not sure why I'm saying these things here. Why do I say them, I don't like to hear them, to hear myself saying them?

TONY: Something about being here makes it OK to say and feel these things, even though you hate hearing yourself?

It occurs to me that there is a part of him that wants (needs), however tentatively, to express these despairing feelings and thoughts. It also occurs to me that my presence here makes it somewhat safe, though not totally safe, to do so. I am full of respect, even admiration for him; this is painful to say the least. That word 'painful' now I look at it again, seems so inadequate.

GEORGE: I don't feel pushed into saying them, but I'm pushing myself to say them . . . to somebody . . . to you. To myself, I suppose. I don't want to jump over the edge, and I don't want just to fall. There's more to say, I feel it. But I don't know what it is.

TONY: It's a big effort to say things out loud, you have to kind of force yourself to do it, and to hear yourself say them to me. I get something like, you don't want to give up on it, and there's more, somewhere.

I have a sense of something changing. I don't feel quite as 'heavy' as I did earlier in the session. I don't want to overestimate it, but is there something in George that's trying to get out now? I don't know. I am tired, even a bit exhausted. This is unusual for me with George. Part of me is glad that the time is up. I think he is glad about that, too.

From the 12th session

GEORGE: I went out on a real binge after last week. I went to a pub in S, a place I don't usually go to. I drank most of the evening, and I got a bottle of Scotch and drank it all when I got home. I just wanted it to stop. After last week, I just felt, fuck it, what is all this about? What's the good of this? All evening, I kept thinking, what's the fucking good of this?

TONY: You mean, what's the good of this . . . coming here, talking about it?

GEORGE: No, I mean what's the good of this sitting around getting pissed half the time. It's all just a waste.

I'm not sure what's happening. He's talked about the pointlessness of drinking before, but not quite like this. He's more animated about it now. He seems more angry.

TONY: Can you say some more? I'm not sure if I get you, really.
GEORGE: I haven't got much more to say. The drinking is a waste of a life . . . my life. But what have I got anyway, what is it I'm wasting? *[Pause of about 8 minutes]*.

There's nothing for me to do and nothing I can say that won't feel intrusive right now. I sit and wait. I try not to let my mind wander. Is he angry with me, with himself, with his family? All three? I don't know. I look at him, I don't want to wander off and leave him on his own, but I don't know how to be with him at this moment.

GEORGE: You know what I'd really like? When I was a kid we went to Cornwall. Me, my mum and dad and one of my sisters. I must have been about six years old. I just remember the sea, the sunshine and the ice-cream. We had chips on the beach. I'd like to sit on the beach and have some chips.

I am listening very carefully. I see a kid on the beach eating chips. I used to do that in Cornwall. Strangely enough, I want to cry.

TONY: Strangely enough, I want to cry.
GEORGE: Me too.
TONY: I have no idea why.
GEORGE: Me neither.
TONY: Do you want to go for a swim?
GEORGE: I'm not allowed to.
TONY: OK.
GEORGE: You're a good bloke.
TONY: Thanks. So are you.

I have no idea what's going on 'technically', but I suddenly sense a real bond between us. The impulse to cry has gone. I remember my dad teaching my sister and me to swim in Cornwall. We used to camp in a field. There were no proper camping sites in those days. It rained a lot.

GEORGE: It rained a lot.
TONY: I know.

Part of me wonders what this is about, but I'm really not concerned too much about the content right now. There's a process going on here that's difficult to make sense of, cognitively speaking. It feels to me like a recognition of the humanity that exists within and between us. On one level, it's just two men sitting together and talking about the past. At another level, this is what I mean by an 'existential encounter'. It's actually good to be with this man at the moment. It's time to end. He looks at me, gets up, and prepares to leave.

GEORGE: See you next week.
TONY: OK.

From the 13ᵗʰ session (last ten or fifteen minutes)

GEORGE: I can't say I'm going to stop drinking. I don't know if I'll ever stop drinking. What I can say is that I don't like drinking. I never liked it. I just do it. I know why I do it, and I know it doesn't work. Look, I'm going on holiday next week, I won't be able to come.
TONY: OK
GEORGE: Believe it or not, I'm going to Cornwall. I don't really know why. I never go anywhere on holiday. I don't like holidays. Maybe I'm not going on holiday. Maybe I'm just going . . . [pause]
TONY: For some chips on the beach?
GEORGE: Yes. Sort of. There's more to it . . . [pause]
TONY: I know.
GEORGE: Part of me is just a kid on a beach all on his own, part of me's just a drunk. God knows where the other bits are, if there are any. I don't believe in all that inner child crap, not really. It might be a big disaster, this chips business. I'm not trying to recapture a golden moment, I don't have any golden moments.
TONY: But it sounds to me like a search for something . . . that might go wrong?
GEORGE: Yes, but not a quest.
TONY: No, not a quest.
GEORGE: You know what I'm talking about, don't you?
TONY: I think so. To go back and start again?
GEORGE: Maybe, to go back, yes. To start again, maybe. I did think, maybe. Is this therapy?
TONY: Cornwall, or here?
GEORGE: Here, both.
TONY: Maybe. Is it?
GEORGE: Yes. There's more to me than beer and chips, I hope. See you in a couple of weeks.
TONY: OK.

What can I make of this? The hour flew by. I was shocked when it was time. I don't know if it was 'therapy'. What I do know was that I experienced myself as simply enjoying his company. He seemed to be enjoying mine. He smiled a couple of times, especially when I said 'chips on the beach'. It's such a poignant image, it had stayed with me all week. Chips on the beach. For me, a kind of paradise for him, I'm still not sure. Certainly not a paradise. A kid on the beach eating chips, not allowed in the sea. A lonely kid eating chips, looking at the sea. After he left, I sat for half an hour before going home, thinking about being a kid in Cornwall. My Dad was fun. He taught me how to use a surf-board until it got too rough and it started to rain. I thought, 'not allowed in the sea, what's the point of being a kid on a beach if you can't go in the sea?' I suddenly thought, 'I know George really well. I hope he goes in the sea.' And then, 'There's more to me than beer and chips, I hope'.

Postscript

George came back after his 'holiday'. He didn't drink at all during the four days he was there, but he did drink from time to time later, sometimes heavily. He did eat chips, and he did walk in the sea. He came for 48 sessions in all. A year later, I got a postcard from him, sent from a town in the Midlands where he now lives. It said, 'The chips are good here. Thanks. George'.

The 'self' that I met in George was of course, complex and consisted of many configurations, in the sense that Mearns and Thorne use that term (see chapter 3). 'George The Drunk' was quiet, defeated, defended, hard to contact. He was never drunk during counselling sessions, though sometimes hung over, but it was as if he were drunk, or at least in that space that alcohol provided for him. He was cut off from himself, he could communicate little about his feelings for himself or for others. He often retreated into 'George The Drunk' when the going got a bit tough. If he started to recognise something painful or threatening he would lapse into what I could only describe to myself as a 'talking coma'. He said things, but somehow I couldn't really understand what they meant to him. He kept me at arm's length, and was sometimes dismissive of my fumbling attempts to empathise with him.

Gradually, I got to know George The Drunk, especially during the first five or six sessions. He was hard to like, and he knew it. He appeared less often as time went by, but when he came back, he did so with a vengeance. This configuration was important and useful to him. It enabled him to switch off whenever he needed to. It was an important defence against the possibility of being overwhelmed by the terror that his isolation might be permanent, that this was all there was. It doesn't seem to me to be an exaggeration to say that George The Drunk kept George alive. This seems bizarre in the light of the fact that drinking to excess, 'binge drinking', was very likely to be doing considerable damage to George's body, including his brain. A bottle of Scotch in one evening, on top of four or five pints of beer, is Hemingway territory.

There are some who might think it irresponsible not to address George's drinking habit directly — to challenge this piece of destructive behaviour. But alcohol, to George, was the only 'friend' he had, a distraction from the terror of living alone, and an anaesthetic against the pain of his isolation. The danger, of course, was that George would become dependent on the alcohol, that he would become 'an alcoholic' if he wasn't one already, and would slide into oblivion permanently. It was important to me to understand the relationship George had with alcohol, and that meant I had to form a relationship with George The Drunk, and value him just as much when in his 'coma' as when out of it.

We never worked explicitly on George's 'alcohol problem'. George's 'problems' were existential: how to be in this world among so many people, yet remain alone, and how to reach out and touch and be touched by others when he had no experience at all of how to do that. In fact, he saw relationships as threatening, dangerous and unpredictable. He once said that his ideal job would be as a palaeontologist working in the basement of the British Museum. Nobody would know he was there, and he could get on with putting bones in boxes, 'Fossil George'.

In the extract, we met another part of George. He called him 'The Kid With The Chips'. This George turned up increasingly often as time went by. When he first emerged, it was as a painful memory of being alone, though accompanied by members of his family, eating his chips and wanting to play in the sea. The Kid With The Chips was quiet, polite, never rebelled, stoic. He expected never to get what he wanted, never even to have his wants heard. He just tagged along. Sometimes, it seemed, The Kid With The Chips just tagged along to counselling. He was a good client, desperately eager to please, but never expecting to get much from it. He never corrected my mistakes in understanding him, and was always grateful for the time I gave him. It was as hard to get to know The Kid With The Chips as it was to get to know George The Drunk, yet when he first emerged in counselling he made us both want to cry.

I should say that it was hard *at first*, to get to know The Kid With The Chips. The temptation for me was to value the Kid more highly than the Drunk, because he was so vulnerable, innocent and appealing. Such an attitude on my part would, however, have been a therapeutic disaster. All of George's 'self-configurations' were equally vital in the business of staying alive. The Kid played his part by staying quiet, not being a nuisance, watching from the wings; the Drunk by retreating from threat and pain to a place of relative safety. Without the Drunk, the Kid couldn't survive, and vice versa. Other aspects of George, or configurations within George's self, were 'George The Manager', the efficient professional who dealt with relationship issues by delegating them to someone else ('good management technique'), and 'Will The Real George Please Stand Up' ('Real George' for short).

It was never the case that one of these 'Georges' should win out against the others. Counselling isn't a fight for supremacy, but a process of integration. In fact, there were not 'multiple Georges', there was only one George. Each aspect of George represented a part of George's experience and his ideas about himself, but they were not dissociated or split-off parts indicating a fragmentation of George's 'self'. Each part was known at some level to George; his 'self' was a consistent, organised whole that adopted different ways of being to cope with and survive the process of living. It both amused and helped George to label these different experiences in this way, and he began to see how his behaviour had become adapted to overcome different kinds of challenges.

The Kid With The Chips, however, became the key for George that slowly began to unlock repressed and half-forgotten experiences and feelings. He began to ask himself, 'How did The Kid With the Chips really feel, deep inside himself, when he become aware that he just wasn't important to anyone?' Crucially, The Kid began to develop some understanding of how life might have been for his parents and for his siblings. It seemed to me that The Kid began to experience some empathy for a struggling, large family, with very little money in a post-war Britain at a time of austerity and shortage. This never entirely neutralised the powerful feeling of being unimportant, but it did introduce a new dimension to his understanding of himself as a child and the role played by his family and environment in his development as a person.

It is not unusual, in my experience, for people gradually to discover more empathy for others through the process of their own counselling. Many people enter counselling understandably concerned with their own problems and issues and their own sense of self. Gradually, once they are on the road to resolving the internal hurts created during destructive relationships with others, people often (though not always) develop a more compassionate and understanding view of those others. Of course, this does not change the past or, in itself, undo the damage, but it is often a signal that even very destructive past relationships are losing their power to control present-day behaviour and attitudes.

My comments (in italics) in the above extract reveal much about my own process as a counsellor with this client. There are times when I lose all sense of this being a 'counselling relationship', and these are the times when I enter into the relationship most wholeheartedly, and without conscious awareness of its therapeutic nature. At these times it is, to me, simply a meeting that touches some of the existential depth I referred to earlier. I use the word 'simply' in its best possible sense here that is, uncluttered by external concerns and uncontaminated by any anxiety of mine. I do not need George to be any different from the way he is able to be right now. I have no goals for him, only for myself — to understand him as deeply as I can, and to be undefended and transparent to him.

The above extracts and the discussion that followed enable us to move forward in our consideration of person-centred counselling and examine more closely two further issues that are receiving renewed attention within the person-centred community. They are, first, work at the 'edge of awareness', and second, the idiosyncratic nature of empathic understanding.

Working at the edge of awareness

In chapter 3, I discussed the person-centred concept of 'self' in some detail, and noted that Mearns and Thorne's (2000) subtle revision of that concept to include 'edge of awareness' material in the self represents something of a departure from hitherto accepted theory.

The generally accepted definition of self, until recently, excludes anything that is not within awareness. For example, Rogers (1951), in his discussion of the nineteen propositions is quite clear that the term 'self', '. . . is here being used in a more restricted sense, namely, the awareness of being, of functioning' (p. 498). Rogers also offered a definition of 'self-concept', a term he used interchangeably with 'self-structure': 'The self-concept, or self-structure, may be thought of as an organized configuration of perceptions of the self which are admissible to awareness' (Rogers, 1951, p 136). (Rogers did concede that this definition, '. . . may change as our exploration of the phenomena of therapy continues' (p. 137).)

An early reference to the edge of awareness is in Rogers (1966),
> . . . *it is not the case that the client-centered therapist responds only to the obvious in the phenomenal world of the client. If that were so, it is doubtful that any movement would ensue in therapy. Indeed there would be no therapy. Instead, the client-centered therapist aims to dip from the pool of* implicit meanings just at the edge of the client's awareness (p. 160, my emphasis).

Here, in stating in very strong terms ('there would be no therapy') a major feature of empathic understanding, i.e. that it is concerned with both the 'obvious' and the partially hidden or obscured, Rogers described a central component of his system of counselling. By responding to edge of awareness material, that material is brought into sharper relief, more fully into awareness and, potentially, incorporated into the configuration of perceptions that constitute the self. He does not say, however, that only the hidden is of psychotherapeutic importance. Responding to 'the obvious' is the means by which counsellors attune themselves to the client's presently experienced internal world, and demonstrate acceptance and understanding of that world. There is no remark to be found anywhere in Rogers' writing that it should be the counsellor's goal actively to seek out the edge of awareness at the expense of all else; instead he indicates that a counsellor who *only* responds to the obvious is unlikely to provide the conditions necessary for growth to occur. There is a deal of difference between 'aiming to dip from the pool of implicit meanings', and viewing 'the obvious' as of only marginal importance or no importance at all.

Person-centred counselling has, throughout its history, included edge of awareness material in its effort empathically to understand a person's experiencing process. Counselling can be regarded as an effort to integrate edge of awareness material into the self-structure, or enable such material to modify or augment the self-structure. Mearns and Thorne imply that edge of awareness material is in some sense already impinging on or influencing the self even though it is not assimilated into or integrated into the self-concept (self-structure), thus echoing Rogers' (1959) remark that 'Behavior is regulated at times by the self and at times by those aspects of the organism's experience which are not included in the self' (p. 226).

In including the term 'behaviour' in his discussion, Rogers reminds us that while counselling is, to a large extent, concerned with how people feel about themselves and how they experience themselves, it is also about how the self-concept is reflected in the world in behavioural terms. With less distortion or denial, clients have more internal resources to negotiate creatively between the promptings of 'actualisation' and the mediating demands of the social world (Mearns and Thorne, 2000, pp. 182–3).

The self-concept is, according to Rogers, 'an organized configuration of perceptions of the self' (op. cit.); to Mearns (1994/2000), it is, '. . . an attitude which is learned like any other attitude' (p. 82), with a cognitive, affective and behavioural component. Mearns goes on to suggest that a feature of the self-concept is its consistency, that it is this consistency that provides '. . . coherence and predictability to the person' (p. 83), and that 'the effect of therapy is to increase the "dissonance" within the client's self concept' (p. 83). Mearns and Thorne's extension of the theory of self implies that material yet to be organised into a configuration or integrated with other existing configurations can still legitimately be regarded as 'elements' of the self, and (following from Rogers, 1959, op. cit.) influences a person's behaviour.

As edge of awareness material becomes increasingly admissible into full awareness, the process of integrating it into the self-concept can proceed. The hesitant recognition of edge of awareness material signals the potential for integration, and if that potential is realised, the configurations of perceptions can be modified to include hitherto denied or distorted experiences. In Mearns' (1994/2000) phrase, edge of awareness material, where it is inconsistent with the existing self-concept, creates dissonance, and, 'The increase of dissonance within therapy is not a comfortable experience because dissonance brings its own tension' (Mearns, op. cit., p. 83). It is possible, then, to conceptualise edge of awareness material as that material, not yet in full awareness but accompanied by tension and/or anxiety, which has the potential to be integrated into existing perceptions of the self, or to modify or even replace existing configurations of perceptions.

The term 'potential for integration' is chosen here because there equally exists the potential for edge of awareness material to be further distorted or denied should the prevailing conditions be unfavourable for constructive personality change to occur. In other words, the existing self-concept can be so powerful that it responds to tension and dissonance with renewed defence. Or the conditions in which tension begins to be felt can be perceived as unsafe or untrustworthy, and the movement from edge of awareness to full awareness is curtailed rather than allowed to reach fruition. The psychotherapeutic conditions that are favourable to this process are, in the person-centred tradition, well known (e.g. Rogers, 1957a), but it is conceivable (and probable) that it also occurs independently of psychotherapy (see Bozarth, 1998, pp. 35–42).

Rogers also introduced the notion of 'levels' of experience (Rogers, 1951). On the one hand, there is 'the total or organismic level', and on the other is the level of 'awareness'. For example, a person may experience fear of inadequacy at an organismic level, but distort the experience at the awareness level into a fear of climbing stairs, since inadequacy contradicts the picture he has of himself, but experiencing a fear of heights does not. The edge of awareness could, then, be conceptualised as experiences held at the organismic level by the defence of distortion or denial, but in the process of reaching the awareness level, though not (yet) in full awareness. Actualisation tends to favour the admission of all experience into awareness, but conditions of worth tend to disfavour the admission of some experience into awareness. When defences begin to dissolve, experiences begin to move from the organismic to the awareness level, a situation accompanied by tension or anxiety, since the self-concept may have to be re-organised to accommodate this new material.

A problem for the person-centred counsellor is that the concept of 'edge of awareness' is uncomfortably close, as Mearns and Thorne (2000) remind us (p. 176, see above), to the psychoanalytic concept of 'the unconscious', as is the term 'organismic level of experience'. Mearns and Thorne remark that person-centred therapy does not 'wander into the unconscious. . .', but 'works within awareness, and . . . the *emerging awareness of the client*' (p. 176, emphasis in original). In person-centred counselling, the location of an experience at the edge of awareness refers operationally to experiences that are subject to the defences of distortion or denial, i.e., those experiences that challenge the currently held self-concept, to such an extent that the experiences are not allowed fully into awareness, but are, nevertheless, in some measure impinging on the client's phenomenal field. In other words, they are making a difference, even though their content is not differentiated sharply enough for a person to describe them.

Rogers refers to three 'sets' or categories of experiences. Firstly, there are those that are ignored,

> *because they are irrelevant to the self-structure . . . They exist in the ground of my phenomenal field, but they do not reinforce or contradict my concept of self, they meet no need related to self, they are ignored . . . It is undoubtedly true that the great majority of our sensory experiences are thus ignored, never raised to the level of conscious symbolization, and exist only as organic sensations, without ever having been related in any way to the organized concept of the self or to the concept of the self in relation to the environment (Rogers, 1951, pp. 503–4).*

Secondly, is that group of experiences '. . . which are accepted into consciousness and organized into some relationship with the self-structure either because they meet a need of the self or because they are consistent with the self-structure and thus reinforce it' (p. 504). There is an element of 'selection' present here; in other words a person '. . . selects from her many sensory experiences those that fit in with her concept of herself' (p. 504). Included in this category are experiences that are symbolised because they are related to the needs of the self. For example, 'I notice a book because it is on a topic I wish to learn about; I perceive neckties when I am preparing to buy one for myself' (p. 504).

These two sets of experiences are, in the main, unproblematic insofar as they represent little or no threat to the self. However, they may present problems to seriously disturbed, catatonic or 'autistic' people who display no evidence of ability to recognise *any* experience, and who are, in Prouty's terms, contact-impaired (e.g. Prouty, 1994, 2000, 2002).

The third group of experiences includes those that are *prevented* from entering into awareness, and Rogers itemises two 'sub-categories' in this group. First, there are those experiences that are denied in a somewhat conscious manner. The person is aware of the experience or perception, but simply denies its importance, significance or truth. Rogers remarks that 'This type of more or less conscious denial of perception is certainly a frequent occurrence with everyone' (p. 505).

Of most significance is that group of experiences that are denied to awareness either entirely or accepted only in a distorted fashion, because 'an adequate conscious representation of it would be entirely inconsistent with the concept of self. Thus, a woman whose concept of self has been deeply influenced by a very strictly moralistic and religious upbringing, experiences strong organic cravings for sexual satisfaction. To symbolise these, to permit them to appear in consciousness, would provide a traumatic contradiction to her concept of self. The organic experience is something which occurs and is an organic fact. But the symbolization of these desires, so that they become part of conscious awareness, is something which the conscious self can and does prevent' (p. 505).

Rogers emphasises that perceptions are excluded not necessarily because they are derogatory, but because they are contradictory. Even a positive perception of self would not be allowed into awareness if it contradicted an existing negative perception. For example, an unexpected examination success might not modify a negative self-concept, but might instead be rationalised into 'a piece of good luck'. The person whose perception of himself as 'useless at exams and an educational failure' might continue to hold on to this perception, even with plenty of objective contradictory evidence.

Counselling at the edge of awareness — a brief example[2]

This brief extract is taken from a counselling interview between Carl Rogers and Ms G, recorded in England in 1983. The client has been talking about the feelings she still has about herself and her parents that originated in early childhood.

CARL: *I wonder what that shaking of your head means . . . It looks like*

---

2. A full transcript from which this extract is taken can be found in Merry (1995). The client gave her permission for the transcript to be published and used for educational purposes. Originally transcribed from videotape by Bob Lusty.

you're saying, 'It isn't possible.'

Ms G: *I was saying, 'Isn't possible', and I was thinking I can't blame, I can't blame it on anybody that . . . and I was thinking I can't . . . um . . . I wanted to tell you a bit about what happened and . . . but then I thought that by telling you I'd kind of be blaming it on something and . . .*

CARL: *It's got to come out so carefully that it doesn't blame anybody or anything, you can't just let it out.*

Ms G: *That's what's so awful about it, I know it reminded . . . I'm running this battle somehow with my emotions, but maybe it is OK to blame and to say, to get it all out, and then when it's all out maybe I can do something with it that makes it OK with everybody concerned, but . . .*

CARL: *So it's quite possible that it's OK to be unreasonable and irrational even, spill things that aren't quite right, because then you might then be able to make it OK afterwards once they were out.*

[Pause]

Ms G: *I just realised something . . . part of the hurt is about not being considered and I'm talking about when I was young and my parents kept on getting back together again and separating and getting back together gain and separating and I went into children's homes and all sorts of things that I wasn't considered, and now what I'm doing is not considering myself. I'm not . . . it's like I can't consider myself, I don't think I'm important enough to be considered.*

CARL: *That childhood experience of being shuttled around and not being considered in the situation . . . er. . . resulted in you not being able to consider and take care of yourself . . . [Pause] . . . and you must have felt very keenly the business of being treated as an object, just put here, put there and not really, not really considered, not really cared about.*

Ms G: *I mean, how can you say what you want when you're four?*

CARL: *How can you possibly say when you're four years old, 'Hey! Look at me, I need to be considered, I need to be thought about.'*

This seems like a good example of a complex set of feelings that are beginning to emerge into full awareness. The dialogue moves on to Ms. G making a pact with herself that 'I think I'll be me for a while', rather than be the way other people seem to want her to be.

Rogers' attitudes and behaviour remain consistent with person-centred theory and practice throughout the interview. At no time can he be observed looking for hidden meanings or trying directly to uncover edge of awareness material, yet such material does begin tentatively to emerge during the interview. In a short time, Rogers has made empathic contact with Ms G, and his responses to her are sensitive to and understanding of the struggle that she is experiencing. By responding to the 'obvious' in Ms G's statements whilst remaining sensitive to the deep complexity that lies behind them, Rogers provides the conditions where the denial of experiences is no longer necessary.

In this extract, it is Ms G's process of actualisation that enables her to uncover and express feelings that hitherto have remained unacknowledged. Rogers' non-intrusive, non-directive attitude, evidenced by his non-judgemental empathic understanding, proves sufficient for edge of awareness material to find some expression.

Idiosyncratic empathy

The term 'idiosyncratic empathy' was coined by Bozarth (1984/2001) partly as a rebuttal of the notion of empathic understanding as a somewhat mechanical process involving the restatement or repetition of clients' words and feelings. To Bozarth, empathy involves, 'a way of being that is unique and idiosyncratic to the therapist, the client and to their particular experiencing of each other' (1984, p. 68). The term 'reflection of feelings', though commonly used in person-centred counselling, does not capture the essence of the empathic process that evolves from the congruence of the counsellor, the quality of the person-to-person encounter in the relationship, and the intuition of the counsellor (Bozarth, 1984, p. 69).

In my understanding of idiosyncratic empathy, I emphasise the non-systematic, non-formulaic process of responding to the client as a person, a process that evolves from a close 'indwelling' into the client's subjective world. Deep attunement to a person's internal frame of reference, an appreciation of that person as an active agent in his or her social world, and an openness to our own flow of experience in relation to that person are the foundations of an empathic experience and response. Such a response may, at first, seem surprising, even tangential to the overt content of a client's statement, and it may be in response to edge of awareness material in either the client or the counsellor. To this extent, I believe that empathy is an emergent property of the relationship itself. The willingness of the client to self-express (however tentatively), together with the counsellor's non-judgemental attention to the self-expressing person, create a relationship from which emerges an experience of empathic understanding, usually (though not exclusively) expressed by the counsellor. In other words, the relationship creates the conditions where empathic understanding becomes available, and may be experienced and expressed either by the counsellor or by the client. The latter case would indicate a process of emerging 'self-empathy' or self-understanding. It may be something of a departure from traditional person-centred theory to suggest that the relationship creates the conditions for self-empathy as much as it creates the conditions for counsellor empathy. Nevertheless, clients often discover and experience a deep level of self-understanding without the counsellor necessarily being aware of its content until expressed directly by the client.

The empathic process is not, then, a logical, sequential series of steps (though it may sometimes have these qualities), especially when the material is at or close to the client's edge of awareness. It is likely that both client and counsellor are only directly aware of a small proportion of the dynamics of the relationship, and the internal dynamics of either of them. More perceptions of the relationship are likely to develop out of the direct awareness of the participants, perhaps at a 'subceived' rather than directly perceived level.

To explore further what I mean by 'idiosyncratic empathy', we can return, briefly, to the extracts with which I started this chapter:

GEORGE: You know what I'd really like? When I was a kid we went to Cornwall. Me, my mum and dad and one of my sisters. I must have been about six years old. I just remember the sea, the sunshine and the ice-cream. We had chips on the beach. I'd like to sit on the beach and have some chips.

I am listening very carefully. I see a kid on the beach eating chips. I used to do that in Cornwall. Strangely enough, I want to cry.

TONY: Strangely enough, I want to cry.
GEORGE: Me too.
TONY: I have no idea why.
GEORGE: Me neither.
TONY: Do you want to go for a swim?
GEORGE: I'm not allowed to.
TONY: OK.
GEORGE: You're a good bloke.
TONY: Thanks. So are you.

I have no idea what's going on 'technically', but I suddenly sense a real bond between us. The impulse to cry has gone. I remember my dad teaching my sister and me to swim in Cornwall. We used to camp in a field. There were no proper camping sites in those days. It rained a lot.

GEORGE: It rained a lot.
TONY: I know.

In this extract there is little or no evidence of the counsellor responding 'systematically' to the client's self-expression. The question, 'Do you want to go for a swim?' does not logically follow from what went before in any obvious manner. The dialogue only begins to make sense when the internal processes and awareness of the counsellor are taken into consideration. There is evidence that the client and counsellor are closely attuned to each other; they are deeply aware of each other and each is making a difference to the other. This is not a client monologue, followed by a response by the counsellor to that monologue; rather, it is a dialogue and an encounter at a deep level.

It is idiosyncratically empathic because it emerges from the meeting of two 'selves' who have developed a keen appreciation of each other and a resonance at an existential level. While the counsellor's responses emerge partly from his awareness of his own process, that process is in harmony with, and embracing of, the client's process. It is an 'intuitive' response because it does not respond only to the spoken words of the client, but represents a more holistic appreciation of the client as a person.

I hope that the contents of this chapter provide some indication of the complexities and subtleties of person-centred counselling. In the next chapter, I give some suggestions and examples of how the variety of attitudes, values and personal qualities discussed so far can be explored in personally meaningful ways. The intention is to bring the theory more to life so that you can experiment with it and directly experience some of it.

Checklist: Relational depth

- Relational depth is most likely to develop when counsellors have integrated person-centred values, qualities and attitudes into their way of being.
- Counsellors who are too anxious to achieve relational depth may inadvertently compromise the essentially non-directive nature of person-centred counselling.
- Working at relational depth with different self-configurations requires counsellors to respect and value all expressions of self and self-experience equally.
- Edge of awareness material emerges as clients experience empathic understanding and positive regard from a congruent counsellor in a relationship relatively free of threat to existing concepts of self.
- Person-centred counselling works within the client's awareness and with the emerging awareness of the client.
- Idiosyncratic empathy refers to the non-formulaic, spontaneous and non-systematic nature of empathic responding that can occur when counsellors are deeply attuned to clients' internal worlds, and are open to their own flow of inner experiencing.

Developing person-centred values, skills, attitudes and personal qualities   7

All counsellors (of whatever school of thought) need to be skilled at listening and communicating if they are to be effective in building and maintaining counselling relationships. Person-centred counsellors need to be able to communicate their empathic understanding, their personal congruence and their willingness to accept and respect their clients with as little judgement as possible. This is best summed up by the phrase *quality of presence*, meaning that it is the underlying attitudes and values of the counsellor that help clients feel safe enough to explore difficult or painful experiences. Counsellors who stick rigidly to a set of rules, or who try to use whatever technique comes to mind, are in danger of making the process mechanical and contrived.

Person-centred counselling depends on the establishment and maintenance of a relationship built on the necessary and sufficient conditions explored in the previous chapters. It does not prescribe any specific behaviours on the part of the counsellor, *including any of the behaviour I discuss in what follows*. There is no formula, or rule-book, or set of instructions about what you, as a counsellor, should *do* in specific terms. Your 'way of being' in the counselling relationship springs from certain *attitudes*, *values* and *personal qualities* you hold about people and the counselling process. 'Qualities' are concerned with distinctive attributes or characteristics, and in the counselling context, these qualities are to do with your personal characteristics and with the relationships you form with your clients. 'Attitudes' are concerned with your way of thinking about something, and the behaviour related to that way of thinking, whilst 'values' are concerned with your judgement about what is and what is not important in a situation. Bayne et al. (1998) suggest asking yourself six questions to help clarify your own values:

- *What are your main values?*
- *Do you act on them?*
- *Do you want to act on any of them more?*
- *If you do, what will you do less of?*
- *Do any of your values conflict with each other?*
- *How do your values affect others?* (p. 160)

This chapter encourages you to do two things. Firstly, it suggests you examine your presently held values and attitudes concerning the counselling process, and the kinds of qualities you bring to it or see as important. Secondly, it suggests ways in which you might experiment with how you communicate your attitudes and values in a counselling context. The questions are: do you communicate what you intend to communicate in ways that others can most readily accept and understand, and are there ways in which your current values and attitudes might be in conflict with what you hope to achieve as a counsellor? Finally, can you communicate your counselling values and attitudes more accurately, so that the quality of the relationship you build with your client is more consistent with your understanding of person-centred values?

All of Rogers' research into what constituted effective counselling concentrated on the skills, qualities, values and attitudes of the counsellor. Except indirectly, he did not concern himself with the part played by clients, other than to say that clients need to perceive and experience the core conditions in order to make use of them, that they would be in psychological contact with their counsellor and that they would, to some degree, be anxious or vulnerable.

However, we do know some things about the ways in which clients affect the process of counselling and its outcomes. For example, clients who seem to benefit most are those who have a belief in the effectiveness of the counselling process, and a belief in their own capacity to change in positive ways.

Other factors include clients' motivation for change, the extent to which they are already able to form close relationships with others, and their expectations of what they might gain from counselling. Of course, these things are not confined to person-centred counselling; they are quite general factors affecting the outcome of all forms of counselling. In other words, counselling consists of a dialogue, and both counsellor and client have a part to play in its success or failure.

Person-centred counselling is concerned to enable individuals to discover from *within themselves* the strength and personal resources they need in order to effect change, including in self-concept, self-esteem and self-regard. Person-centred counselling is not a process of change arising from sources external to the client, and does not rely on external suggestion or persuasion of any form. It aims to re-create the conditions most likely to promote optimal functioning motivated by the client's actualising tendency.

In this book I am concerned with ways in which we can become more effective in our efforts to help our clients discover their own psychological resources, and to make the kinds of changes in their lives that they see as important. Creating the kind of environment in which this is likely to happen requires a combination of facilitative values, attitudes and personal qualities, coupled with sensitive and skilled communication.

One way of thinking about skills is that they are ways to put attitudes and values into practice through behaviour. It is possible to become more skilled in listening and communicating so that what we mean is what we say, and how we are with our clients is how we like to be with them.

What follows concentrates on the skills, values, attitudes and personal qualities that contribute to all good relationships, not only those between clients and their counsellors. Though they are appropriate not only in counselling, they are probably more evident in the counselling hour because the counsellor tries to communicate them and 'be' them in a concentrated and disciplined way.

Exercise: Your current 'model' or approach to counselling

Before you go any further, take a look at the statements below. All of them have been said about counselling at one time or another. Some of them could be said, accurately, about person-centred counselling, others probably not.

Aims of the exercise
To help you identify what you presently think is the purpose of counselling, and what are the priorities of the counsellor. To help you work towards developing your own counselling 'model'.

What to do
STEP 1: Read the following statements about counselling, and write down the ones you think to be true, or approximately true for you. If you think of other statements not included here, jot them down also.

STEP 2: When you have finished, share your results with your group if you have one. Do your statements constitute a 'model' of counselling? Are there any statements in your model or approximate model that conflict with each other?

- *Counselling is about helping people to solve problems.*
- *Counselling is where you listen carefully to your client so that you can give them good advice about how to become more fulfilled.*
- *Counsellors need to be very knowledgeable about human development before they can be of much use to their clients.*
- *Counselling is about bringing the unconscious into awareness.*
- *Counselling is about helping people come to terms with their feelings.*
- *Counsellors need to develop a wide repertoire of techniques so they can help as many different kinds of people as possible.*
- *Counselling is for normal neurotics, psychotherapy is for the mentally ill.*
- *Counsellors stay in the 'here and now', but psychotherapists work with the past.*

- *Counsellors offer suggestions and directions so that people can find alternative ways of understanding themselves.*
- *Counselling is about developing self-esteem.*
- *Counsellors act as 'mirrors' so their clients can see themselves more clearly reflected in the way their counsellor responds to them.*
- *Counselling is for people experiencing a crisis of some kind.*
- *Counsellors help people become more self-aware.*
- *Counselling helps people come to terms with insoluble problems.*
- *Counsellors need to be well adjusted and content so they do not use their clients for their own unmet needs.*
- *Counsellors' first priority is to identify their clients' problems so they can devise ways of helping clients to overcome them.*
- *Counsellors need to experience counselling for themselves before they start practising.*
- *Counselling is a process consisting of a number of stages. Counsellors need the appropriate skills to be able to handle each stage.*
- *People are too complex to be explained by any one theory. Counsellors should combine aspects of different theories to ensure a more complete appreciation of the person.*

Next, I identify some of the characteristics of counselling presented under three main headings (empathic understanding, congruence and unconditional positive regard) that reflect the core conditions of person-centred counselling, and the discussion offers further ideas and perspectives for understanding them. I also identify some possible ways in which these core conditions can be communicated, either directly or indirectly, to our clients, and I give some ideas about how you might explore what the core conditions mean to you. The important thing is for you to find your own authentic ways of 'living' the core conditions in your relationships with your clients.

Empathic understanding

In everyday life we tend to listen only partially; sometimes we may be rehearsing a response, or trying to construct an argument or in other ways paying only limited attention to what we are hearing.

In counselling, a different, more active and focused listening is required. Empathic understanding involves a process of listening to understand a person's own perspective, point of view and feelings, etc. It means entering into the other person's world, suspending our own interpretations and judgements and trying to see things as our clients see them. Although we may be feeling sympathetic to our client, empathy goes beyond sympathy in that empathy requires a deep understanding of a client's experience, whereas sympathy may not always be accompanied by understanding. Empathic understanding includes a deep and close attention to our client's inner, subjective experiencing, and in so doing we communicate our non-judgemental regard for them as persons. This is not something we can learn as a technique, or even a skill, unless it is accompanied by a genuine trust in, and respect for, the client's process of change and growth.

Carl Rogers (1980), in his book *A Way of Being*, put it this way:

> *It means entering the private perceptual world of the other and becoming thoroughly at home in it. It involves being sensitive, moment by moment, to the changing felt meanings which flow in this other person, to the fear or rage or tenderness or confusion or whatever that he or she is experiencing. It means temporarily living in the other's life, moving about in it delicately without making judgements* (p. 142).

It is the process of communicating our empathic understanding to our clients that makes this form of listening active and involving. But in person-centred counselling we do not listen and respond with empathy in order to achieve any particular counselling goal. This might seem paradoxical at first, but we are not trying to bring about change in our clients directly, we are trying to establish the conditions in which the client's own powers of self-healing can become activated. Reference to person-centred theory, discussed in previous chapters, helps us to understand this. It is the client's actualising tendency that motivates change, and this tendency effects more constructive ends in a relationship free of threat, and thus free of the need to distort or deny experience into awareness. Taking this approach is extremely liberating for us as counsellors. We do not change our clients, they change themselves to whatever degree and in whatever direction they are able at this present point in their lives. This is also an expression of the generally non-authoritarian and non-directive attitude of person-centred counselling. It places the expertise about the client's life in the client's hands, and it trusts in each person's capacity to grow towards integration and fulfilment, rather than placing trust in the counsellor's effectiveness at directing the client's experiencing process.

Exploring empathic understanding

Effective counselling responses, those that enable clients to feel understood and encouraged to explore more deeply, are based in the counsellor's respect for the client's self-resources, arise from the counsellor's close empathic understanding of the client's internal frame of reference, and may have some or all of the following characteristics:

• **Accuracy:** The counsellor responds in a way that accurately captures at least some of the meaning the client appears to be expressing.
Example
   CLIENT: My sister and I have never got on. I've always been jealous of her, especially when my mother bought her all the best things and I got

hand-me-downs. I'm glad she's moved away now, I could never compete anyway.

COUNSELLOR: *There was always trouble between you and your sister. You feel better now you don't have to live with her.*

• **Accuracy and basic empathy**: The counsellor's response shows an understanding of the more easily accessible feelings and meanings, especially the emotional meanings, of the client's inner world at that time.

Example

CLIENT: *(same statement as above)*

COUNSELLOR: *You were jealous for a long time, and now it's a relief not to have to compete any longer? Is that it?*

• **Deeper empathy**: The counsellor senses more than just surface meanings and emotions. There is an awareness of client's feelings that may be lying just below the surface, and the counsellor is able to respond to them with respect and sensitivity.

Example

CLIENT: I often feel that I have missed out on so much. I mean, I love my kids and everything, but I've had to work so hard to get things for them. When I look back to my childhood there wasn't much fun, not many good times when I could just be carefree. I've tried to make sure life isn't like that for them, but I never got much of anything — it was all work and worry, still is.

COUNSELLOR: *You never got the kind of childhood you want for your own kids, is that what you mean? It's like you missed out on the joy of just being a kid, having fun. I guess it feels like quite a big gap there, is that right?*

As a client feels understood and accepted without judgement, he or she is likely to begin expressing deeper feelings. It is not the counsellor's role to try to find deeper meaning or to get beyond a client's level of awareness. Consistently moving beyond a client's current level of awareness tends to direct the process, we risk the client losing his or her sense of self-determination, and the counsellor is perceived as having the expertise about the client rather than the client him or herself. However, we do need to take into account the suggestion that Rogers and others have made regarding working with 'edge of awareness' material. I have already discussed this concept, but it might be a good idea to go back and review what was said about it.

• **Tentativeness**: The counsellor is sensitive and exploratory. He or she is not diagnosing or interpreting, but checking the extent to which understanding is developing.

• **Economy:** Counsellor responses are economical when they communicate directly, and do not include lengthy explanations or descriptions. Being economical is a skill that can be developed using metaphors, similes or figures of speech for example, to express complex things briefly and understandably. This is not to say that counsellor responses *should* be 'economical' before they can successfully communicate what we intend to communicate. This is not a mechanical exercise in which our responses have to conform to some standard or formula. Here, I am suggesting that we can look at the ways in which we say things to see the extent to which we can be clearer and more accurate. I do not want to stifle genuineness or spontaneity.

Example
> CLIENT: It feels like no matter what I do, I never get anywhere. I try and try, but I make no impression. I seem to put so much time and energy in, but it gets nowhere, all I end up with is a headache. *(Laughs)* There is a funny side to it, keeping on and on struggling like this, bashing my head against a brick wall, I feel dazed by it.
> COUNSELLOR: (with warmth and humour) *Like a woodpecker on a concrete post.*
> CLIENT: *(Laughs, then seriously)* Yes, exactly, you can imagine how *that* must feel!

• **Warmth:** The counsellor communicates respect and a prizing of the client as unique, worthwhile and to be valued, but please remember what was said earlier about 'warmth' not necessarily being the same thing as 'affection', and it does not include being over-friendly.

• **Rapport:** Establishing rapport is a matter of being sensitive to the client's way of being and respecting and valuing it. This does *not* mean, however, that you should mimic your clients, or adopt their words and way of speaking! An important characteristic of your responses is that they are genuine for you; again, they shouldn't conform to any particular formula at the expense of being authentic for you.

• **Immediacy:** The counsellor is able to use the present situation, the existing feelings within the client and within him or herself as part of the process of establishing a relationship with the client. Present, 'here and now' feelings are not denied or avoided, but talked about openly and appropriately. This results from the counsellor's close attention to the client's experiencing, not because it is 'good counselling technique' to make good use of immediacy.

Example
> CLIENT: I have always had trouble with people I see as being in authority, people with some power over me. I find it really hard to talk to them without feeling small or stupid. I feel it with you sometimes. I'm

feeling like that now a bit, and it really annoys me, that I still haven't got over that.

Counsellor: *So, for a long time it's been hard to meet people who might put you down, or something, and even with me that feeling comes up, and I guess you might be saying, 'Why haven't I grown out of that?'*

In other approaches to counselling, particularly psychodynamic ones, this exchange would be seen as an example of transference. In other words, the client is behaving towards the counsellor in ways that are derived from past experiences with others, without being conscious of it. In person-centred counselling such feelings or behaviours are not treated any differently from other feelings and behaviours, i.e. they are accepted and understood without judgement or evaluation.

• **Purposefulness**: Counselling is more than a conversation — it is a genuine exploration of meanings and experiences. Good counsellors are concentrated and focused. They do not drift off into rambling and meandering small talk.

Blocks to communication

No matter how hard we try to listen attentively, actively and empathically, there often seem to be things which interfere with this process, when we suddenly realise that for a while we have not been listening very well at all. It *is* difficult to maintain a high level of empathy for long periods of time. Even the most experienced counsellors occasionally find their attention wandering, or misunderstand what someone has said to them.

Empathy is a vital component of good counselling, but we can take great comfort from the fact that often the genuine *attempt* to understand, even if we don't quite make it, is enough for clients to feel taken seriously, valued and encouraged.

What follows are some ways of experimenting with your own listening, and getting to know more about it.

Exercise: Listening

Aims of the exercise
To understand more about how you listen to people.

What to do
Before going any further with this chapter, take some time to think about ways in which you normally listen to people.

Step 1: Recall situations in which you haven't really understood what was being said. What was happening within you at the time? Were you thinking of something else, trying to win an argument, thinking about what you should say next, etc?

STEP 2: Now think of occasions when someone has been listening to you. What was it about their behaviour that helped you feel understood, or not? When you felt misunderstood, what feelings arose in you? Try to remember when you felt clearly understood by someone important to you. What feelings did that experience stimulate in you?

STEP 3: Make a list of behaviour which helped you feel understood. In the past, people have come up with ideas like: 'she looked straight at me and nodded from time to time', 'she didn't seem distracted by things happening outside', 'the things she said back were to the point, connected with what I was trying to say', and 'she didn't interrupt all the time'.

STEP 4: When you have finished this exercise, compare your ideas with what follows and see how many of them you experience when trying to be more empathic.

• **Being preoccupied**
   No matter how hard you try, you cannot stop thinking about something else. It might be an important engagement later that day, a letter you have to write, or it might even be a continuous worrying about how empathic you are being!

• **Being defensive**
   Your client may be challenging your competence, and you find you begin to justify yourself, or you might simply be worried that your client sees you as someone of less competence than they expected. This, and similar things, can sometimes lead to us becoming closed and defensive, which always interferes with our ability to listen.

• **Being inappropriately sympathetic**
   Clients sometimes tell us about very unhappy, even tragic events in their lives. If we find ourselves becoming too sympathetic it can lead us into trying to reassure or make things better. When this happens, we cease to listen properly, and we may become over-concerned with our own emotional state. Sympathy, whilst being a normal reaction to another person's distress, is not, as I said above, the same thing as empathic understanding. It is often helpful to share sympathetic feelings with our clients, a process which can enable us to return to experiencing empathic understanding.

• **Feeling dislike**
   Person-centred counsellors are only human, with human likes and dislikes. If we feel antipathy towards a client, we probably won't be able to listen with acceptance and without judgement. We should

explore what it is about this client that leads us to feeling this way. If, as time goes by, we find ourselves still actively disliking this client, we have met a personal limitation. It is honest and professional to admit this to oneself, and we may have to cease giving counselling to this person.

• **Identifying with others**
Identifying sometimes happens when clients talk about experiences that are familiar to us. We begin to recall these experiences and the feelings that went with them. This is natural, but the danger is in assuming that because we felt a certain way, this client must be feeling the same way, and we begin to relate to clients as if they are having these feelings.

• **Feeling uncomfortable, shocked or embarrassed**
Sometimes clients need to talk about very intimate things, or things that lie quite outside our own experience. This can be particularly true when it comes to talking about sex or sexuality. If clients detect that we are uncomfortable talking about these things, they may try and protect us, and themselves, by avoiding them, which can mean that important therapeutic opportunities are missed.
In training, we can confront issues which are personally difficult for us so that our discomfort does not lead us to being unable to listen openly to clients in the future.

• **The need for reward**
We all need to feel that we are doing a good job, really making a positive difference to our clients in helping them lead more satisfying lives. Paradoxically, the need to be a good counsellor can become so strong that we try too hard and become anxious, and this affects our capacity to relax and listen. This can also happen if we have an excessive need to be liked and respected by our clients.

• **Forming theories**
It can be very tempting to pay more attention to your own process of forming theories about clients than actually to listening to them. Theories might include speculations about how 'disturbed' this person is, whether the client has had a very unhappy childhood, whether the client is telling the truth or not, and so on. It is much more productive to attend to your clients' descriptions of themselves, and let them tell you, gradually, what is troubling them, than it is to jump to conclusions.
One danger of theories is that you might start believing they are true, and then you might start to relate to your clients as if you knew the truth about them when the chances are that you do not.

Now we have reviewed some of the things that interfere with our ability to listen, we can concentrate on ways of developing more empathic listening behaviour. Some of the exercises that follow are tried and tested ways of focusing on listening with more understanding and insight, others are aimed at developing the communication skills we need to make our empathy known to our clients.

Use the exercises as ways of introducing yourself to the kinds of skills, attitudes and personal qualities that add up to effective counselling.

Exercise: Developing empathy (The empathy lab)

Aims of the exercise
To develop skills in active, empathic listening by experimenting with a variety of ways of listening and responding.

What to do
This needs three people — a talker, a listener and an observer. The talker and listener should sit opposite each other, and the observer should sit close by, but out of the direct line of sight of the talker and listener so as not to distract them.

THE TALKER should speak of something that has some real meaning. It needn't be a problem, though it could be. The important thing is not to make something up, but to talk about some real experience or feeling. For example, you could talk about your relationships at home, or at work, or about something you did recently that made an impression on you, like visiting somewhere new, or meeting new people.
THE LISTENER should try to listen as actively and attentively as possible. Become aware of the emotions and feelings in the talker's voice. Ask yourself, 'What is this person saying to me, and what does it mean for her?

Try to show the talker that you are really listening and trying to understand. Find your own ways of doing this that feel natural and authentic to you. Try not to have a list of things in your head that you should try to do. Experiment a bit.

If you do not understand something the talker says, you can ask for it to be repeated, or expressed in different words.

When you have made some kind of response to the talker, allow yourself and the talker some time — it can be difficult to be comfortable with silences, but they are important.

* *Giving someone your full attention like this may seem a bit awkward at first, maybe even a bit mechanical, but as you become more used to it you will find it easier. Eventually, you will find it becomes second*

> *nature to listen with greater attention.*
> • *Notice how your mind wanders — how you drift off sometimes and miss something, how you find yourself getting a response ready, how you sometimes get some thought triggered off and follow that instead of listening, and so on.*

THE OBSERVER should look at the way the listener pays attention. Does the listener maintain good contact with the talker? What is the listener's body language like? Are the listener's responses accurate, or off the mark? Are they tentative and exploratory or dogmatic?

Try this, at first, for five or ten minutes. Then debrief with the talker saying how well understood he or she felt, and how well listened to.

Try to be as specific as you can in your feedback, 'I felt very well understood when you nodded and said . . .', or, 'I don't think you understood me when you said . . .', or 'When you yawned and looked out of the window I didn't feel you were really with me!'

THE OBSERVER can take notes during the exercise, and be ready to give feedback to the listener, not to the talker!

Then swap roles and go through the exercise again. When everyone has had a turn at each role, you can increase the time — up to 30 minutes is something to aim for.

I used to have a checklist to accompany the above exercise, but I now think it does more harm than good. The important thing is to discover better ways of communicating for yourself that are based in your own experience, rather than try to conform to some external notion of what is effective and what is not. Let the feedback guide you about what is effective — and what is not — about your own 'style' and way of being empathic.

Exercise: Experiencing empathy yourself

Aim of the exercise
To learn to appreciate the power of empathy first-hand.

What to do
Of all the ways I know to learn to be more empathic, being deeply understood ourselves is the best. Being a client with an understanding, empathic counsellor, or spending time with a naturally empathic friend, is a very enriching experience. It teaches us how valuable empathy is in any good relationship, and this somehow triggers off our own empathic abilities.

Exercise: Using a tape recorder

Aim of the exercise
A variation on the empathy lab. Adds an extra dimension to the feedback and discussion.

What to do
You can use a tape recorder in an empathy lab instead of, or as well as, an observer. The tape will enable you to check specific incidents, and will help you to examine your listening behaviour much more accurately. Tape-record an empathy lab and when you play it back, stop it from time to time and recall what you were feeling as the listener — what was going on inside. You might be able to say to the talker, 'When you were saying that, I was feeling such and such a thing,' and you can discuss what effect it might have had if you had shared that feeling with the talker — and possibly explore the reasons you chose not to share it.

Exercise: Using metaphors and similes

Aim of the exercise
To practise being economical with language, and to enhance the communication of empathy.

Metaphors and other figures of speech help us to communicate complicated things in almost visual ways. For example, the complex feelings associated with being lost, without direction, wandering without purpose, seeming to have no meaning, going through life without any real goals, could be summed up by the phrase 'I am a ship without a rudder'.

Using metaphors and similes can feel quite awkward at first, especially if your normal use of language does not include many of them. You have to experiment and find your own style. The important thing is for it to feel and be natural for you. There can be nothing worse than a well-meant metaphor sounding out of place or clichéd.

What to do
Make a list of common metaphors or similes that express feelings and emotions, for example:

- Leaving no stone unturned   • Like a broken record
- Like banging your head against a brick wall
- Like a straw in the wind   • Like a dog with two tails
- She was the cat who had the cream

Whenever you hear a new metaphor or simile that seems to express a feeling or emotion accurately and sensitively, make a note of it. Use them more freely in your everyday language until they become much more a natural part of it.

Exercise: Using transcripts

Aim of the exercise
To understand the differences between effective and ineffective counselling. A word of caution — listening to tapes of other counsellors at work or reading transcripts is not a 'how to do it' instruction.

Different people communicate the core conditions in different ways. This exercise will help you appreciate that diversity. It is not a substitute for you finding your own way of being with people and communicating, through your attitudes and behaviour, your way of creating relationships based on the core conditions.

What to do
Sometimes training courses provide transcripts of counselling interviews, or you can find them in books and journals. There are a number in Rogers' *Client-Centered Therapy*, (1951) and *On Becoming a Person* (1961). A complete transcript of a 30-minute counselling session can be found in *Invitation to Person-Centred Psychology* (Merry, 1995). Read what the client has said, and then, before you read the counsellor's response, try to imagine what you might have said had you been the counsellor. Imagine that you are sitting in front of this client, hearing these things. What do you feel about what the client said? How would you have responded? Write it down, or use a tape recorder.

Check your responses against what the counsellor actually said. Notice the different things that different people focus on, and the variety of ways in which the same statements can be heard and understood. You may find your responses better or worse, although that is not the main aim of this exercise. This exercise can sometimes feel too mechanical or contrived, but it can also be a useful way into thinking about what counselling involves.

Exercise: Doing it all wrong

Aim of the exercise
To experience the frustration of bad listening.

What to do
This can be quite fun, but it also has a serious side to it. Get into an empathy lab, but this time, instead of listening well and responding well, do everything you can to show you are **not** listening. Look out of the window, yawn a lot, fall asleep if you can, make up ridiculously inappropriate responses, give a lot of very bad advice. This exercise often leads to a lot of laughter, which is always helpful. It certainly shows up the differences between being listened to and not listened to.

Exercise: Empathy in everyday life

Aim of the exercise
To incorporate more empathic understanding in all relationships.

What to do
Next time you are with someone, especially if you care for them, try to listen to them with more attention. Try to put aside your own thoughts and needs and concentrate instead on really trying to understand this person in a new way. This will involve you in trying to sense what life is like for them, and to see things through their eyes. Try to let them know that you have understood them, or at least are trying to understand them more deeply. You may find qualities in them that you had not noticed before, and you may be surprised at how much richer the relationship becomes. This is especially important, and often very rewarding, with children.

Next time you are with someone you dislike, or cannot feel any warmth for, try to put aside the feelings that come up. Try to listen as if it were for the first time, and you may find things in the other person that you can warm towards, or at least you may begin to understand more about why you feel such dislike!

Exercise: Listening to yourself

Aim of the exercise
To become more aware of your own internal communication.

What to do
Empathy involves a sensitive awareness to the feelings and emotions of others but how well do you listen to yourself? How often are you really aware of your own feelings?

In different situations try to become more aware of the flow and complexity of your thoughts and feelings. You can try this when you are with someone you like or love, or when you feel yourself to be in a difficult or stressful situation.

A good experience is to find somewhere secluded and put on a favourite piece of music. As the music plays, pay attention to the feelings that come up and say them to yourself, 'Now I feel warm and calm like on a quiet beach in the sunshine, now I feel disturbed like I'm expecting something to happen, now I feel sadness . . . ' and so on. It is important that you *name* the feelings as you become aware of them so you really notice them and acknowledge them.

The more empathic you can be with yourself, the easier you will find it to be empathic with others.

Congruence

In person-centred counselling it is necessary for us to be as clear as possible in our relationships with clients. Personal, unresolved issues are always present in all of us, but they are less likely to become intrusive if we have spent some time on our own personal growth and psychological health. A helpful way to do this is through our own counselling, and this also has the advantage of letting us know what it feels like to be a client.

Being aware of our feelings towards others is one aspect of congruence. Another is the ability to communicate in ways that reveal us as people, not as just experts or technicians. If we are to be authentic it means we cannot hide behind roles or masks. We have to come out into the open and meet others openly and non-defensively. This can be quite a hard thing to do, and often it takes some courage to reveal ourselves and our feelings.

Congruence is not something that happens overnight, but we do not need to be a hundred per cent congruent (even if that were possible), before we can be effective counsellors. The development of congruence is a process, probably a lifelong one that we need to nurture. The more authentic we can become, the more we are able to offer our clients the quality of presence I mentioned earlier.

The communication of congruence to clients is largely an indirect process. In other words, congruence is not a matter of reporting to our clients the way we are feeling about them, and whilst a self-disclosure (e.g. 'I am feeling confused') might represent accurately a counsellor's present experiencing, the condition of congruence is met when a counsellor is aware of his or her current feelings, and does not distort them or deny them. Whether or not directly to disclose a feeling is a matter of choice, taking into account the client's present experiencing (a disclosure may be distracting), and the extent to which a counsellor's feelings may be interfering with his or her ability to experience empathic understanding.

Exploring congruence

Technically, congruence is much more than just being aware of feelings, though this is definitely part of it. I regard the exercises that follow as experiments in congruence and communication.

Exercise: Say how you felt

Aims of the exercise
To explore what congruence means to you.

What to do
This needs two people. Recall a recent event that had some meaning for you. It might be an argument or disagreement with a loved one, or a difficult situation at work — anything that made an impression on you.

As you go through the story try to be as clear as you can about what you were feeling at the time, and how you feel about it now. Go a little further than you would normally; instead of saying, 'I felt angry', say what it was in particular that made you angry, and say what you feel about anger itself. Do you have difficulty in expressing anger, for example, or do you get angry easily?

Also, notice more about the people in your story. Do they remind you of others from your past? For example, do you get angry more easily with some kinds of people than others? Why do you think this might be?

Example
> *The more I tried to talk to my doctor about what was wrong with me, the more irritated and angry I got. What really made me angry was that he hardly looked at me. All he did was scribble things down on a pad, and look at his watch. I tried to keep cool, but he hardly seemed to be listening to me at all. At one point I wanted to throw something at him, but I didn't. He reminded me of my maths teacher at school. I would do the best I could, but he used to treat me as if I didn't exist, he wrote me off as useless. I would try and tell him what I didn't understand, but he couldn't care less. Whenever I get that feeling now, that someone is writing me off, I want to shout, but I never do, in case I get into trouble, I suppose.*

Whilst you are doing this, your friend or colleague can be practising their counselling attitudes, helping you to be clearer about your feelings by listening, reflecting and summarising.

Exercise: Keeping a journal

Aim of the exercise
To become aware of themes and patterns in your life, and to explore them.

What to do
Keeping a journal can be a powerful way of helping you notice more about yourself. Keep a record of people and events and concentrate on recalling and describing what you were feeling. It can be useful to include a record of your dreams in your journal, again concentrating on the feelings that were part of the dream.

A journal can be a small notebook that you keep with you to jot things down as they occur to you, or a thick, hardbacked book that you keep up to date, if not every day, then at least once a week.

Don't restrict yourself only to writing things. Make sketches or drawings as well. You can also keep pictures and stories that mean something to you from papers or magazines, for example. The point is to keep a record of the changes you notice in yourself, and others around you, and the way you feel you are developing more awareness of yourself. After keeping the journal for some weeks or months you might begin to notice themes and patterns that you were unaware of before.

Keeping a record of dreams can be difficult, because dreams are so easily forgotten very quickly. One way to overcome this is to keep by your bed a small notebook and pencil that you can reach easily in the dark. Whenever you wake up with a dream in your mind, stay still for a moment or two and recall as much detail of the dream as you can; only then should you write down as much as you can remember.

After a few weeks or more you might discover common themes and patterns in your dreams, and it is worth exploring what they might mean to you.

Exercise: Non-verbal communication

Aim of the exercise
To develop awareness of congruent and incongruent behaviour in yourself and others.

What to do
One thing to be aware of in communication is the extent to which a person's verbal and non-verbal communication match up.

Remember, it is not necessarily because they are lying that people's behaviour doesn't always seem appropriate to what they are saying.

Try to observe people's behaviour more closely when they speak. If someone is saying they feel comfortable and relaxed, why does he keep fidgeting and looking out of the window? If someone says she is not angry, why is she raising her voice and tearing up bits of paper? Be careful, however, not to slip into too much interpretation of what you observe.

Making a videotape of an empathy lab, and then looking at the non-verbal aspect, is a good way to become more aware of the different ways people express themselves other than with words alone.

This is all to do with how much a person's feelings are reflected in their observable non-verbal (and verbal) behaviour. If you are in a group, you can ask for feedback and observations from others about how far your behaviour matches what you say you are feeling.

Understanding more about your own non-verbal behaviour is a good place to start. When you are with a client or in a practice session with a colleague, you may feel you are getting tense or vaguely uncomfortable, for example. The signals your body is sending you can help you get clearer about how you are feeling emotionally.

A word of warning though. People's behaviour is complex and contains many layers of meaning. It is not easy to tell what someone is really feeling just by watching what they do.

Unconditional positive regard

Unconditional positive regard is a matter of personal values and attitudes rather than a skill or a single piece of behaviour. Our acceptance of our clients is communicated by our way of being with them, rather than by anything in particular we may say or do. If we *feel* judgemental, we are likely to *be* judgemental, no matter how much we try to hide it, and hiding our judgementalism would conflict with our aim of being congruent. Being empathic with someone, giving them close attention and doing our best to understand them is one way of communicating respect and positive regard. The communication of unconditional positive regard is, like congruence, an indirect rather than a direct process. Communicating unconditional positive regard does not imply offering evaluations of a client (e.g. 'You are a good mother', or 'You did well to confront your partner with your anxieties'). Unconditional positive regard, when experienced by counsellors, is communicated to clients through a general attitude of respect for and understanding of them as individual people, and being supportive of them is best achieved through a process of empathic understanding without judgement.

Unconditional positive regard does not mean that we have to adopt an attitude of being 'nice', or over-friendly, or behaving in any way that is false. To do this would be a therapeutic disaster. It probably does make the process easier if we like our clients as people, and even feel great affection for them, but it is not a *condition* of counselling that you *must* like everybody. It is true that there are some people whom we like on first sight, with others it may take longer, or it may not happen at all.

It is worth remembering that we care about our clients as people in the process of change, rather than about examples of their behaviour or presently held attitudes. If we find our feelings are inconsistent with our wish to be accepting, it is important to allow full awareness of the discrepancy so we can later discuss it in supervision.

We all know of people whose behaviour and attitudes we deplore, and we may feel we could never be their counsellor because we would always be feeling judgemental about them, or even actively disliking them. This is something we must all consider very carefully. Could you be a counsellor to someone you knew to be a child abuser, for example? If you couldn't, what would you do if a client revealed him or herself as one?

Yet often it is the very people about whom we feel most judgemental who need our help, or someone's help, more than anyone. In my experience, people who have done terrible things have themselves experienced terrible things being done to them. Elsewhere in this book I talk about 'conditions of worth', and you might find that section helps with unconditional positive regard, which at first sight appears to be an impossible thing to ask of anyone, including person-centred counsellors.

Exploring unconditional positive regard

Unconditional positive regard is an attitude or set of values towards others that cannot be directly taught or learned. We are all conditioned, in some way or another, to be able to accept some things about people more easily than others. And we all probably have internalised attitudes towards others that, on closer examination, turn out to be irrational or founded more on prejudice than reality.

Our early experiences with people are very powerful in shaping the kinds of attitudes we hold, and often we are quite unconscious of our prejudices. It is possible to spend some time revealing our own prejudices, likes and dislikes, and seeing how far we need to hold on to the prejudices we have and the stereotypes we have unconsciously made a part of ourselves.

Exercise: Stereotype bashing

Aims of the exercise
To explore what unconditional positive regard means for you. To test the limits of your positive regard. To develop more awareness of yourself and others. To examine stereotyping and prejudice.

What to do

As it is very important in person-centred counselling to be able to deal with issues of power openly, it is crucial that counsellors confront and deal with their own racism, sexism and other prejudices to the extent they have these problems.

All good training courses include the examination of racist and sexist attitudes and help would-be counsellors to overcome them. You can supplement this by going on good racism and sexism awareness workshops, and by really paying attention to the attitudes and values you may hold.

In the meantime, you can start the process yourself by becoming more aware of some of the stereotypes and prejudices you hold, and beginning to re-examine them. First, don't be afraid of being prejudiced or view it as a matter of shame, but you do need to be open to change and to re-evaluating the views and opinions you hold about people.

Stereotyping happens because it is too complicated to see everything in individual terms, and we need general categories to help us make sense of all the complexities of human life. It obviously is not helpful in counselling, though, to hang on to stereotypes that prevent us from seeing people as individuals, with unique experiences, feelings and needs, even though they seem to be members of particular groups.

Prejudices arise mainly through fear of the unknown or fear of differences that we do not understand. They are often composed of subtle (and not so subtle) messages that have become taken for granted, and passed on in attitudes, media images, 'jokes' and stories.

Write down a list of groups and 'types', like :
Women, black people, Muslims, Scottish people, Irish people, Jewish people, Catholics, disabled people, English people, football supporters, teenagers, the elderly, Americans, northerners, men, southerners.

Next to each heading, write down a list of words or phrases that come immediately into your mind, for example :
Americans: rich, hospitable, superficial, violent, consumers, overweight, meat-eaters, warm, fitness fanatics, 'have a nice day', friendly, creative.
English people: cool, reserved, stiff, unfriendly, inefficient, conservative, repressed, sincere, inventive, cultured.

When you have got as complete a list as you can manage, share and compare it with a partner's list, preferably someone in a different 'group' from yourself. You will probably find that some of the words in your list contradict each other, like 'overweight' and 'fitness fanatics'. Explore the words and phrases against each of the headings. How many of them are actually true as far as you can see, and how many of them are clearly prejudices, biases and stereotypes?

Exercise: Valuing yourself

One way to become more accepting of others is to become more accepting of yourself. What parts of you do you dislike, or would like to change for the better? Do you have a healthy level of self-esteem? Do you value the good things about yourself?

Do you blame yourself for your imperfections? Do you find it easy to forgive yourself when you do something you dislike or regret later?

Many of us find it easier to admit to our faults and the things we do not like about ourselves, than to acknowledge and value our good, positive sides. This exercise is designed to focus on your positive, creative and likeable characteristics, and to admit to them and share them with others.

Aim of the exercise
To learn to appreciate and value your positive characteristics.

What to do
Write down 'ten things I really value about myself'.
For example:
- I really value the way I talk to my kids.
- I really value the way I can entertain people.
- I really value the way I listen to people.
- I really value the way I care about the people close to me.
- I really value my sense of humour.

You can now share your list with a partner or with your group. Learn to recognise and appreciate the positive things in yourself — they are what you build on in your relationships with others, including your clients.

It is helpful to balance this exercise by considering those things about yourself that you do not value or like. Constructive self-criticism is an important part of the process too.

Exercise: Making judgements

Sometimes, when we are quick to make judgements about others, we find that the things we dislike in them are the same things we dislike in ourselves. When you find yourself being judgemental, ask yourself, 'What is it about this person that reminds me of things I dislike in myself?' This process of seeing in others elements of ourselves is called 'projection'.

Aim of the exercise
To become aware of some ways in which we project parts of ourselves onto others.

What to do
Write down a list of people you dislike or feel wary of. They may be people you know personally, or people you have heard about through others. Next to each name, write down the things about them that you dislike or make you feel uncomfortable.

Now, with a partner or group, look closely at the list you have made, and talk through the ways in which you might also have some of those characteristics.

Alternatively, write down as much detail as you can about someone who makes you feel uncomfortable. Either role-play that person yourself with your group and talk afterwards about what it felt like to be that person, or have another member of your group role-play the person as a client for whom you are the counsellor. Again, talk through what it felt like to be that person's counsellor, and how you might try to see beyond the dislikeable characteristics to other aspects of the person.

Exercise: Things from the past

Sometimes we find ourselves disliking particular kinds of people, though rationally there seems to be no good reason why this should be so. It may be that some people remind us, in some way, of unhappy experiences we once had, and those experiences can get restimulated without us being fully aware of it.

Aims of the exercise
To bring some of the past into the present, and to become aware of how we might relate to people today based on past experiences.

What to do
Think of groups of people you dislike and write down the things about them you imagine to be so dislikeable. For example :

- *Police officers, because they are too powerful and authoritarian.*
- *Doctors, because they never listen to what you say.*

Now either write down, or recount to a partner or group, whatever you can recall from your past experiences with these people. Take it in turns to explore incidents, memories, vague impressions and more vivid memories. Concentrate especially on what you felt while these things were taking place, and notice how far you have extended characteristics that might have been true about an individual person to include the whole group he or she represents.

Exercise: Hurt people do hurtful things

Something for all counsellors to remember is that people who themselves have experienced great hurt often turn out to do hurtful and destructive things to others. This does not mean that we have to condone or excuse their actions, but it does help us to work with such people.

It's also worth remembering that when such people come for counselling they are sometimes implicitly recognising their hurtful behaviour and are wanting to do something about it.

Aim of the exercise
To understand how previous hurtful experiences can affect present-day behaviour.

What to do
When you next come across someone who behaves in destructive, even violent ways, or whenever you read about such people, ask yourself what kinds of experiences that person might have had as a very young child, that may have led to this behaviour.

Practice counselling

Experimenting with and exploring the three core conditions in the way we have done so far can help us become familiar with what they each mean, but in practice the core conditions need to be present in the relationship as a configuration of values, personal qualities and attitudes, not as separate entities. I have already described the core conditions as a unity or *gestalt* and the task for counsellors is to integrate this unity of personal qualities, values and attitudes into their way of being with clients.

The only way to experiment safely with counselling relationships based on the core conditions is to practise 'living' them in a consistent way with people whose need for counselling is not overwhelming and who are willing to contribute to the counsellor's development by offering themselves as practice clients. On any properly organised counsellor training programme there should be plenty of opportunities to practise counselling in a controlled and relatively safe environment, and most people are willing to take turns at being client and counsellor.

In effect, practice counselling sessions are an extension of the 'empathy lab' idea. The difference is that the empathy lab is an opportunity to focus on ways of communicating empathic understanding, and to get feedback from others on our effectiveness at achieving that. Practice counselling sessions require the focus to be on the qualities of the relationship in all its aspects, not only on the level of empathy present, but also on the ability of the counsellor to remain congruent, non-judgemental and non-directive in the way I previously defined those terms.

A problem with practice counselling sessions during training is that trainee counsellors, whilst they can accumulate some useful experience, often find that experience to be limited to a series of 'one-off' or first interviews. It is more difficult to gain experience of more long-term counselling relationships. To overcome this, I suggest that trainees form pairs in which one person agrees to be counsellor, and the other, client, and that this arrangement continues over a period of some months. This gives the relationship a chance to develop, and gives both client and counsellor experience of a more established counselling relationship. In any training group, each person should, in this way, have the opportunity to counsel the same 'client' for (say) 20 sessions, and it also gives each 'client' an experience of being in that role for the same number of sessions with a 'counsellor' who is, of course, a different person from their 'client'.

The following exercise gives some suggestions about the organisation of practice counselling sessions and outlines some ways of making best use of the learning opportunities available.

Learning from the experience of practice counselling

A number of options are open to you for making the most from the experience. To simulate real conditions it is probably best not to include an observer, but if you have the necessary equipment, you can videotape or audiotape some or all of the sessions for review later. If it is possible, you could agree with another group member to act as 'supervisor', and use that person in exactly the same way as you would with a 'real' supervisor once your counselling practice has begun (see chapter 9).

Take notes immediately after the session, concentrating on how you felt about the experience, where you feel things went well and where you felt less effective. After a number of sessions, you might be able to discern patterns and recurring themes that you can think about and explore in supervision, remembering to protect confidentiality. This latter point is just as important as it is with 'real' clients, and nothing that takes place during practice counselling sessions should ever become common knowledge among the other group members, unless you have permission to make it so from the client concerned.

Reviewing the video- or audiotapes can be especially helpful, either on your own or with a colleague (or staff member), providing you have the client's permission to do so. If your client is willing, his or her input at this stage can be particularly useful, especially if the client can give you direct feedback about how well he or she felt understood, and how he or she experienced the relationship as a whole.

There may be some difficulties in using practice clients to give feedback in this way. If the sessions cover difficult or painful experiences, clients may be unwilling to 'relive' them in the more objective way that giving feedback requires. Or people may be resistant to dealing with

Exercise: Practice counselling

Aim of the exercise
To develop experience of ongoing counselling relationships.

What to do
STEP 1: Find a partner with whom you think you can work for about 20 sessions (or as many as time will allow). Begin with an 'agreement setting' session of the kind you would conduct with a 'real' client, arranging when and where to meet, for how long, and for how many sessions in the first instance. I suggest that you work towards 50 minute or one hour sessions, perhaps starting with 30 minutes at first. The same rules of confidentiality should apply in exactly the same way as with 'real' clients. It is important that neither client nor counsellor 'role-plays' any more than is necessary to imitate 'real' conditions. It is best if both people approach this not only as an exercise, but also as an opportunity for authentic experience, working on real (not imaginary) client 'issues'.

STEP 2: Review each session as soon after completing it as possible. I suggest you first read through my suggestions (below) about ways of getting the most from review and feedback.

Getting started
Beginning to counsel 'for real' is a different experience from taking part in structured or semi-structured exercises of the kind included in this book. Rather than exploring yourself and your values, or experimenting separately with the various attitudes, skills and personal qualities I have described, you are now trying to put all that learning into practice.

Person-centred counselling does not follow a particular formula, and the idea that counselling is a 'way of being' with someone, rather than a 'way of doing' something, can be a bit daunting at first. I don't want to provide a prescription for what you should do, but person-centred counselling is a disciplined process, not an 'anything goes' process. Brodley (1993) has suggested a set of guidelines that you might want to bear in mind when you first set out to provide the kind of experience for your client that is required of person-centred counselling. One way of using the guidelines is to refer to them when you are reviewing a tape of yourself or during a feedback session. What follows is a summary of the main points suggested by Brodley:

- Absorb the meanings which the client is expressing to you. What is the client succeeding at 'getting at', or what is she or he trying to 'get at'?
- When you express your tentative understanding, think of yourself as trying to check whether or not you have, in fact, understood.

You may express your tentativeness with introductory statements such as: 'Is this right?', or 'Is this what you mean?'

- Avoid introductions to your empathic responses which suggest you are trying to interpret the client or that your task is to discover or elicit 'deeper' meanings. Introductions which sometimes create such misunderstandings are, 'I sense you are really feeling . . . or 'You sound like you . . .'

- Stay completely within the client's frame of reference. As you are listening, try to grasp the client's viewpoint together with the meanings and feelings that are the client's at that time. Try to absorb those things into yourself — without the reservations and interferences of scepticism or criticism. Put aside any doubts or critical feelings about the client's statements and try to understand the client's point of view and feelings.

- If you don't understand what the client has been expressing, simply say you haven't understood yet, and ask the client to state in a different way what she or he was expressing.

- After you make an empathic understanding response, allow your client to initiate the next response. Allow silence. Relax and allow yourself and your client a chance to think and feel further — to reflect upon the experiences that are being expressed between you.

- Do not ask leading or probing questions such as, 'How do you feel about that?', or, 'Tell me more about . . . ', 'What do you think he or she would feel about that?' or 'Can you tell me more about your relationship to X?'

- Do not ask your client questions that involve assumptions or theories that are not part of those directly expressed or clearly implied in what your client has been saying. Examples are, 'Do you remember how you felt when your brother was born?', 'How do you feel when someone has authority over you?'

- Avoid interpretations of any kind.

- Avoid agreement (or disagreement) with what the client is saying.

- Avoid suggestions or guidance of any kind.

- Avoid praise or criticism of the client or of the client's behaviour.

- If your client indicates she or he feels stopped and doesn't know how to proceed and asks for your help, a relatively non-directive response that is often helpful is to say something such as, 'Sometimes, if one gives oneself a bit more time, some thoughts or direction will come to mind', or, 'I feel there's no hurry, so if you can, try and let yourself relax to give yourself a chance to see if something comes to you.'

- If the client asks for more help, then you can suggest she or he takes more time, or say something like, 'Sometimes it helps to think back over the concerns that brought you in.' The best guidance is usually the encouragement to take time for the client to search his or her experience and thoughts.

- If the client has lost his or her train of thought, avoid prompting or reminding the client unless she or he asks for help. Scattered thoughts and discontinuity of theme should be accepted in the same manner as developed and coherent thoughts.
- Avoid integrating for the client, e.g., 'That sounds like it may be related to the problem you have with your mother.' Empathic interviews often result in integration, but it is not the counsellor's responsibility to find or direct such connections.
- Avoid volunteering comments about the client's apparent feelings, state or other experiences, e.g. 'You seem to have a lot of emotions around that topic', or 'It seems you have an issue with abandonment or loss.' Of course, these examples may be similar to empathic responses, if the client has been expressing any of these ideas.
- If your client asks you a question,
  (a) give yourself a chance to absorb the question,
  (b) ask for further clarification of the question if you need it,
  (c) respond to the question in a direct, person-to-person manner. This can mean different things, depending upon the nature of the question, your own knowledge and expertise in the arena being inquired about, your own personal feelings about self-disclosure and your personal feelings about expressing opinions.

This may seem a lot to remember and, as I said above, I do not mean it as a list of instructions. The point to emphasise is that your responses to your client need to focus on your developing empathic understanding of your client's expression, not on attempts to direct the process or suggest ways in which your client might express his or her feelings. Brodley's guidelines can be a useful way of thinking through particular incidents with your client, especially where you felt you may have been distracted from your attempts to understand and communicate your understanding.

difficult issues in their counselling sessions if they think that they will have to go over them a second time. To overcome difficulties such as these, you can make an agreement with the client not to include some sessions, or parts of sessions, in the feedback discussions, but this does mean that some learning opportunities may be lost.

One way of making the exploration of a practice counselling session more fruitful is through a system called *Interpersonal Process Recall* (Kagan, 1984). This involves playing back a video- or audiotape to help you recall what was happening at the time. The process of recall is helped by the presence of a third person who was not involved in the original experience, known as the *Inquirer*. While listening to — or watching — the recording, the Inquirer waits until the counsellor decides to stop the tape, and then invites the counsellor, through a series of non-interpretive, neutral questions, to recall and think through the experience more deeply. The control over when to stop the tape rests with the original counsellor, so the counsellor maintains power within the recall process and becomes responsible for his or her own learning.

The Inquirer needs to be non-judgemental, to ask brief, open-ended questions, and to accept that the counsellor can choose to respond or not to any question. Some questions from Kagan's checklist include:

- What were you thinking at that moment?
- What were you feeling?
- What did you think the other person was feeling?
- Was there anything you wanted to say but couldn't find appropriate words for?
- What had you hoped would happen next?
- Had you any goals or intentions at that point?
- What prevented you from saying what you really wanted to say?

Before returning to the tape, the Inquirer might ask:

- Did the setting affect you?
- How did you feel about your own behaviour?
- What things have you learnt from this recall?

For a more detailed discussion of IPR, and the variation that includes involving the client in the process, see Bayne et. al. (1999).

Whether you choose to use the structured form of IPR, or something less formal, or Brodley's guidelines (above), it is important to remember that practice counselling sessions are of most value when they are followed by some kind of review. In this way you can gradually develop more insight into your own way of practising counselling, where you are most effective and where you experience most difficulty.

Some different approaches to counselling

The exercises and ideas given above are designed to help you become familiar with the process of engaging directly with people to understand them empathically without judgement and test out your understanding with them, a process that contributes to the formation of a relationship rich in the core conditions.

It can help to contrast the person-centred way of being with clients with other approaches to highlight the differences. To this end, we can look again at some of Jack's statements (see chapter 5) but this time to respond to them in ways that do not conform to person-centred theory.

CLIENT: Well, there are so many things. I don't know if you can help with them . . . It just seems that everything gets on top of me so easily these days, much more than they used to. I suppose I have been having a bad time lately. I don't seem to get on with my teenage daughter like I used to . . . I feel very unhappy at work, maybe I've been there too long. My wife and I seem to be at each other's throats . . . I don't know . . . coming to a counsellor seems like a last resort, but I can't keep going like this much longer.

COUNSELLOR: *You're very tense. I think we should try some relaxation exercises later, you might find them useful at work. Could you say more about your relationship with your daughter?*

• Here, the counsellor has told Jack how he is feeling, and has suggested a solution to this 'problem'. The counsellor has also begun to direct the process by suggesting Jack talk about his daughter.

CLIENT: I do feel a bit on my own. In fact I feel alone a lot of the time. Because there isn't anything specific, I can't really talk much about it. My wife says I'm moody and closed off . . . but how do you talk about something and nothing? It all seems a bit futile.

COUNSELLOR: *Your feeling of being alone probably stems from the breakdown of your relationships at home. How does your wife feel about you at the moment . . . have her feelings for you changed?*

• The counsellor is really beginning to interpret and diagnose Jack now, then neatly, but unhelpfully, removes Jack from his own feelings and gets him to speculate about the feelings of someone else!

CLIENT: I just feel like I'm complaining when I have no real right to. I've got everything I need . . . why do I feel so, so unhappy?

COUNSELLOR: *That sounds like an old tape you're playing there. Did your parents say those kinds of things to you? What was your relationship with your parents like?*

• This is a bit of Transactional Analysis coupled with more than a hint of Freud. The counsellor is not concentrating on understanding Jack from Jack's point of view, but leading him into a discussion of his childhood. In person-centred counselling, Jack will do this when he sees it as important, and in his own way. What this counsellor is doing is formulating Jack's problems for him, and suggesting the solution.

CLIENT: No, it doesn't. I usually just keep these things to myself. Most people would never suspect I feel this way. I know my wife knows I'm unhappy. I think she's a bit scared of it, as if it's something to do with her. I want to tell her it isn't, but if we do start to talk about it we end up rowing, or I deny there's anything wrong.

COUNSELLOR: *People who have difficulty expressing their feelings often feel depressed and unhappy, just like you do. Let's try an experiment. Imagine your wife is in the empty chair next to you, and you are able to talk to her. What is it that you'd really like to say to her? If you practise it here it'll be easier to do it in reality. Would you like to try this for a while?*

• The first remark tells the client what is wrong with him. It is not very accepting or understanding of Jack's present feelings about himself. Next, the counsellor takes complete charge. This technique (a psychodrama and gestalt technique) may be very useful in some circumstances, but it removes the possibility for Jack to explore his feelings in his own way, developing his own resources, and places responsibility for the counselling squarely on the counsellor. In gestalt counselling this technique would be introduced sensitively as an integral part of an ongoing process, not suddenly and sharply stuck in like this. Jack could decline the invitation, but many clients find it very hard to resist po*werful suggestions like this.*

CLIENT: When I think about that, about what I just said, it does feel like there's another person in me, or perhaps it's another bit of me, who has kept quiet for a long time, and not really been happy with what's going on. I mean, the main bit of me is successful and all that, but . . . I need to think about this more . . .

COUNSELLOR: *It seems there are parts of you not very well integrated, sort of split off. Try not to think so much and get more in touch with what you are feeling. Let's try and get acquainted with that quiet person and find out what he wants.*

• This response is very interpretive and diagnostic — 'You have a split personality' — and it would be a very difficult thing for a client to hear and make some sense of. Next, it devalues Jack's need to take time and think, and admonishes him for not being a 'feeling enough' person — very judgemental! Finally, it offers a solution to what the counsellor assumes to be the problem.

Other techniques

You will have noticed that I do not describe techniques like relaxation, guided fantasy, or role playing etc. as part of the counselling process, though I think such techniques can be useful in developing more awareness of ourselves, in training groups for example. In my experience, person-centred counsellors tend to use very few techniques like these, if any at all. Carl Rogers' view was that they may be useful only in so far as they help to establish a relationship built on the three core conditions of empathy, congruence and unconditional positive regard.

A problem in person-centred counselling (and all other counselling) occurs when the counsellor reaches for a technique either when the going gets tough (when the client seems 'stuck' for example), or simply because the counsellor knows a lot of techniques and wants to use them. It would be better to ask ourselves about the quality of empathy we are giving, the degree to which we are being congruent, and the extent to which we are being judgemental, before opting for a technique that might gloss over these problems.

Techniques are not person-centred if they serve to remove the focus of the counselling away from the client's inner world to that of the counsellor, or if they divert clients' attention away from what they are presently feeling towards something the counsellor thinks they ought to feel. As I said before, person-centred counsellors take the view that the client is the one and only expert. It is the client who knows what hurts, and it is only the client who has the resources and power for change. The counsellor's role is to help provide the conditions of security and trust that enable clients to discover, develop and use their own resources.

Some concluding comments to this chapter

There are many ways of being authentically person-centred, but all of them require a great deal of self-knowledge and a disciplined rather than haphazard approach to the counselling process. Because the person-centred approach does not rely on learning particular strategies to respond to particular client issues it is often described as one of the more difficult approaches to understand fully. Mearns (1997), for example, suggests that person-centred counselling:

> ... *probably requires more training and a greater intensity of training than most other mainstream counselling approaches because of the daunting personal development objectives which require to be met* (p. x).

This chapter has focused on some of those 'daunting personal development objectives', and has treated 'skills' as the means by which we put our values, personal qualities and attitudes into practice with our clients. The next chapter discusses some of the issues you are likely to meet when you first begin to work with clients. It also takes our discussion of self-development a stage further by briefly reviewing the advantages of experiencing your own counselling, and I have some ideas about developing deeper levels of congruence through working in groups. Before leaving this chapter, I suggest you work through the following checklist.

Checklist: Values, skills, personal qualities and attitudes

- Person-centred counselling revolves around a client/counsellor relationship of definable qualities.
- Person-centred counselling enables the self-resources of clients to become available for the purposes of change.
- Empathic understanding, congruence and unconditional positive regard are attitudes and core personal qualities, not skills or techniques.
- Empathic understanding is an active process involving close attention to a client's experiencing process, and should not be confused with sympathy or identification.
- The development of a counsellor's empathic abilities involves a close examination of a counsellor's values and self-awareness as well as the acquisition of communication skills.
- A congruent counsellor is one who is aware of his or her feelings in relationships with clients, and whose outward communication and behaviour matches his or her inner experiencing.
- The communication of congruence to clients is normally an indirect process and does not necessarily involve self-disclosure on the part of the counsellor.
- Congruent self-disclosure by the counsellor may, at times, be helpful, especially when doing so enables the counsellor to experience deeper levels of empathic understanding and unconditional positive regard.
- Unconditional positive regard involves respect for individual people and a trust in their capacity for self-development. It does not involve offering unsolicited evaluations, either negative or positive, of clients' experiencing.
- The development of a counsellor's unconditional positive regard involves high levels of self-awareness and a willingness to question personally held beliefs, prejudices and assumptions.
- A problem with incorporating techniques from other approaches is that they may be inconsistent with a trust in the client's actualising tendency and self-resources.

Training issues: client work and personal development

8

This chapter is written mainly for students on training courses in person-centred counselling, and for those organising such courses (or planning to do so). It offers some ideas and perspectives concerning client work while in training, and, more briefly, discusses some issues concerning the need for counsellors at all levels of experience to attend to on-going self-development needs.

There is a natural limit to the usefulness of practice counselling sessions with fellow students. As I have said several times in this book, person-centred counselling is less concerned with skills and techniques, and more concerned with the development and personal ownership of a set of values, personal qualities and attitudes. Giving verbal expression to empathic understanding does, of course, involve the acquisition and refinement of clear and sensitive communication skills, and this is a vital aspect of all counsellor training programmes. But polishing 'communication skills' in the safety of a training course has, at some appropriate point, to give way to the reality of sitting face to face with 'real' clients whose needs are unpredictable.

This next section is designed for those who are beginning to work with real clients. This can be both exciting and, at times, provoke some anxiety. It is important for many trainees that they feel supported and understood during the transition between training and practice, and the resources of the training group, both staff and students, are most important here. Peer support groups, small group sessions and supervision all have their part to play in providing opportunities for you to discuss the problems you may be facing, and the successes and satisfaction to be gained from being in close relationship with clients. This chapter discusses some of the issues that you might face when embarking on a placement with a counselling agency, and it makes some suggestions about how to get more from training placement experiences. In this context, I discuss the advantages and disadvantages of offering brief counselling or time-limited counselling because many counselling agencies restrict the number of sessions allowed to each client.

Next, I offer some discussion and suggestions about personal counselling for the trainee counsellor, particularly because BACP requires that all trainees should experience being a client themselves before they can be individually accredited. Finally, we explore some of the advantages of working on personal development objectives in groups.

The training placement

An established and essential part of all counsellor training is working with clients under appropriate supervision. Plans for starting to work with clients will usually be made in consultation with the course staff once everyone involved is satisfied that you are ready to start working with clients. Usually, this decision will be based on evidence of competence on the course itself, and normally involves some kind of formal or informal assessment process. Depending upon the demands of the specific course, you will normally have to complete a certain number of supervised hours working with clients before you can complete the course, usually in the region of 100 to 150 hours with a range of clients. Some of those clients need to be medium- or long-term clients, which, for training purposes, is usually regarded as being more than 6 sessions. A series of 'one-offs' is generally not considered adequate.

BACP advise that trainee counsellors gain their counselling experience working within a counselling agency, and not in private practice. This is principally with the care and protection of the client in mind — agencies should provide a safe environment which the client can trust, but also should be protective of and nurturing to the trainee. Although there are different kinds of agencies offering placements, many are within voluntary organisations which may provide free or low-cost counselling for people who request the service.

Some ideas about where placements can be found include:
- Specialist voluntary services e.g. bereavement, alcohol and drug counselling, young people's counselling services, etc.
- Primary healthcare settings such as GP surgeries.
- College counselling services.
- Agencies for the care of survivors of child sexual abuse, victims of domestic violence, HIV/AIDS centres, etc.
- Organisations caring for the homeless.
- Church or ministry organisations offering pastoral services.
- Mental health agencies, e.g. MIND.
- Organisations for carers of the disabled or those with mental health problems.

More unusual placements, though still appropriate for person-centred trainees, might include:
- Prisons and other custodial settings.
- Social services settings working with adults with learning disabilities.
- Psychiatric day-care units.

You should be careful to make sure that the agency you work for provides opportunities for counselling, rather than the use of counselling skills or befriending, for example. The current availability of suitable placements for trainees and the apparently ever-increasing demand for them means that ideally tailored situations are hard to find.

Placements may take a considerable time to organise. Agencies may need to recruit through a selection process, and after selection may require counsellors to complete their own training programme to make sure they can provide the kind of work to which the counselling service is committed. There may be a delay of up to six months from the initial application to beginning to work with a new client.

There may also be no guarantee that you will be accepted for the placement, even after going through the orientation training, so you may be best advised to put in two or three applications to different agencies, hoping that at least one will be successful.

For you, as a person-centred trainee, it is important to determine how far the agency will:

- enable you to work exclusively using the person-centred approach
- enable you to receive person-centred supervision
- provide a secure organisational framework from which you can practise
- allow casework material to be available for assessment if necessary.

In addition, it is best to clarify whether or not the agency will allow tape-recording of clients, especially if there is a need to do this as part of the course assessment procedures. You should also be familiar with the agency's various policies on, for example, the number of sessions allowed, rules of confidentiality, supervision requirements, referral and record-keeping and note-taking. You should also clarify that the agency can provide whatever written reports your training course requires (if any) and what the lines of communication are between the agency and your training course. Dryden et al. (1995) recommend a 'three-way contract' between yourself, the agency and your course that incorporates the points we make above, but which also includes clarification concerning who takes clinical responsibility for your counselling work, and what happens in the case of difficulties or disputes between you and the agency, including concerns about the quality and ethics of your work.

Counselling approaches of the agency

Some agencies welcome trainees from a variety of theoretical approaches and will allow you to practise using your preferred approach. Others expect you to conform to a specific approach, and you need to clarify this at the start. There is no point in offering person-centred counselling if the agency is a psychodynamic one, for example.

Many agencies provide their own initial training courses in their specialist field, e.g. counselling people with addictions or those who have been bereaved. Some of the content of these courses may conflict with your person-centred training. This may or may not be a problem for you, but you do need to clarify how far the expectations of the agency are different from what you may be willing and able to offer. The agency may expect you to attend regular in-house supervision sessions with other counsellors, not all of whom will be trainees, and again, some aspects of the supervision provided may not be consistent with your person-centred model.

Agencies may limit the number of sessions available to clients because of the scale of the demand for its services and length of waiting time, on the basis of policy or resources available. Others may have no time limits or, more commonly, limit the time to anywhere between four sessions and 20 in total. The policy of the agency in this respect may well be a critical factor for you as very restricted counselling may not be appropriate for training purposes and you could feel constrained by the agency's policies.

Supervision arrangements

Some organisations may have funds available to provide you with an individual supervisor of your choice. Others provide individual or group supervision for their counsellors (not all of whom will be students). Person-centred trainees may be dependent on receiving person-centred supervision to meet the requirements of their training programmes and this may not be provided by the agency, even though trainees are able to work in a person-centred way with their clients. This could lead to a conflict between the requirements of the agency and the requirements of your training course. To meet the latter, you may have to find person-centred supervision outside the agency (provided the confidentiality boundaries of the agency allow clients' cases to be discussed outside of the agency) at your own expense. There is additionally the dilemma and confusion that can be experienced when receiving two sets of supervision. I know of one person-centred trainee who received compulsory non-person-centred group supervision, and found it so confusing that she held back and revealed as little of herself and her work as possible. She did not experience the supervision as helpful to her development as a person-centred counsellor, and had to find an alternative source of person-centred supervision once she had discussed her situation with both the agency and her training course.

Organisational framework

Well-run agencies provide a secure organisational framework in which you can develop as a counsellor by providing the necessary administrative backup and suitable accommodation. They may also have an arrangement for making an initial assessment of the client's needs and for emergency support, should it be needed.

In training it can be useful for you if organisational details are the responsibility of the agency, so that you can focus specifically on the development of your counselling relationships with your clients, without the need to be concerned with administrative problems that might interfere with the relationship.

Examples of some issues that might be relevant here include:

- Time. (The length of the sessions.) What happens when the client arrives early or late?
- Space. (The counselling accommodation.) Is the setting confidential? Additional complications may arise if the client is counselled at home.
- Assessment issues. What can be expected by both client and counsellor at the first meeting?
- Content. Does the agency expect the counsellor to be involved in advice-giving?
- Fees. How are fees paid, and to whom? Is there a 'sliding scale' of fees? How are issues of payment made clear to clients, and who takes responsibility for this?
- Complaints. How are complaints by clients dealt with?
- Insurance. Is there a need for personal indemnity insurance?

Initial assessment of clients

The role of initial assessment for a person-centred practitioner is open to debate (see Bozarth, 1998), but safety and competency issues are often considered by the agency to be paramount. Furthermore, some selection is sometimes considered necessary to ensure that the resources of the agency are sufficient for the (likely) psychological and emotional needs of prospective clients. An initial assessment is usually performed by a qualified and experienced counsellor and the client then allocated to a trainee.

The process of allocation will vary according to the needs and ethos of the agency. In some agencies an assessment form is provided for the trainee counsellor to complete, or for the client to complete, during the first sessions.

Issues for you to consider here include:

- Why has this client been allocated to me?
- Do I need to read the assessment notes?
- Will I be competent enough?
- Will the client stay in counselling?
- Will I be able to have unconditional positive regard for this client?
- Will I be able to sustain a relationship?
- Will I get the contracting right?
- Will I manage the time boundaries satisfactorily?
- Will I be able to cope with the responsibility of working with a real client — am I confident enough?
- What should I do if clients do not show up?

There may be a variety of reasons why an agency allocates particular clients to particular counsellors. For example, clients may have preferences about the gender of their counsellor, or their ethnic group, or the agency may decide that some clients problems are beyond the scope and experience of trainees. It will help if you clarify with the agency what their various policies are, if they have any, so that you do not find yourself only allocated clients of a specific kind, or only with specific problems.

Keeping a log

If you are on an accredited training course, you will almost certainly be expected to keep a log of your client work which is likely to be used in some way towards your assessment. There are at least two good reasons why keeping a log is a good way to support your learning as a counsellor. First, it provides you with a record of your client work and details the range of clients with whom you work. Second, it provides opportunities to reflect on your work, how you see yourself developing as a counsellor, where you experience particular difficulties and how you make use of your supervision time.

To be most useful, then, a log needs to be much more than simply a record or diary. Getting used to evaluating and appraising your work for yourself helps you to develop as a reflective practitioner, that is — someone who can identify what they are learning from their experience and can feed that learning back into their ongoing practice. Each time you enter into a counselling relationship with a client you are, in effect, testing the theory of person-centred counselling and exploring its limits. You are also constantly testing your own limits as a counsellor — perhaps certain kinds of clients or client issues cause you particular problems, for example. Or, perhaps, you feel particularly effective with some clients, or with some issues. Either way, a productive means of continuing your development as a counsellor is through the process of reflection and being open to self-criticism, an important part of the development of your 'internal supervisor' (see chapter 9).

Different courses have differing requirements for professional logs, some asking for more detail than others, but the overall aims remain constant — to encourage self-appraisal and the taking of responsibility yourself for your own learning.

Finally, the training process is much enhanced through sharing with other trainees the experience of working with real clients. Courses where client work begins only when skills and theory work have finished miss these opportunities, and the benefits of reflecting on practice and linking practice with theory in a supportive training environment are lost.

Checklist: client work

- Establish the number of supervised counselling hours you need to satisfy course requirements.
- Establish what your course means by 'ongoing counselling relationships' (the minimum number of sessions expected with each client, or some clients), and if you are expected to work with a variety of clients.
- Establish early on in your course what counselling opportunities are available to you locally.

- When approaching a counselling agency for a possible placement, establish that you will be involved in counselling, not using counselling skills.
- Establish what role (if any) the agency plays in your course assessment.
- Clarify the lines of communication between you, the agency and your course.
- Clarify any counselling agency requirements for in-house training.
- Clarify agency guidelines and requirements for supervision.
- Clarify agency policy (if any) on confidentiality and tape-recording.
- Clarify the process by which the agency allocates clients to you.
- Keep a log of your counselling hours in which you reflect on your experience.

Time-limited work

A common dilemma for counsellors working within agencies occurs when the agency limits the number of sessions allowed with each client. In the person-centred tradition the decision about when to end counselling is a matter for discussion, with the lead being taken by the client. Ideally, counselling finishes when the client's sense of self has developed to the point where he or she no longer experiences a current need for self-exploration. Time-limited work is becoming more common generally with the development of Employee Assistance Programmes, insurance cover and so on. Counsellors who work in medical settings, such as within a group general medical practice, may also be limited in the number of sessions they can offer each client.

Limitations on numbers of sessions can be because the agency concerned believes in the effectiveness of working within strict time boundaries, or it perceives itself as working only with very closely defined problem areas, such as bereavement, and discourages more general self-exploration outside of those boundaries. An agency may also define itself as offering a service only to people experiencing an immediate crisis, with more longer-term work being left to others. Additionally, an agency may feel under pressure to offer its services to a large number of people and 'ration' its time and other resources to make this possible.

Attitudes towards time in counselling are complex. It is not a simplistic matter of 'more means better', and opinions vary about what constitutes 'brief counselling'. For example, Feltham (1997a) thinks of brief counselling as between six and 20 sessions, and Dryden and Feltham (1992) report on surveys of UK student counselling services where average attendance was between two and five sessions. Bayne et al. (1999) remark, 'These findings [of Dryden and Feltham] indicate brief counselling by default rather than by design' (p. 19).

The issue of time-limited or brief counselling has something of a history within the PCA. A paper by Shlien (1957), for example, researched the theoretical and practical implications of offering time-limited client-centred (person-centred) counselling at the University of Chicago Counseling Center. In this paper, Shlien discussed the attitude taken towards time by the psychotherapist Otto Rank who had, indirectly, some significant influence on Rogers as he developed person-centred counselling. Rank, according to Shlien, 'deliberately used the device of "end setting" . . . to "project the end phase forward" . . . mainly to mobilize the constructive force of the "will conflict"'. (Rogers never adopted this 'strategy' concerning time, and took the view that the length of time spent in counselling was a matter for the individuals concerned. For Rogers, deliberately limiting time in this way would have been a misuse of the counsellor's power). Furthermore, Jessie Taft, a therapist and Rank's translator, amplified the significance of time limits. She called them 'one of the most valuable tools ever introduced into therapy', and argued that time is the supremely representative symbol of all limitations in living. Shlien then quoted a passage from Taft (1933):

> *If there is no therapeutic understanding and use of one interview, many interviews equally barren cannot help. In the single interview, if that is all I allow myself to count upon, if I am willing to take that one hour in and for itself, there is not time to hide behind material, no time to explore the past or future. I myself am the remedy at this moment if there is any and I can no longer escape my responsibility, not for the client, but for myself and my role in the situation. Here is just one hour to be lived through as it goes, one hour of present immediate relationship, however limited, with another human being who has brought himself to the point of asking for help* (p. 11).

The issue here is one of quality rather than quantity. Taft argued that when counselling is limited to a single session, there is a powerful incentive to engage in a relationship in which the counsellor's authenticity and presence are of most significance. Taft was writing before person-centred counselling was developed, but her identification of herself as 'the remedy at this moment if there is any' was later to become echoed in Rogers' work, particularly concerning issues of congruence, authenticity and the counsellor's close attention to the client's frame of reference.

Shlien's research detailed counselling limited to 20 interviews:

> *From comparisons on most of the instruments and measures, we know that it compares very favorably with, and often exceeds, results of longer unlimited therapy* (p. 321).

However, Shlien introduced a note of caution:

> *In a blind analysis . . . the brief time-limited cases show sharp decline in a theoretically describable score (affective*

complexity) during the follow-up period six months after
therapy ends (p. 321).

The indications from Shlien's work were that relatively brief periods of person-centred counselling resulted in successful outcomes equalling and in some cases exceeding the results of longer term counselling. There was, however, a diminishing of the positive effects of brief counselling after a six month period.

Shlien's work was inspired, at least in part, by pragmatic considerations:

The project stems from a practical problem faced by many
clinical agencies — a demand for service exceeding the supply
... (p. 318).

Much more recently, Thorne (1999) has returned to the same theme. He reports on an 'experiment' at his university counselling centre in which he offered very brief counselling opportunities of three sessions only. Thorne reports being excited and encouraged by the results of his experiment:

I did not find myself being in the least bit coercive but was able
to marvel at the client's ability to stay single-mindedly within
the area of most concern. Again it was as if the limited time
ensured that the client quickly established an agenda and did
not deviate from it even if deep water flooded in after half an
hour ...

... Perhaps most surprising of all, I found myself bonding with
these short-term clients in a deep but uncomplicated way. It
was as if they had taken the decision to trust me and the process
and then jumped in with both feet. There was no agonising
testing out the relationship nor was there great pain at its
ending ... (pp. 10–11).

At first sight, Thorne appears enthusiastic about the benefits of brief person-centred counselling. The discipline imposed by limited time seemed to have had a positive effect. Reminiscent of Taft's writing over 40 years previously, Thorne remarked:

I remember the buzz of being on full psychological alert
through every minute of every session. I became the very
embodiment of the core conditions and allowed my energy no
respite. It was as if the relationship with each client was so
precious that not a moment of it could be squandered. We
person-centred therapists often talk about being fully present
in the here and now, and here, it seemed, was a structure which
aided this vibrant co-presence of counsellor and client (p. 10).

However, towards the end of his 1999 article, Thorne's attitude changes considerably:

> *Having described the challenge and how both I and my clients rose to it in triumphant fashion, can I now face that part of me which says it was a charade, an abject capitulation to a mad world? What, after all, was the challenge? The challenge was to cut down the appalling waiting list and, at the same time, to demonstrate to the University at large that the Counselling Service could be endlessly inventive in finding new ways of mopping up the psychologically and emotionally wounded. It had little to do with discovering new ways of responding to human distress. Brief therapy in this context was a pragmatic answer to escalating misery in a dysfunctional institution strapped for money* (p. 11).

Contained within the above quote is the reservation felt by many person-centred (and other) counsellors about time-limited counselling. The pressure to restrict clients to a limited number of sessions is, in many instances, not derived from experience or reliable research into the effectiveness or otherwise of brief therapy, but is driven by a perceived economic necessity and, in Thorne's phrase, '. . . the powerful allure of the short-term reward and allied to it the fear of commitment' (p. 11).

Counsellors who have sympathy with Thorne's view, that, '. . . it is the therapy for a world which is constantly on the hoof, where individuals are for ever seeking to be a jump ahead of the next person, where instant knowledge is the key to survival, where to stand still or fall by the wayside is to court annihilation' (p. 11), are faced with a difficult personal dilemma. Since counselling positions are not in unlimited supply, many counsellors are driven by market forces into accepting employment where attitudes towards time-limited counselling conflict with their own value systems. For many, the situation is time-limited counselling or no counselling at all, and under these circumstances many counsellors find themselves uncomfortably fitting in with the demands of an employer for quick results, whilst knowing that what they can offer their clients may be less than they need or deserve.

Many counselling agencies are acutely aware of this dilemma, and respond as flexibly as resources allow, by enabling counsellors in some circumstances to continue beyond the normally allowable number of sessions, for example. Many others, however, do not, and person-centred counsellors in these situations can find themselves in particular difficulties, and there are, of course, no simple solutions or easy answers.

One unhelpful by-product of time-limited counselling, especially (but not only) for inexperienced person-centred counsellors, is to assume that less available time implies a more directive counsellor. This may result from the pressure of the counselling agency for measurable (and quick) 'results' — the solving of a problem, or the lifting of a depression, for example. The temptation under pressure to direct the client's attention to a specific, apparently manageable problem, and so to produce a 'result' can become very difficult to resist. It is essential, however, in person-centred counselling, to resist this temptation vigorously, though it is easily understandable why counsellors sometimes give way to it.

My belief, and my experience, points in exactly the opposite direction. Fewer available sessions implies a determination to be present in a non-directive and non-authoritarian manner in exactly the same way as when time is not limited. A real danger in adopting a more directive approach, apart from the fact that such an approach would be entirely theoretically inconsistent, is the danger of further disempowering an already disempowered client. In other words, a grave danger, as far as person-centred counselling goes, lies in inadvertently communicating the impression that clients' self-resources and tendency towards actualisation are not to be trusted, and this can have the effect of strengthening a client's external locus of evaluation — the client experiences the message that the resources for change lie outside of him or herself and with the counsellor. An unintended consequence is for clients to absorb the message that they are dependent on others for the solution to life's problems, rather than experiencing a strengthened appreciation of their own resources.

A further point concerns the counsellor's respect for clients' realistic assumptions about what is and what is not possible in a limited time. My experience shows me that most clients, unless very seriously disturbed, are able to appreciate that while time-limited counselling can be of some significant help, it may not be all that is required, and indeed this may also represent the reality of time-unlimited counselling. My experience with brief counselling informs me to attend to a number of issues at the beginning of counselling, and at the end of it. For example, openly discussing with clients the fact that sessions are limited helps both client and counsellor take the restricted time into consideration, and to be aware that some client issues may not be fully addressed or not addressed at all. Discussing where the client might go for further help if needed at the end of the allowed sessions also communicates respect for the client's needs as he or she expresses them.

In this book, I do not set out to resolve complex issues such as those created by the ever-increasing demands for time-limited work. I can, however, offer some ideas and perspectives from a person-centred standpoint that may help you find a way of working that diminishes their impact, and helps you to deliver effective counselling in less than ideal circumstances. You may, then, like to consider some of the following points in thinking through your attitude towards offering time-limited counselling.

Checklist: Time-limited work

- Many clients benefit significantly from brief counselling experiences, and many would remain only for a limited number of sessions anyway.
- Any person-centred counselling help, however time-limited, providing it involves a strong therapeutic relationship rich in the core conditions, can make a real and lasting contribution to a client's process of self-understanding.
- The quality of the counselling relationship is the most significant factor. Many sessions of a poor quality relationship are likely to be of less benefit than fewer sessions where the quality of the relationship is high.
- Limiting the number of sessions may have some positive outcomes. It may, for example, enable you to focus in a more disciplined and concentrated way on trying to understand your client as deeply as you can.
- Restricted time availability does not require a more directive approach. Rather, it requires a disciplined undertaking to focus exclusively and empathically on the client's frame of reference in the same way as with time-unlimited counselling.
- Adopting a more directive approach undermines trust in the client's self-resources and risks strengthening a client's external locus of evaluation and dependency on the counsellor.
- When approaching a counselling agency for work as a counsellor or trainee counsellor, check the agency's attitude towards time-limited work, particularly the degree of flexibility they allow.

Personal counselling for the counsellor

Attitudes towards trainees experiencing their own personal counselling during a training course vary from one organisation to another (Dryden and Thorne, 1991). Some training courses require a certain number of hours; other recommend counselling during training and some leave it up to the individuals concerned. The situation has become a little clearer since BACP adopted, in 1998, the requirement that all people applying for accreditation should have experienced a minimum of 40 hours of personal counselling, or an equivalent experience of 'being in the client role' (see Bayne et al. 1999, p. 131).

Advantages of experiencing your own counselling include 'inside knowledge' of what it is like to be a client, and some opportunity to experience at least one practitioner offering the service for which you are training or have trained. Other more general benefits are also possibilities, like enhanced self-awareness, and personal congruence.

Whilst it may seem obvious on an intuitive level that personal counselling is likely to result in you being a more effective counsellor, there is no clear research evidence that points in that direction (Bergin and Garfield, 1994; Macran and Shapiro, 1998). However, effective person-centred counselling demands a great deal of commitment to an ongoing process of personal development, and getting your own counselling is one way to keep up with that commitment. It is consistent with person-centred values that you should have the freedom to decide for yourself when, and under what circumstances, your own counselling is appropriate, and personal counselling during training is not always the best option for some people. For example, I am reminded of a trainee who had completed over 300 hours of counselling immediately prior to undertaking a training course. For this person, a further 40 hours spent in counselling simply because it was a course requirement would have been superfluous.

An argument against personal counselling during person-centred training involves the expectation that personal development will play the central role in training. Working on personal issues during and as a crucial part of training can be undermined if a person is already engaging in deep internal exploration elsewhere. Some trainees have found the intensity of training leaves little emotional energy for further personal work as an individual client, and others have found that personal counselling leaves little room for exploring personal concerns in their training group. I am aware of trainees whose level of engagement with training group processes fell dramatically once they had begun individual counselling, and opportunities for learning were lost.

On the other hand, some trainees discover that personal counselling during training helps them to focus more deeply on issues that have arisen during and resulting from their training experiences. They report the advantage of having personal time to reflect on training experience more intensely than they would have been able to otherwise. Experiencing your own counselling at some point before you begin to see clients, and at times during your career, helps you to continue with your personal development and can enable you to form deep and effective relationships with your clients and others.

The arguments for and against personal counselling during training are not, then, conclusive. (For a more detailed discussion, see Wilkins, 1997, pp. 65–80.) Person-centred training, as emphasised in this book, is, in large part, a process of personal development, and there are many ways of attending to personal development other than through individual counselling. Many of the exercises described in this book offer opportunities for personal development work, but an effective way of developing higher levels of self-awareness and personal congruence is through being in a group dedicated to exploring personal development and interpersonal relationships.

Personal development through group work

In a training context, group work takes many forms — most of the exercises in this book, for example, are best done in small groups of three to six people, but this section is concerned with the use of larger, relatively unstructured groups that play an important part in many person-centred counsellor training programmes. 'Unstructured' refers to the fact that such groups tend to have little in the way of formal agendas or tasks, but are designed to enable participants to explore their relationships with each other and/or to develop higher levels of self-awareness in a generally supportive group environment.

In the 1960s, Rogers became well known for his development of a form of unstructured group that became known as 'basic encounter' (Rogers, 1970; Bozarth, 1998, pp. 143–48). Basic encounter groups can involve any number of participants (up to several hundred on occasion, see Wood, 1999), but for most purposes, encounter groups usually involve between twelve and thirty members. Originally, encounter groups were offered to people who wanted an intensive group experience that would enable them to explore and understand how they formed relationships with others, or who wanted a personal development experience other than individual counselling or therapy. More recently, large encounter groups have been organised to explore aspects of cross cultural communication and other cultural factors, (see, for example, Sanford, 1999; Wood, 1999). Lago and MacMillan (1999) report on the history of group work in the PCA and give many examples of contemporary use of groups in a variety of settings.

Counsellor training courses in the person-centred tradition tend to make extensive use of groups, often labelling them 'community groups', or 'personal development groups', rather than 'encounter groups', in which all members of the training course (including the staff) meet together (often for several hours) without a fixed or pre-determined agenda. These groups offer distinct and powerful opportunities for the clarification of relationships between course members, and for the personal development of individual members. Fairhurst and Merry (1999) describe ways in which a course group can use 'community meetings' to explore issues of cultural diversity and conflict, and give examples of some of the ways individuals have used group settings to further personal development needs. Mearns (1994) argues that unstructured groups play a vital role in counsellor training because they enable people to move beyond what he describes as the 'portrayal of empathic and acceptant ways of being' (p. 42), which is difficult to sustain and likely to be challenged in a group setting, towards more authentic expression.

Groups without a predetermined agenda can be difficult to understand at first, especially by people whose experience of the PCA is limited, and they can sometimes feel uncomfortable or, at times, threatening. In everyday life we are used to groups being convened for clear purposes; there is usually an agenda and someone taking the lead or acting as 'chair', so it is unusual for a group to be convened without such formal organisation. But it is this very lack of a formal agenda that makes the group a potent context for personal growth because people are free to express themselves and find ways of relating to each other without the pressure of having to produce a specified result or come to a decision.

Brodley and Merry (1995) describe person-centred peer groups (those without formally designated leaders or 'facilitators'), as:

> ... *created primarily for students to explore person-centred psychology and practice, but they also function to foster the personal development of participants, to serve individual and group determined goals and, at times, may function to provide individual therapeutic experiences* (p. 17).

Whilst describing an aim of person-centred peer groups as the creation of 'an optimal interpersonal and psychological climate, based on Rogers' therapeutic attitudes within the group' (p. 17), they acknowledge that the goal of freedom and psychological safety in a group context is likely to be imperfect:

> *Freedom and psychological safety in a group setting ... are necessarily qualified or approximated freedom and safety. This is because the pursuit of individual freedom cannot ethically involve 'an attempt to deprive others of theirs' (Mill, 1859). In person-centred groups, freedom is further qualified by the pursuit of psychological safety for all participants. In order for such a climate to be perceived and experienced by participants in the group, each participant's freedom must ideally be expressed without producing threat, hurt or insult in the experience of others. Regardless of the care taken by participants, it is very unlikely, if not impossible, to prevent all experiences of threat, hurt or insult* (pp. 17–18).

Some people find this 'freedom and psychological safety' unnerving and disorienting, especially at first, and it does often take time to become comfortable with this unfamiliar environment and discover how best to make use of it. Brodley and Merry have offered some suggestions and 'guidelines' in an effort to help people make better use of the opportunities for personal development that groups provide, and to minimise the risk of inadvertent 'threat, hurt or insult'. They make the point that the underlying values of the PCA — respect for persons and trust in their capability to be self-directed, self-regulating and constructive — can be maintained in a group context, just as in the context of individual counselling, but they suggest the additional concept of 'courtesy' as a guiding attitude towards others when relating to them in a group context:

> *The English speaking concept of 'courtesy' is very close in meaning to the person-centred values of respect and trust, but courtesy also suggests familiar forms of behaviour that express consideration and respect. Commonly understood behavioural associations to the idea of courtesy may give some immediate,*

*in-the-moment guidance, when self-representing and when
assisting in the group. The thought, 'I am trying to act
courteously', or, 'I want to act courteously' may help people
choose their words in ways that have a likelihood of resulting
in perceptions and experiences of psychological safety in the
group* (p. 19).

Brodley and Merry's guidelines are offered as examples of the kind of
behaviours that are likely to promote freedom and safety within a group
context, and less likely to produce unintended hurt or threat to others.
The guidelines are not intended comprehensively to cover all possible ways
of participating in groups and are not intended to be treated as 'rules'.
They are presented in three categories: (1) general guidelines; (2) guidelines
for self-representation and pursuit of personal goals including self-
disclosures, expression of wants and desires, self-reflective and therapeutic
process, emotional expression, reactions to and observations about other
persons in the group, expression of ideas, etc; and (3) guidelines for
assisting in the group, including interactions to assist exploration of
conflicts and misunderstandings among other participants, acts of
acknowledgement or invitation towards others, assisting in the sharing of
time during sessions, time keeping, etc.

1. General guidelines for personal learning in groups

1   Allow silences and try to relax and reflect inwardly during periods of
    silence.
2   When you speak, take time to centre yourself, and take your time as
    you speak to help yourself remain centred.
3   If you begin to feel that your remarks are taking too long, stop and
    ask the group if they are still willing to listen.
4   Ask for responses if you particularly want them, and make clear
    whether you want validation of being understood or you want
    reactions from the frame of reference of other participants.
5   If you make a mistake, or you realise you have misunderstood, or
    you lose control, you can, when the opportunity presents itself, make
    corrections.

2. Guidelines for self-representation and pursuit of personal goals in groups

1   When you start, give the group an idea of what kind of thing you are
    going to say (offer a suggestion, ask for something, express and idea
    or point of view, tell something of a very personal or emotional nature,
    etc.).
2   Ask the group if they are willing to attend to the kind of thing you are
    going to be saying at that time.
3   If you want to express thoughts or feelings to another person, ask for
    consent before you begin.
4   If your remarks are a reaction to something the other person has said

or done, before stating your reactions, describe the behaviour or summarise what has been said. Then ask if you have observed or understood accurately. Be open to corrections.

5 If your remarks are reactions to another person, be careful to discriminate your feelings and emotions in reaction to that person, from your observations and interpretations. Make your observations and interpretations explicit as interpreted by you. Avoid accusational language. Avoid blaming language. If your reactions are complex, go slowly through your separate points and ask if you are being understood. When finished, ask for the kind of responses you want and from whom you want them.

6 When self-revealing or self-disclosing, pause from time to time to give others who may need to check their understandings an opportunity to do so. When you have completed your disclosures, let the group know what kinds of response you particularly want and from whom.

7 Make empathic responses to find out if you have accurately understood other persons when you are quite unsure of understanding.

3. Guidelines for assisting in the group

1 Keep the therapeutic attitudes in mind as you listen to and respond to other participants.

2 Attempt to clarify when the interaction between others seems to involve misunderstandings. For example, you may say you have the impression that there is some misunderstanding, or request restatements, or may ask the interacting persons whether or not they feel understood by each other, or may ask the others in the group if they feel the communication has been understood, or may summarise the misunderstanding as you perceive it.

3 Attempt to find out if the focus of the group is satisfactory to participants.

4 Attempt to support participants' desires to speak in the group. For example, ask if there is someone who has so far in the session not spoken who wants to do so, or ask a specific person, or comment that a specific person had earlier started to speak but may not have finished, or if someone is interrupted, when possible, ask if they had finished.

5 Assist in the time keeping and sharing of time in the group. For example, ask if there is anything any participant wants to be sure to talk about during the present session, or remind the group that a participant had stated a wish to talk about something but has not done so, or remind the group of the amount of time left before the end of the session.

6 Try to respond to requests from others. Seek clarification for yourself from the person making the request if it is not clear to you.

7 Try to contribute your point of view if someone is seeking group

consensus about matters of group structure or group goals.

8 Try to remain aware of people in the group who come from a different culture or background from yourself. Different people have different experiences and expectations of groups, and behaviour within groups; misunderstandings can sometimes occur because of this. If you think this may be happening, you can check it out and clarify it with the person or people involved.

Finally, whatever opportunities you have for working and being in groups either as part of your training or not, you might like to consider the checklist overleaf to help clarify your attitudes towards groups, and how well you are making the most of the opportunities for personal development they can offer.

Checklist: Experiencing groups

- What am I experiencing physically, emotionally, intellectually in the group?
- Am I clear about what is going on for me or am I confused?
- Do I feel in control of my feelings or are my feelings in control of me?
- Am I afraid of some of my feelings?
- What prevents me from having empathy or experiencing uncondi tional positive regard for other group members?
- Do I hold other members of the group responsible for some of my feelings?
- How far do I take responsibility for my own learning in the group?
- Do I feel judged my other members of the group, and if so, how does this affect the way I express myself in the group?
- How free do I feel to express myself as I am in the group?
- What do I think is affecting my freedom?
- What happens to me when strong negative or positive emotions are expressed in the group?
- How far do I feel able to take risks in the group?
- How well do I express my feelings towards others in the group, or towards the group as a whole?
- How do I take care not to cause inadvertent hurt or threat to others whilst expressing myself in the group?

Supervision 9

Supervision is the process by which you get support for your counselling work, usually in a one-to-one relationship with a more experienced counsellor, but sometimes as part of a small group. Supervision consists of a formal arrangement between you and a supervisor in terms of frequency of meetings and fees, etc., much in the same way as your formal arrangements with your clients. It is normal for trainee or inexperienced counsellors to need more supervision than more experienced counsellors, but in the UK supervision is an on-going commitment throughout a counsellor's professional life. The BACP considers it unethical for a counsellor to be in practice without adequate supervision.

Person-centred supervision is concerned with how you, the counsellor, form relationships with your clients, and how you can deepen your empathic understanding of them whilst remaining as congruent as you can and experiencing unconditional positive regard towards them.

This places the onus on you to be as open and non-defensive as you can be in talking through the ways you think and feel about yourself in relationship with your clients. Supervision is about you as a person working with those who have come to you for help, and this means that your supervisor, if he or she is to be effective in person-centred terms, needs to work towards establishing a relationship with you that has the same qualities as the relationships you try to provide for your clients. Put briefly, the supervisory relationship should mirror the client/counsellor relationship in that it values the qualities of empathic understanding, congruence and unconditional positive regard and takes these as core conditions for effective supervision.

Different approaches to counselling naturally enough take different approaches to supervision. In the psychodynamic traditions, for example, more emphasis is placed on issues concerning counter-transference, but in the person-centred approach the accent is likely to be on the qualities of the relationships between you and your clients. It is seen as more fruitful to think about the contributions you make in those relationships than it is to speculate about what your client may be experiencing or to interpret your client's behaviour. Surprisingly, little has been written about person-centred supervision. Some examples are Mearns (1997), Hackney and Goodyear (1984), Patterson (1997), Worrall (2001), and Merry (2001).

If you are a counsellor in training, your training organisation will probably have expectations about how often you should be in supervision, and with whom. Some organisations insist that your supervisor is trained in the same counselling approach as you, others are more flexible. Normally, trainees are expected to have at least one hour of individual supervision for every five or six hours of client work, and this conforms to BACP guidelines about the amount and frequency of supervision required on BACP accredited courses. Usually, individual supervision for client work is an extra expense for trainees which is often not included in the course fee. On the completion of training, BACP expects counsellors to have at least one and a half hours' individual supervision every month.

All aspects of counselling practice can be discussed in supervision including ethical dilemmas, the referral of clients to other forms of help, as well as 'technical' matters such as the payment of fees, issues of confidentiality, the suitability or otherwise of counselling premises, and so on. It is important that whatever arrangements you make for supervision it provides you with the support and stimulation you need. Supervision, then, is considered a very significant part of counselling training, and an essential part of on-going, ethical and professional practice. The rest of this chapter explores supervision in some detail, and provides some suggestions about how you can get the best out of it and put the most into it.

I asked a group of trainee counsellors what experience they had of supervision, and how they had responded to it. The discussions revealed a wide range of experiences, and they brainstormed some keywords that they felt described some of their experience. Before you go any further, I suggest you try the following exercise

---

Exercise: Images of supervision

Aims of the exercise
To explore experience of supervision and to compare your experience so far with others.

What to do
STEP 1: If you are in a small group, brainstorm some key words about supervisors that reflect the experience of supervision you have had so far, if any. If you have yet to experience supervision, what concerns do you have about it?

STEP 2: Compare your list with the one that follows. Generally, is most experience positive or negative?

How I experienced my supervisor:
- As a detective
- As a police officer

- As a master craftsman
- As a confessor
- As a guru
- As a lifeguard
- As a judge
- As a counsellor
- As a mechanic who tried to 'fix' me
- As a parent
- As a teacher
- As a companion
- As a witness
- As a supporter
- As a training coach

These trainee counsellors had mixed experience of supervision, some of it good and some of it unhelpful. It ranged from perceiving their supervisor as someone who tried to catch them out doing something wrong, to being a teacher of counselling theory and practice, to someone providing support, expertise and encouragement.

Next, I asked them to brainstorm some keywords that described their feelings about themselves as 'supervisees'. I suggest that, before you read their list, you try it for yourself in the next exercise.

Exercise: Images of being a supervisee

Aim of the exercise
To share and compare experience of being a supervisee.

What to do
STEP 1: Brainstorm some keywords that best describe your experience and perceptions of being a supervisee.
STEP 2: Compare your list with the one that follows.

I experienced myself in supervision:
- As a suspect
- As an apprentice
- As a sinner
- As a follower
- As guilty
- As a trusted person
- As a person
- As a potential law-breaker
- As a child
- As a pupil
- As 'out of my depth'
- As a client
- As a competent person
- As a learner

As you can see, some of these trainees had negative experiences of being in supervision. At its best, supervision enabled them to feel trusted and respected as people gaining more confidence and knowledge. At its worst, they experienced themselves as under some kind of scrutiny, or even as plain wrong.

A person-centred approach to supervision

In previous chapters of this book I examined a number of principles that underpin the person-centred approach to counselling, and it is from these same principles that a person-centred approach to supervision is derived. As noted above, an effective supervisory relationship needs to be built on the core conditions of empathic understanding, congruence and unconditional positive regard, and these are all qualities or attitudes experienced by the supervisor for the supervisee. In the same way, supervision proceeds on the basis that it is the counsellor's perceptions of, and meanings attributed to, counselling relationships that guide the way they behave.

Supervision, then, provides opportunities for supervisees (counsellors) to experience a relationship that is free of threat, and is supportive and understanding so that they can explore non-defensively what the counselling process means to them, and how they experience themselves in relationship with their clients. This is the major function of person-centred supervision, and that function is served by the supervisor and supervisee exploring cooperatively how supervisees express their empathic understanding and how they are able to remain both congruent and non-judgemental. Whilst there are many areas of overlap between counselling relationships and supervisory relationships, a major difference is that supervision needs to attend to particular issues and so it has an agenda in a way that counselling relationships do not.

Supervision as 'collaborative inquiry'

A useful way to think about supervision is to regard it as a form of research or inquiry in which two people (the supervisor and the counsellor) collaborate or co-operate in an effort to understand what is going on within the counselling relationship and within the counsellor (see also Merry, 2001). This moves the emphasis away from 'doing things right or wrong' (which seems to be the case in some approaches to supervision) to 'how is the counsellor being, and how is that way of being contributing to the development of a counselling relationship based on the core conditions?' A feature of collaborative research or inquiry (see, for example, Heron, 1971, 1981; Reason, 1988) is that it works towards equalising the power distribution in the relationship, and both supervisor and supervisee have particular, important contributions to make to the process, each depending equally on the other.

A parallel can be drawn here with the person-centred approach to research described by Mearns and McLeod (1984). Their discussion showed how person-centred values can be incorporated into research by, for example, treating people with respect and sensitivity, viewing them as participants rather than 'subjects', and being concerned with their frames of reference.

In order to explore the application of a collaborative inquiry method to supervision we need first to establish some of its general principles:

- Humans have the capacity to choose how they will act and have an ability to be self-directing. A collaborative inquiry approach to supervision acknowledges that both people involved are self-directed and both can contribute equally to the process.
- A collaborative approach is democratic in that it does not assume one person (usually the supervisor) to be more influential in the process than the other (usually, the supervisee). Both are equally influential, though in different ways, and each has a valid perspective to bring.
- The process enables a deeper engagement with counselling issues because it values all forms of knowledge as equally legitimate. In other words, the counsellor's and the supervisor's subjective experience of counselling, and the counsellor's and the supervisor's intuition and emotional responses to the material, are just as important as the objective 'facts'. Both cognitive and intuitive forms of knowing are available and can be explored.
- Once a supervisory relationship based on the core conditions has been established, counsellors are more likely to discuss difficult issues because the need to be defensive is dissolved. Evaluations of the quality of the counselling relationship can be made jointly because the counsellor does not feel threatened as a person, but supported as an individual trying to make good counselling relationships, often under trying circumstances.
- The supervisor can be perceived as a 'co-worker' able to offer expertise, knowledge and experience in the pursuit of deeper understanding, rather than as a judge or police officer.

To illustrate these principles, what follows is an example of part of a supervision session involving an experienced (male) counsellor/ supervisor and a counsellor (also male) in the latter stages of a training course. Though a reconstruction rather than a transcript, what follows accurately represents the discussion.

A supervision session

SUPERVISOR (S): OK, what have you brought for us today?

COUNSELLOR (C): Several things, which seem, at least on the surface, to be connected in some way. At the moment, I am seeing four clients a week. I have been seeing two of them for about ten weeks; one is a young woman, about 28 years old, and the other a man a year or two older. I have talked about them both to you before, so you'll remember I see them both at the counselling agency where I work. There are no restrictions on the number of sessions allowed, but they encourage us to review after eight to ten sessions. The agency doesn't specialise in any particular client group, but we don't see people under the age of

18. Most clients are self-referred, but we do have arrangements with several local GP practices, so many clients come to us on their recommendations. Let me say something about the woman to start with, who was a self-referral. She came with feelings of anxiety about her relationship with her boyfriend. You'll remember I found it difficult at first to feel as if I was really in a relationship with her. She found it very difficult to talk to me and when she did the talk seemed to be about very superficial things. It's about time for a review of our work, and I'm not sure if I'm the right counsellor for her, and I'm thinking maybe I should refer her to someone else.

S: I remember. We decided you were trying to go too fast, and to be content to let her take her time. You were feeling impatient with her, and also you felt a bit deskilled in that nothing seemed to get through to her.

C: That's right. But lately my feeling has changed. Now it's more like I find it difficult to listen to her. In fact, she does touch on some deeper areas, and I've got the feeling that I don't really respond with similar depth. It's like my responses are superficial, rather than what she says always being superficial.

S: OK. That's interesting. Now you're saying maybe it's you keeping things on a surface level, rather than her. You find it hard to listen, rather than she finds it hard to talk, is that what you mean?

C: Well, it's a bit of both. I think she does still find it hard to talk, and I am finding it hard to listen. It's like we're in it together, both of us keeping things superficial, at least most of the time, in different ways. I don't know how to explain it, but there seems to be something in me that stops things happening. It's a struggle . . . I'm struggling.

S: You're struggling with something in yourself, as much as, if not more than, anything in her, is that it, or close to it? And you seem to see it as a kind of conspiracy to prevent any depth.

C: Something like that. She'll say something, and I'll know it wasn't easy for her, but I can't seem to find the words I need so that she will know I've understood her, or even heard her.

S: So you are aware that she is expressing some parts of herself, and that it isn't easy for her, but that's as far as it goes for you? Can you give me an example, perhaps?

C: I did make some notes after the last session. I wish I'd tape-recorded it. She said something like, 'When Peter (her partner) tries to get close, physically close, I pretend not to notice. I'll say something trivial, but inside I'm feeling, 'don't keep trying to touch me'. I try and deflect it most of the time. It's not that I don't have feelings for him, but his physical touching makes me withdraw, and I don't know why.' I said, and these were my exact words, 'You don't welcome his approaches.' As soon as I'd said it, I realised first that it was an obvious thing to say, and second that it hadn't gone any way towards recognising the complexity of her feelings. It just felt trivial and even a bit dismissive. At the time I almost felt ashamed I'd said it.

S: OK, you feel like you missed the point, or rather you oversimplified it, you did understand her but didn't respond with any real understanding, something like that?

C: That's just it. I think I did understand her quite well . . .

S: . . . but you couldn't find a way to express it? What did you understand, can you recall?

C: I understood that she did feel physically OK with him at times, but that there was something that happened when he showed his feelings directly that made her recoil from him, and she had no idea why she did that, but it seemed automatic, a kind of reflex.

S: And you sort of toned it all down to that phrase 'you don't welcome him'? You understood quite a bit more than you said?

C: What I said was a cliché. What I thought was, 'Poor guy, he does his best and gets rejected.' I guess I felt sorry for him.

S: So your feelings were felt towards him, rather than towards her.

C: Yes, I suppose so. If I'd seen it from her point of view I might have understood something of the struggle going on in her. From other things she's said I know she does want physical intimacy, but she often sabotages her chances of getting it. There is something about the other person making it clear that makes her withdraw.

S: So how can you get yourself more centred on her world and her experiences, and less concerned with Peter's?

C: Well, I guess that's become my question to myself now. Have I got more sympathy for Peter than I have empathy for her? Now I'm thinking about that, I wish there was a simple explanation, like this is what has happened to me or something, but that isn't true.

S: If I understand you now, you are wondering about to what extent you are getting drawn into what you imagine Peter to be feeling, and there isn't an obvious reason why you might be doing that.

C: I think I might be doing that quite a lot with her, now I come to think about it. I find myself sort of commenting on the other people in her story, rather than staying with her. What is it about her that makes me do that?

S: It seems you think this might go on quite a bit. Another question might be, 'What is it about you that makes you do that?'

C: Well, that's a better question. I don't know the answer to that right now. She doesn't remind me of anyone in particular or any situations I remember. I feel uncomfortable at the moment, like you asked an uncomfortable question.

S: There's something a bit troubling about me asking you to look into yourself?

C: Yes. I'd rather talk about her and what she's doing, rather than about me and what I'm doing. But I know it's the right question. I'd rather you talk about her than me.

S: This might seem a bit obvious, but, like you'd rather think about Peter than about her?

C: I'd thought about that too. I think what I'm doing is not admitting to myself what I do feel about her. It seems risky.

S: It feels dangerous to acknowledge your feelings about her to yourself?

C: Yes. To be honest, I'm not sure what it is I'm feeling, except I do know I don't feel much warmth for her. I find her difficult and a bit rejecting. I don't get much feeling that I am doing any good for her, or being much help. Again, it seems too obvious, but she does to me what she says she does to Peter but in a different way. She says 'help me' to me, but when I try to she kind of doesn't notice. It's frustrating.

S: Right. Now you're saying you feel your attempts to understand her are deflected, she deflects them, at least, you feel deflected, and you don't feel much liking for her.

C: I'm a bit ashamed to admit that I don't actually like her. I think this dislike might be a cover-up for something more extreme. I'll put it like this, I'm afraid that my dislike for her might involve a part of me that I don't like much in myself. I don't know where to go with this.

S: Earlier, you used the word 'struggle', and I can really sense a struggle going on in you at the moment. It's difficult to admit you don't like one of your clients, especially as you feel there might be something else involved even stronger, and there's fear that you might be about to discover something you won't want to accept in yourself, is that right? And the feeling of 'where do I go with it all?' really troubles you? The question is, can you find a way through this so that you can be with her in a more helpful or understanding way?

C: Or should I just admit that maybe I'm not the right counsellor for her? What do I do with the feeling of dislike? I'm not ready to admit defeat, there are things about her that I admire.

S: OK, so one option is to give up, but you don't seem ready to do that right away, especially as there are some things you feel OK about.

C: And what about congruence? Theoretically, shouldn't I be disclosing my feelings for her to her? They seem to be getting in the way of any empathy, and I couldn't say I'm experiencing positive regard for her, conditional or otherwise.

S: Well, at least you are now aware of your negative feelings for her, which you didn't seem to be a few minutes ago, and that's one crucial aspect of congruence. Sometimes just being aware of a feeling helps you to do something with it, and the theory doesn't mean that because you are aware of a feeling in yourself you have to disclose it. We shouldn't rule out disclosing your feeling to her at some time, or referring her to someone else, but I think both would be a bit hasty right now. If you decide to do either, we really need to spend a lot of time with it first, I would say. Things seem to have changed a bit to me, now you are saying you think it might be something in you that is at the bottom of this, is that what you mean? How do you feel about exploring this a bit more with your counsellor?

C: I'd feel OK about that. Are you suggesting it?

S: Yes, I think I am. We don't have the time to go much further with it here.

C: OK, I think you are right. I'll have at least two sessions with my counsellor before I next see you. Can we talk about it more then?

S: OK. We can leave it until then. In the meantime, I understand you to want to focus more on trying to understand her world, rather than Peter's, and pay more attention to what is going on in you when you are next with her. Did you say you had two clients, and that things with them seemed to be connected somehow?

C: Yes, but things with the other one seem a bit clearer now as well. The connection is the superficiality bit. I realise that with both clients I am tending to focus on other people rather than on the clients themselves. This seems to be a bit of a pattern at the moment.

This is a good example of a person-centred supervision session in which the counsellor felt able to explore some complex and difficult issues, and there is a marked co-operative, collaborative feel to it. The supervisor's main concerns are to clarify and understand how this counsellor is experiencing his relationships with his clients, and what sense or meaning he is making from those experiences, and there are a number of similarities between this session and the counselling session given in chapter 5. For example, the supervisor is concerned to communicate the extent of his empathic understanding of the counsellor, and there are several good instances of this. Examples are:

You're struggling with something in yourself, as much as, if not more than, anything in her, is that it, or close to it? And you seem to see it as a kind of conspiracy to prevent any depth; and: If I understand you now, you are wondering about to what extent you are getting drawn in to what you imagine Peter to be feeling, and there isn't an obvious reason why you might be doing that.

Notice also that the supervisor does not judge the counsellor as a person as he recounts his relationship with his client, but tries to understand the counsellor's experience as he struggles with his own feelings. A good example of this comes when the counsellor admits to feeling dislike for his client, and the supervisor responds:

It's difficult to admit you don't like one of your clients, especially as you feel there might be something else involved even stronger, and there's fear that you might be about to discover something you won't want to accept in yourself, is that right? And the feeling of 'where do I go with it all?' really troubles you?

There are also some differences between this session and the counselling session given in chapter 5. One difference is that the supervisor asks more questions, and another is that he offers some suggestions for further action by the counsellor:

What did you understand?; What is it about you that makes you do that?, and How do you feel about exploring this a bit more with your counsellor?

These questions and suggestions indicate that there is an agenda for supervision that goes beyond the agenda for counselling. Supervision needs to be both supportive and, at times, directly (though sensitively) challenging because part of its function is to encourage the counsellor to think about what he is doing and how he is being in relation to his clients. In other words, supervision is also an opportunity to explore the theory of counselling and how that theory is translated into practice. The importance of theory is illustrated in this extract when the counsellor questions the role of 'congruence' in this relationship, and the supervisor reminds him that one aspect of congruence is the awareness of feelings, and another is concerned with the direct communication of feelings to the client.

Some supervisors and supervisees prefer to make the various components of supervision explicit through agreeing to a fairly formal (though not rigid) contract. This contract can cover both organisational issues, like payment of fees, times and frequency of meetings and so on, and other functions like 'support', 'challenge', 'theory' and 'ethics'. One way of doing that which is consistent with the collaborative inquiry model is for both people to make clear to each other what their concerns are, what they see their various roles to be and what expectations they have of supervision, and then to translate the results of that process into a contract or agreement. Below, I give an example of how one supervisor and one supervisee went about this process.

Supervisor's concerns, roles and expectations

- I expect us to meet every two weeks for 90 minutes each time.
- The fee per session is £35. I expect you to be reasonably well organised and to think about the issues you might want to discuss beforehand.
- I will try to offer you a supervisory relationship in which you feel OK about bringing your client work for discussion. My main concern will be with trying to understand you as best as I can.
- I will be as straightforward and congruent with you as possible and, if I feel the need to be critical, it will be of aspects of your work rather than of you as a person.
- If necessary and appropriate, I will offer you my way of doing things by way of comparison, not as instructions.
- I am as concerned as you are that your clients get good, safe, effective and ethical counselling. If I have any doubts about any of this, I will discuss them with you openly.
- I will provide your training organisation with whatever reports they request, but I will always discuss them with you first and show you what I have written before I send it.
- I am prepared to discuss aspects of counselling theory with you whenever appropriate, but I am not your counselling trainer. If you are having particular problems with theory I would prefer you to deal with them in your training group.
- Your emotional well-being is an important factor determining the effectiveness of your counselling, and I am willing to help you explore emotional difficulties that arise through your work. But I am not your counsellor, and I would prefer you to talk difficult issues through with your counsellor rather than with me if they seem to be taking over the supervision sessions.
- As we both work in a multi-cultural society, I expect us both to take this into account when talking about your work as a counsellor.

Supervisee's concerns, roles and expectations

- I hope you will try to understand my concerns from my point of view, whilst offering your own point of view whenever necessary.
- I expect you to make your experience available to me, but I hope you won't insist that I do things your way.
- I am unsure about some aspects of person-centred theory; I hope you will be able to help me clear some of them up.
- I expect you to supply my training organisation with confirmation of our supervision hours and to write whatever reports they ask for after discussing them with me.
- 'Boundaries' sometimes confuse me. I hope we can discuss boundary issues openly.
- I find some counselling work emotionally challenging. I hope to be able to express this in supervision, but I don't expect you to be my full-time counsellor.
- I expect you to be supportive of me when I need it, but also to point out weaknesses when you see them.
- I am particularly concerned about certain issues within my practice, including working with different cultural groups, the depth of my empathic understanding, and congruence. Other issues are to do with endings and making referrals.

When they had completed this part of the exercise, this supervisee and supervisor went on to draw up the following contract. (They called it an 'agreement'.)

Supervision agreement between X (supervisor) and Y (supervisee)

- We will meet on every second Tuesday of each month between 6.00 pm and 7.30 pm. Whenever possible, at least three days' notice should be given if one or other is unable to attend.
- The fee is £35 for the 90-minutes supervision, payable at the end of each session.
- Supervision requires openness and mutual respect, and we both undertake to work towards a relationship of trust and understanding. We will work together towards a relationship that is both challenging and supportive.
- Whilst the supervisor is concerned about the quality of counselling delivered to clients, he does not take 'clinical responsibility' for the counsellor's work. The counsellor will clarify with his training organisation and his 'placement' who takes responsibility for what.
- The supervisor will supply the counsellor's training organisation with whatever reports are required, after discussion with the counsellor.
- Supervisor and counsellor are concerned to ensure the counsellor's work falls within the BACP Code of Ethics. If ethical problems or issues arise,

these will be discussed as openly as possible and any action agreed on as far as possible.
- The counsellor will take care to protect the anonymity of his clients. Supervision is regarded as confidential, unless ethical considerations override this. Reports and feedback to the training organisation will be discussed with the counsellor.
- The counsellor's emotional well-being is a supervision issue, but if there is a need for formal counselling, the supervisee will not expect the supervisor to provide it.
- Supervisor and counsellor recognise that counselling takes place within a multi-cultural social context, and will ensure that issues of multi-culturalism inform all aspects of supervision.
- We agree to take particular note of issues concerning working with difference, endings, empathy, congruence, some counselling theory and making referrals.
- This agreement is unlikely to be perfect, and it is agreed to review it periodically and to alter it if necessary.

This agreement has a number of distinct advantages. Firstly, it makes explicit what otherwise might have remained implicit, and so open to misunderstanding. Secondly, it establishes the boundaries of the supervisory relationship — not too much (but some) 'teaching' of counselling theory, and an agreement that difficult personal issues might be best addressed in a counselling relationship with someone else, rather than in supervision, although provision is made for the exploration of emotional issues arising from the counsellor's practice. Thirdly, it establishes supervision as a joint and collaborative activity, rather than as something the supervisor does to the counsellor. The importance of a supervisory relationship built on the core conditions is established right at the start, and both people know what their responsibilities are and where they end.

Other models of supervision

So far, I have discussed only individual, one-to-one supervision. My experience is that this is the best form of supervision for trainee or relatively inexperienced counsellors. Its most obvious advantage is that the time available can be spent focused on the work of one person without distractions. This, however, is also its main disadvantage. Individual supervision does not enable perspectives to be included from a variety of people, probably with different backgrounds, strengths and weaknesses.

Three other models of supervision are worth considering, each with advantages and disadvantages:

Peer-group supervision
Peer supervision, in small groups of four or five, is more suitable for relatively experienced counsellors, or those in the final stages of training,

or as a supplement to individual supervision. In this model, people take turns at presenting issues for discussion and feedback from others in the group. More than one point of view can be helpful, but also runs the risk of being confusing. Its advantages are that it is cost-free, and it can be experienced as supportive and encouraging. There is also a lot of learning available from listening to the experiences of others in counselling. Its disadvantages include the possibility that it lacks the challenge provided by a more experienced practitioner, and that some people are more confident, or more willing to be open about mistakes or misgivings, whereas others can be less confident and may tend to hide. Another disadvantage concerns the amount of time each person has available, and the fact that each person's turn at presenting may come around only once in two or three sessions. You may also find that accrediting bodies, like BACP, do not count peer-group supervision for the purposes of individual accreditation. Attention may also have to be given to the interpersonal dynamics of the group if difficult personal issues arise within it, and this is not always easy without a facilitator.

Facilitated group supervision
Here, an experienced counsellor or supervisor offers group supervision to four or five people who again take turns at presenting issues. The advantages here include the prospect of more challenge, though there is no reason why such a group should not be both challenging and supportive. People gain the advantage of hearing different points of view, and the facilitator can help the presenting person towards clarifying what he or she can learn from different perspectives without becoming confused by them. As in the previous model, time may be a problem, and the frequency of opportunity to present issues may also cause difficulties. In any form of group supervision, it is helpful to allow time at the beginning for 'emergencies' to be dealt with so that a participant experiencing a crisis or serious difficulty doesn't have to wait for several weeks. As with peer-group supervision, only the time spent actually presenting your own material can be counted as supervision time for the purposes of BACP accreditation. Both forms of group supervision are best viewed as supplementing individual supervision, rather than replacing it entirely.

Co-supervision
In this model, two people agree to supervise each other and take turns at presenting material for discussion and exploration. This model is probably most suited to experienced counsellors, though there is no reason why this approach could not supplement individual or group supervision for trainee or inexperienced counsellors. The advantages of this model include the fact that it is cost-free and can be a convenient arrangement for busy people — one long (three hour) session a month shared equally between the two people involved can provide enough supervision time to satisfy the ethical requirements of the counselling profession. There are, however, some serious disadvantages. For example, it is inadvisable for co-

supervisors to be working for the same organisation, as other work relationships may impinge on the counselling work and it might be difficult to talk them through with a co-worker. There is also the danger that the relationship becomes somewhat 'cosy' and lacking in challenge. Co-supervision is probably a good arrangement in areas where finding a suitably qualified and experienced supervisor is difficult, but even so it is a useful idea for the two co-supervisors to arrange to meet periodically with a third person to ensure that the supervision is maintaining a healthy level of challenge and is not becoming too much of a social event.

Presenting material for supervision

Some thought and preparation put into what you are going to present for supervision will help to ensure you get the most from it. Some training organisations, and some supervisors, have specific requirements with which you should be familiar and the general guidelines I offer here might have to be adapted to suit your particular needs.

There are three areas that deserve some thought in preparing yourself for supervision: the general context of your work, some details of the client or issue you plan to present, and yourself and your thoughts and feelings in relation to the client or the issue.

General context
This includes some background about the organisation in which your counselling takes place, how your client was referred to you, any 'rules' concerning the number of allowed sessions if such rules exist, the number of sessions so far, and information about any relevant client 'types' or issues. For example:

> *This work takes place within an agency that specialises in helping young people, between the ages of 16 and 21, deal with a wide range of problems, from difficulties with parents and school or college, to unwanted pregnancies and drug use. The agency offers an initial six sessions which can be extended up to 15 in certain cases. The client I am presenting is a young woman, 18 years old, who has left home because of family violence and is living with her boyfriend in a 'squat'. She came on the advice of a doctor who treated her for a prolonged chest infection. She is depressed and anxious, has trouble sleeping, and is beginning to increase her use of illegal drugs. I have seen her five times, and I want to continue with her up to the maximum number of sessions allowed.*

Client details
It will help if your supervisor or supervision group can be given some details of the client work you want to talk through. Take care to protect your client's identity, and stick to factual information, rather than speculations or guesswork.

> *The client, who I shall call Sue, has left home several times before and dropped out of school as soon as she could without gaining any*

qualifications. She has had occasional bouts of fairly heavy drinking, but has not used drugs before. She is unsure what she feels about her boyfriend who is a heavy drugs user, and who has suggested she take up prostitution to finance his habit. She impresses me as an intelligent and resourceful person who is beginning to see the need to break out of her current lifestyle and find something more fulfilling for herself. So far, she has talked quite openly about her feelings for both her parents, and has expressed a lot of anger towards them. She works hard as a client, even though she sometimes finds it difficult to express some feelings because she thinks of it as 'blaming others for her problems'.

Yourself and your thoughts and feelings

Try to identify, as far as you can, how you feel about your client, and whether or not your feelings change when she talks about different things. How well do you think you understand her? Do you have any inclination to judge some parts of her or her 'story', either positively or negatively? How open and congruent do you feel in relation to her? Why are you bringing this client to supervision — are there particular problems or issues you can identify in yourself or with the counselling process?

I feel warm towards her, and I find I have sympathetic feelings for her, and I think I understand how difficult she sometimes finds it to explore incidents from her past, partly because she feels some shame about them. I feel I am a good listener with her, and I think she feels understood by me a good deal of the time. The problem for me at the moment is trying to understand how she could even contemplate becoming a prostitute, though I understand how desperate she must be feeling. I find my feelings of anger are being directed at her boyfriend, though she doesn't feel any anger for him, at least she has never expressed any. I am afraid that if she leaves counselling now she'll just drift into prostitution and more drug-use herself. I am torn between wanting to persuade her to stay, and respecting her decision to leave if that's what she decides to do, and I'm afraid that the boyfriend is putting pressure on her to leave. If she does leave, I will think of it as a failure on my part to help her sufficiently.

With this kind of background information your supervisor (or group) will be better able to help you explore your relationships with your clients. Remember that the supervision needs to focus on you and your feelings and thoughts, rather than drift off into speculations about how your client might behave in the future, or what drove her to counselling in the first place.

Bayne et al. (1999), offer two contrasting suggestions about how to present clients in supervision. One consists of a brief series of general prompts, such as, What do I wish to accomplish with this client?, What am I doing well with this client?, and What could I do better with this client? The other is a much more detailed scheme that addresses a series of questions and issues, such as problem definition, assessment, therapeutic plan and specific aspects of the relationship. This second scheme is probably less appropriate for person-centred supervision because it tends to focus on technical issues, rather than on the qualities of the counselling relationship. Whichever one you choose, or if you develop your own method, supervision is likely to be more fruitful than if you simply rely on 'whatever comes up' (though this can be useful sometimes).

Talking about your client work in this way can be very valuable, but it has one inherent limitation — everything is 'second-hand', relying on your memory for both general impressions and specific detail. You will find it very helpful if you can make some notes immediately after each session to remind you of your thoughts and feelings during the session, but your notes are bound to be selective. This limitation can be significantly overcome if you can tape-record some or all of your sessions with your clients, but there are advantages and disadvantages with taping, some of which we explore next.

Using a tape recorder

The obvious advantage of a tape recorder is that you have a detailed and reliable record of the event. The ways in which you communicate, including your tone of voice, emphasis, and so on as well as what you communicate are available to you and your supervisor. You will be able to notice any patterns, any issues or feelings that you seem to miss and any mistakes in understanding you make, and if you tend to de-emphasise strong feelings, for instance, or exaggerate them. For example, if your client says, 'I hate the sight of my father and I wish I could be rid of him', and your response is, 'You're really not very fond of him', you will notice immediately that you are 'downgrading' a strong feeling into a much more neutral one. This is the kind of thing that is very difficult to notice in oneself, and you may not be aware of it as you talk about your counselling, or make notes about it.

The tape recorder can help you focus exactly on what you say and how you say it. It is a rich source of material for supervision, and is likely to make your supervision more effective and, in turn, your work with your clients. There are, however, some disadvantages to tape-recording.

Firstly, it is obviously necessary to get your client's permission to use a tape recorder, and to discuss with your client what the recording is for, who will listen to it, and what will happen to it after it has been heard. Some clients may give their permission because they are reluctant to disappoint you, even though they feel uneasy about it. You will need to listen very carefully to your client's response to your suggestion to tape-record, and be prepared to abandon the idea if necessary. Letting your clients know they can switch off the tape any time they feel like it during a session often helps to reassure them. Some clients even appreciate being given the tape so they can listen to it themselves.

It is possible to overstate the problems caused to clients by counsellors asking them permission to use a tape recorder. Most objections to taping are made in terms of breaking confidentiality or worrying clients unnecessarily about who will listen to the tape and what will happen to it.

However, as Mearns (1995) has pointed out, ' . . . clients rarely feel uncomfortable and much more often feel that they are being valued by a process that takes the counsellor's supervision so seriously'.

Secondly, a tape recorder can sometimes be obtrusive, especially if it makes noises when switched on, or if you have to turn the tape over in the middle of a session. It helps if you make sure your tape recorder is small and reliable. It can be very distracting if you have to fiddle with a machine at the start or half way through a session.

Perhaps the most serious disadvantage of using a tape recorder is that it has a tendency to concentrate attention on the micro-skills of counselling, rather than on the overall quality of the relationships you develop with your clients. Discussing specific words and phrases can seem useful at the time, but the extent to which this helps you find ways of being spontaneous, authentic and empathic is often questionable. It will help if you can draw your supervisor's attention to 'passages' of your counselling; where you seem to be in particular difficulty, for example. If you take some responsibility for reviewing the tape before supervision and using it to focus on particular issues you have identified, you are likely to find it more useful.

Finally, taping a session doesn't necessarily guarantee making supervision more useful than not taping. Best use of a tape, or any other way of supervision, requires a non-judgemental and supportive relationship with your supervisor. If this relationship is not established first, you are less likely to provide a tape of yourself experiencing severe difficulties, just as you are less likely to talk about difficult or risky experiences without a tape.

Developing your 'internal supervisor'
Supervision is obviously an important source of external support. It can provide a sense of security in times of stress or difficulty, and it enables you to reflect on and develop your practice. As important as external support, however, is the capacity to monitor yourself, and to evolve your own sense of ethical behaviour. This process reflects the concept (discussed in earlier chapters) of developing an internal, rather than an external, locus of evaluation. In counselling sessions, your only immediate source of support and guidance is yourself, and learning to listen to yourself and be guided by your own values is part of the process of becoming a confident and ethical practitioner.

You can help yourself to develop your internal supervisor in a number of ways. Firstly, you can make sure you are familiar with the BACP Ethical Framework for Good Practice in Counselling and Psychotherapy and you can think through the issues it represents and talk them through with your group, if you have one. The point here is to come to your own conclusions about what you consider to be an ethical approach to counselling, and what your own attitudes and values are, rather than simply relying on a set of externally given 'rules'.

Secondly, you can monitor your own practice by keeping a professional journal that is more than just a record of what you are doing, but goes on to evaluate and appraise your ideas about your own effectiveness. Most counsellor training courses require students to do something like this whilst in training, but there is no reason why you should not continue the practice throughout your professional life.

Finally, it is unhelpful for any counsellor, no matter how experienced, to consider themselves as fully trained. Developing your own internal supervisor helps you to identify areas where you are less confident or knowledgeable, and prompts you to seek further training or exploration. Becoming more congruent means, in part, that more of your feelings are available to your awareness without distortion, and this heightened awareness allows you to monitor your work more realistically. 'Working on yourself' represents a commitment to an on-going process of development, and your capacity to be your own supervisor is an important part of that development.

Checklist: Supervision

- Formal supervision provides support for client work.
- Regular supervision is a requirement of ethical practice.
- Person-centred supervision is concerned with how counsellors form and maintain relationships based on the core conditions.
- Person-centred supervision may be thought of as a form of collaborative inquiry.
- A collaborative inquiry model views both supervisor and supervisee as equally influential in the search for meaning.
- Clear agreements between supervisors and supervisees help make supervision more useful.
- Group supervision can be equally as effective as individual supervision, but both forms have advantages and disadvantages.
- Organisation of client work for presentation in supervision helps make supervision more effective.
- Tape-recording counselling sessions helps supervision focus on detailed aspects of the client/counsellor relationship.
- The development of the 'internal supervisor' helps counsellors stay aware of the quality of their counselling relationships.

Resources

10

Counselling and counselling psychology have seen rapid growth in the UK and elsewhere over the last ten to fifteen years. There are now many books and journals devoted to aspects of counselling generally, and person-centred counselling in particular, and finding one's way through this expanding literature can be a daunting prospect.

I cannot offer a comprehensive list of books concerning the person-centred approach, but below I suggest a number of publications with which students of the PCA should be familiar. I also suggest a number of books that are not specifically about the person-centred approach, but which should be useful to students and others studying counselling and related topics.

Person-centred books

Most people find the various books by Carl Rogers provide the best places to start, and valuable reference sources during training and beyond. The most popular are *On Becoming a Person* (Houghton Mifflin, 1961), and *A Way of Being* (Houghton Mifflin, 1980), but probably the most systematic exploration of theory is found in *Client-Centered Therapy: Its Current Practice, Implications and Theory* (Houghton Mifflin, 1951).

Two earlier books by Carl Rogers, *The Clinical Treatment of the Problem Child* (Houghton Mifflin, 1939), and *Counseling and Psychotherapy: Newer Concepts in Practice* (Houghton Mifflin, 1942), are difficult to find, and probably only of historical interest now. Similarly *Carl Rogers on Encounter Groups* (Harper and Row, 1970), is no longer widely available, but it includes some useful material from the time when Rogers' interest in group work was an important theme in his work.

The collection of papers, *The Carl Rogers Reader* (Houghton Mifflin, 1989), edited by Kirschenbaum and Henderson, incorporates all of Rogers most important theoretical statements, including the 1957 paper, *The Necessary and Sufficient Conditions of Therapeutic Personality Change*, and (in abridged form) the 1959 paper, *A Theory of Therapy, Personality, and Interpersonal Relationships, As Developed in the Client-Centered*

Framework. A second volume edited by Kirschenbaum and Henderson, *The Carl Rogers Dialogues* (Houghton Mifflin, 1989), includes transcripts and discussions of meetings between Rogers and some of the leading figures in psychology of the day, including B. F. Skinner.

Three other books by Carl Rogers, *Becoming Partners: Marriage and its Alternatives* (Constable, 1973), *Freedom to Learn for the Eighties* (Charles Merrill, 1983), and *On Personal Power* (Constable, 1978), deal with subjects other than counselling. All three now appear somewhat dated, but the chapter on actualisation from *On Personal Power* is still worth reading. Jackie Hill's *Person-Centred Approaches in Schools* (PCCS Books, 1994), is a more contemporary, though less detailed, view of the PCA in educational settings than *Freedom to Learn for the Eighties*.

Person to Person, edited by Carl Rogers and Barry Stevens (Real People Press, 1967) is still of interest because it contains some person-centred writing on working with 'schizophrenics'. Particularly recommended is John Shlien's chapter *A Client-Centered Approach to Schizophrenia: First Approximations*, which includes some brief transcripts from counselling sessions with 'Mike', a hospitalised patient. There is a real flavour here of a deeply sensitive and empathic person-centred therapeutic relationship.

Difficult to find, but still worth searching for, is R. F. Levant and J. M. Shlien's edited volume, *Client-Centered Therapy and the Person-Centered Approach: New Directions in Theory, Research and Practice* (New York: Praeger and London: Sage, 1984). This volume contains the provocative chapter from Shlien, *A Countertheory of Transference*, one of the few examples of writing on this topic from a person-centred perspective. This paper, along with over 50 others from the important, but now discontinued, journal, *Person-Centered Review* have been published by PCCS Books as *Classics in the Person-centred Approach* edited by David Cain (2002).

For those interested in Natalie Rogers' development of 'Expressive Therapy', the best introduction is to be found in *The Creative Connection: Expressive Arts as Healing* (USA: Science and Behavior Books, 1993, UK: PCCS Books, 2000). An extended interview with Natalie Rogers, *Counselling and Creativity: an interview with Natalie Rogers* appears in the *British Journal of Guidance and Counselling*, 1997, *25*, pp. 263–73.

The book edited by Barry Farber, Debora Brink and Patricia Raskin, *The Psychotherapy of Carl Rogers: Cases and Commentary* (Guilford Press, 1996), takes a number of published counselling interviews between Rogers and various clients and subjects them to some searching examination. In the second section of the book, practitioners from other orientations provide critical analysis.

The book by Godfrey Barrett-Lennard, *Carl Rogers' Helping System: Journey and Substance* (Sage, 1998), is probably the single most important book on the Person-Centred Approach to have appeared in recent times. It provides a comprehensive review of the history and development of the approach and carefully documents the most significant research on person-centred counselling and other applications of the PCA. The book moves the evolution of the PCA into new territory, and is indispensable for the serious student. Similarly indispensable is the collection of papers from C. H. Patterson, published by PCCS Books as, *Understanding Psychotherapy: Fifty Years of Client-Centred Theory and Practice*. Patterson's lifetime contribution to the development of person-centred theory and practice is second to none, and it is something of a mystery to me why his books are not more widely read.

The book by the British authors, David Mearns and Brian Thorne, *Person-Centred Counselling in Action* (Sage, second edition, 1999) has proved one of the most popular books on person-centred counselling during the last dozen years or so. It appears on most, if not all, booklists of recommended reading on person-centred and other counselling courses. The latest book from Mearns and Thorne, *Person Centred Therapy Today: New Frontiers in Theory and Practice*, London: Sage (2000), is an essential reader for serious students of the PCA. Of general interest is Thorne and Lambers (eds), *Person-Centred Therapy: A European Perspective* (Sage, 1998).

Tony Merry's book, *Invitation to Person-Centred Psychology* (Whurr, 1995), provides some background and context for the PCA. It outlines the basic theory and philosophy of the approach and discusses its application to counselling, group work and education. *A Dictionary of Person-Centred Psychology* by Keith Tudor and Tony Merry (Whurr, 2002), provides definitions and discussions of all of the terms currently in use in the PCA.

Jerold Bozarth's *Person-Centered Therapy: A Revolutionary Paradigm* (PCCS Books, 1998), takes a detailed and scholarly look at contemporary issues in person-centred psychology. It has clear discussions of, for example, the core conditions, actualisation, encounter and research.

Two publications by David Mearns, *Person-Centred Counselling Training* (Sage, 1997), and *Developing Person-Centred Counselling* (Sage, 1994), provide good discussions on theory and explore issues of importance to counsellors in training.

For a thorough account of Carl Rogers the person, there is none better than Brian Thorne's *Carl Rogers* (Sage, 1992). Here you will find a detailed account of Rogers' life, and good discussion of his major contributions to the counselling field. Some of the main criticisms of Rogers' work are given and answered persuasively. In 2002, a book comprising an extended interview with Carl Rogers, *Carl Rogers the Quiet Revolutionary: An Oral History* (Rogers and Russell, published by Penmarin Books, 2002) is close to being an autobiography. As part of the same project, Natalie Rogers (Carl Rogers daughter) has produced an impressive CD-ROM (*Carl Rogers: A Daughter's Tribute*) for use in computers. It includes video-clips, text exerpts, bibliographies and dozens of photographs spanning the life and career of Carl Rogers.

Also by Brian Thorne, *Person-Centred Counselling: Therapeutic and Spiritual Dimensions* (Whurr, 1991) and *Person-Centred Counselling and Christian Spirituality: The Secular and the Holy* (Whurr, 1998), explore person-centred counselling from a Christian spiritual perspective, and are essential reading for those interested in this aspect of counselling. The latest book on this topic from Brian Thorne, *The Mystical Power of Person-*

Centred Therapy: Hope Beyond Despair (Whurr, 2002), is a powerful book that will delight some readers and surprise others.

Another recent book, *Person-Centred Counselling: An Experiential Approach* (Sage, 1998) by David Rennie offers a radically different perspective on person-centred counselling. Rennie departs from basic person-centred theory and philosophy in his discussion, and readers will be aware of how some of his ideas run counter to those of Rogers. Also representing a departure from mainstream person-centred theory is Richard Worsley's *Process Work in Person-Centred Therapy: Phenomenological and Existential Perspectives* (Palgrave, 2002).

A series of four volumes appeared in 2001 and 2002 (series editor, Gill Wyatt) dealing with Rogers therapeutic conditions: Vol. 1 *Congruence*, Vol. 2. *Empathy*, Vol 3. *Unconditional Positive Regard*, and Vol. 4 *Contact and Perception* (PCCS Books). This series contains contributions of both historical and contemporary interest from most of the best known writers in the person-centred world, and is a rich source of research, perspectives and informed discussion.

Person-centred work with families is an underrepresented area in the literature, but Ned Gaylin's *Family, Self and Psychotherapy: A Person-Centred Perspective* (PCCS Books, 2001), goes a long way towards filling the gap. It is rare to find a book written with a person-centred perspective to particular problems, but an exception is *Counselling the Person Beyond the Alcohol Problem*, by Richard Bryant-Jeffries (Jessica Kingsley, 2001). Peggy Natiello's, *The Person-Centred Approach: A Passionate Presence* (PCCS Books, 2001), is especially good for issues to do with power in helping relationships, groups and communities and the training of person-centred practitioners. Marlis P´örtner's book, *Trust and Understanding: The Person-Centred Approach to Everyday Care for People with Special Needs* (PCCS Books, 2000) shows how the PCA can be used to help people with challenging needs outside of the therapy room.

Few books have appeared on group work within the PCA since the publication of *Carl Rogers on Encounter Groups* (Harper and Row, 1970). An exception is the collection, edited by Colin Lago and Mhairi MacMillan, *Experiences in Relatedness: Groupwork and the Person-Centred Approach* (PCCS Books, 1999). Although not specifically concerned with counselling, this book contains a great deal of discussion on the application of person-centred theory and philosophy to group contexts of various kinds.

List of suggested person-centred books

Easily available

Barrett-Lennard, G. T. (1998) *Carl Rogers' Helping System: Journey and Substance*. London: Sage.

Bozarth, J. (1998) *Person-Centered Therapy: A Revolutionary Paradigm*. Ross-on-Wye: PCCS Books.

Bozarth, J. and Wilkins, P. (eds.) (2001) *Rogers' Therapeutic Conditions:*

Evolution, Theory and Practice. Vol. 3: Unconditional Positive Regard. Ross-on-Wye: PCCS Books.

Bryant-Jeffries, R. (2001) *Counselling the Person Beyond the Alcohol Problem.* London: Jessica Kingsley.

Farber, B., Brink, D. and Raskin, P. (1996) *The Psychotherapy of Carl Rogers: Cases and Commentary.* New York: Guilford Press.

Gaylin, N. (2001) *Family, Self and Psychotherapy: A Person-Centred Perspective.* Ross-on-Wye: PCCS Books.

Haugh, S. and Merry T. (eds.) (2001). *Rogers' Therapeutic Conditions: Evolution, Theory and Practice. Vol. 2: Empathy.* Ross-on-Wye: PCCS Books.

Hill, J. (1994) *Person-Centred Approaches in Schools.* Manchester: PCCS Books.

Kirschenbaum, H. and Henderson, V. (eds.) (1989) *The Carl Rogers Reader.* Boston: Houghton Mifflin.

Kirschenbaum, H. and Henderson, V. (eds.) (1989) *The Carl Rogers Dialogues.* Boston: Houghton Mifflin.

Lago, C. and MacMillan, M. (eds.) (1999) *Experiences in Relatedness: Groupwork and the Person-Centred Approach.* Ross-on-Wye: PCCS Books.

Mearns, D. (1994) *Developing Person-Centred Counselling.* London: Sage.

Mearns, D. (1997) *Person-Centred Counselling Training.* London: Sage.

Mearns, D. and Thorne, B. (1999) *Person-Centred Counselling in Action.* 2nd edition. London: Sage.

Mearns, D. and Thorne, B. (2000) *Person-Centred Therapy Today: New Frontiers in Theory and Practice.* London: Sage.

Merry, T. (1995) *Invitation to Person-Centred Psychology.* London: Whurr.

Natiello, P. (2001). *The Person-Centred Approach: A Passionate Presence.* Ross-on-Wye: PCCS Books.

Patterson, C. H. (2000) *Understanding Psychotherapy: Fifty Years of Client-Centred Theory and Practice.* Ross-on-Wye: PCCS Books.

Pörtner, M. (2000) *Trust and Understanding: The Person-Centred Approach to Everyday Care for People with Special Needs.* Ross-on-Wye: PCCS Books.

Rennie, D. (1998) *Person-Centred Counselling: An Experiential Approach.* London: Sage.

Rogers, C.R. (1951) *Client-Centered Therapy: Its Current Practice, Implications and Theory.* Boston: Houghton Mifflin. (Currently published by Constable.)

Rogers, C.R. (1961) *On Becoming a Person.* Boston: Houghton Mifflin. (Currently published by Constable.)

Rogers, C.R. (1972) *Becoming Partners: Marriage and its Alternatives.* New York: Delacorte. (Currently published by Constable.)

Rogers, C.R. (1977) *Carl Rogers On Personal Power.* New York: Delacorte. (Currently published by Constable.)

Rogers, C.R. (1980) *A Way of Being.* Boston: Houghton Mifflin.

Rogers, C.R. (1983) *Freedom to Learn for the Eighties.* Columbus, OH: Charles Merrill.

Rogers, C.R. and Stevens, B. (1967) *Person to Person.* Palo Alto, CA: Real

People Press.

Rogers, N. (1993) *The Creative Connection: Expressive Arts as Healing.* Palo Alto, CA: Science and Behavior Books.

Thorne, B. (1991) *Person-Centred Counselling: Therapeutic and Spiritual Dimensions.* London: Whurr.

Thorne, B. (1992) *Carl Rogers.* London: Sage.

Thorne, B. (1998) *Person-Centred Counselling and Christian Spirituality.* London: Whurr

Thorne, B. (2002) *The Mystical Power of Person-Centred Therapy: Hope Beyond Despair.* London: Whurr.

Thorne, B. and Lambers, E. (1998) *Person-Centred Therapy a European Perspective.* London: Sage.

Tudor, K. and Merry, T. (2002) *Dictionary of Person-Centred Psychology.* London: Whurr.

Worsley, R. (2002) *Process Work in Person-Centred Therapy.* London: Palgrave.

Wyatt, G. (ed.) (2001) *Rogers' Therapeutic Conditions: Evolution, Theory and Practice. Vol. 1: Congruence.* Ross-on-Wye: PCCS Books.

Wyatt, G. and Sanders, P. (eds.) (2002) *Rogers' Therapeutic Conditions: Evolution, Theory and Practice. Vol. 4: Contact and Perception.* Ross-on-Wye: PCCS Books.

CD-ROM

Carl Rogers: A Daughter's Tribute (2002) available from www.mindgardenmedia.com

Out of print or otherwise difficult to obtain person-centred books

Levant, R. F. and Shlien, J. M. (eds.) (1984) *Client-Centered Therapy and the Person-Centered Approach: New Directions in Theory, Research and Practice.* New York: Praeger.

Rogers, C.R. (1939) *The Clinical Treatment of the Problem Child.* Boston: Houghton Mifflin.

Rogers, C.R. (1942) *Counseling and Psychotherapy: Newer Concepts in Practice.* Boston: Houghton Mifflin.

Rogers, C.R. (1970) *Carl Rogers on Encounter Groups.* New York: Harper and Row.

Other useful books on counselling and counselling psychology

Of the hundreds of books now available on counselling, psychotherapy and counselling psychology, I have chosen a limited number that I think might be most useful to counselling students.

Now in its fifth edition, *Theories of Psychotherapy*, by Cecil Patterson (the fifth edition with E. C. Watkins Jnr.) contains very clear and detailed descriptions of a number of therapeutic models. Since Patterson's ideas are heavily influenced by Rogers' work, the sections on client-centred therapy are excellent. John Mcleod's, *An Introduction to Counselling* (2nd edition, 1998, Open University Press), provides a comprehensive review of a number of approaches to counselling, including person-centred counselling, coupled with detailed and scholarly discussions of general themes in counselling, such as integration and eclecticism, research, etc. An excellent book to keep as reference or to 'dip into' for general interest, writing essays, etc, as is Colin Feltham's *What is Counselling?* (Sage, 1995).

A useful book for trainee and experienced counsellors alike is *The Counsellor's Handbook* (Stanley Thornes, 2nd edition, 1999) by Rowan Bayne, Ian Horton, Tony Merry, Elizabeth Noyes and Gladeana MacMahon. It offers short discussions and advice on practical and theoretical issues. For example, there are entries on empathy, email counselling, referrals, advertising, multicultural issues, psychological type, supervision, endings, contracting, etc.

A very popular and useful book is *First Steps in Counselling* by Pete Sanders (PCCS Books, 3rd edition, 2002). It is heavily influenced by person-centred ideas and is suitable for people embarking on a training course in counselling, whether person-centred or not.

A concise description of person-centred counselling is given by Brian Thorne in *Individual Therapy: A Handbook* (ed. Windy Dryden, Open University Press, 1990). This book is particularly useful for its clear explanations of a number of counselling approaches, helpful to those wanting to compare and contrast different counselling systems.

Contemporary Psychotherapies: Models and Methods (Charles Merrill, 1985), edited by Steven Lynn and John Garske, has chapters on a variety of counselling approaches. The chapter on client-centred counselling is by Nat Raskin and is another useful book for comparing and contrasting different approaches.

Two books on working with children from a perspective sympathetic to the person-centred approach are Virginia Axline's *Dibs: in Search of Self* (Victor Gollancz, 1966), and *Play Therapy* (Longman, 1989). Axline's 'non-directive play therapy' is, as she acknowledges, based on Carl Rogers' work.

Maurice Friedman's book, *Dialogue and the Human Image: Beyond Humanistic Psychology* (Sage, 1992), examines Humanistic Psychology, and discusses the work of Rogers, Maslow and others. A useful book for those wanting a constructive critique.

Moira Walker's edited volume, *Peta: A Feminist's Problem with Men* (Open University Press, 1995), contains a chapter by Judy Moore who explains how, as a person-centred therapist, she would approach working with the client described in the book. It provides a useful comparison with other counselling approaches, including Gestalt, cognitive behaviour therapy and feminist therapy.

Another helpful book in comparing different approaches is Michael Kahn's *Between Therapist and Client: The New Relationship* (Freeman and Co., 1991). Here, the author discusses possible reconciliations between different approaches to counselling, including those of Carl Rogers' person-centred perspective and Heinz Kohut's psychoanalytic one.

For those contemplating running counsellor training courses, Windy Dryden, Ian Horton and Dave Mearns, in *Issues in Professional Counsellor Training* (Cassell, 1995) provide useful insights, advice and guidance. In *The Management of Counselling and Psychotherapy Agencies* (Sage, 1998), Colin Lago and Duncan Kitchin give useful and practical advice and guidelines to those running or planning counselling services.

Colin Lago (in collaboration with Joyce Thompson) in *Race, Culture and Counselling* (Open University, 1996) provides comprehensive coverage of sensitive and complex issues, offering a wide range of theories, perspectives and models to illustrate the different ways in which people from different backgrounds communicate. A useful book for all counsellors working in a multi-cultural context.

Pink Therapy (Open University Press, 1996) edited by Dominic Davies and Charles Neal, is a guide for counsellors working with people who are lesbian, gay or bisexual, and proposes a model of gay affirmative therapy. Following the success of this volume, the same editors have compiled *Therapeutic Perspectives in Working with Lesbian, Gay and Bisexual Clients* (Open University Press, 1999), which explores these issues from ten different therapeutic orientations, including the person-centred approach.

Paul Wilkins in *Personal and Professional Development for Counsellors* (Sage, 1997) offers thoughtful discussion and suggestions about how counsellors can continue to develop as persons throughout their counselling careers. The chapter on the therapeutic relationship in person-centred counselling in Colin Feltham's edited book, *Understanding the Counselling Relationship* (Sage, 1999), is also by Paul Wilkins and provides a useful, straightforward account of the person-centred relationship to compare and contrast with others in the same volume.

Arthur Combs' *A Theory of Therapy: Guidelines for Counselling Practice* (Sage, 1989) provides some additional perspectives and original material, particularly concerning the characteristics of effective and ineffective 'helpers'.

Three books that provide some critical perspectives on wider 'mental health' issues are, *This is Madness* (Newnes, Holmes and Dunn, eds., PCCS Books, 1999) *This is Madness Too* (same editors and publishers, 2001), and *Implausible Professions* (House and Totton, eds., PCCS Books, 1997).

Finally, three books that deal with some important issues for all counsellors of all approaches are *Surviving Complaints Against Counsellors and Psychotherapists* (R. Casemore, ed., PCCS Books, 2001), *The Dynamics of Power in Counselling and Psychotherapy* (G. Proctor, PCCS Books, 2002), and *Ethics: Working with Ethical and Moral Dilemmas in Psychotherapy* (P. Clarkson, Whurr, 2000).

Any selection of books is bound to reflect the preferences and biases of the compiler, and others would, no doubt, have made very different choices. I see my selection as a place to start in dealing with a vast and ever-expanding literature, rather than a comprehensive review of what is currently available.

List of other useful counselling books

Axline, V. (1966) *Dibs: in Search of Self.* London: Victor Gollancz.
Axline, V. (1989) *Play Therapy.* London: Longman
Bayne, R., Horton, I., Merry, T., Noyes. and MacMahon, G. (1999) *The Counsellor's Handbook.* 2nd edition. Cheltenham: Stanley Thornes.
Casemore, R. (ed.) (2001) *Surviving Complaints Against Counsellors and Psychotherapists.* Ross-on-Wye: PCCS Books.
Clarkson, P. (ed.) (2000) *Ethics: Working with Ethical and Moral Dilemmas in Psychotherapy.* London: Whurr.
Combs, A. (1989) *A Theory of Therapy: Guidelines for Counselling Practice.* London: Sage.
Davies, D. and Neal, C. (eds.) (1996) *Pink Therapy.* Milton Keynes: Open University Press.
Davies, D. and Neal, C. (eds.) (1999) *Therapeutic Perspectives in Working with Lesbian, Gay and Bisexual Clients.* Milton Keynes: Open University Press.
Dryden, W. (ed.) (1990) *Individual Therapy: A Handbook.* Milton Keynes: Open University Press.
Dryden, W., Horton, I. and Mearns, D. (1995) *Issues in Professional Counsellor Training.* London: Cassell.
Feltham, C. (1995) *What is Counselling?* London: Sage.
Feltham, C. (ed.) (1999) *Understanding the Counselling Relationship.* London: Sage.
Friedman, M. (1992) *Dialogue and the Human Image: Beyond Humanistic Psychology.* London: Sage.
House, R. and Totton (eds) (1997). *Implausible Professions: Arguments for Pluralism and Autonomy in Psychotherapy and Counselling.* Ross-on-Wye: PCCS Books.
Kahn, M. (1991) *Between Therapist and Client: The New Relationship.* New York: Freeman and Co.
Lago, C. (in collaboration with Joyce Thompson) (1996) *Race, Culture and Counselling.* Milton Keynes: Open University Press.
Lago, C. and Kitchin, D. (1998) *The Management of Counselling and Psychotherapy Agencies.* London: Sage.
Lynn, S. and Garske, J. (eds.) (1985) *Contemporary Psychotherapies: Models and Methods.* Columbus, OH: Charles Merrill.
Mcleod, J. (1998) *An Introduction to Counselling.* 2nd edition. Milton Keynes: Open University Press.
Newnes, C., Holmes, G. and Dunn, C. (eds.) (1999). *This is Madness.* Ross-on-Wye: PCCS Books.
Newnes, C., Holmes, G. and Dunn, C. (eds.) (2001) *This is Madness Too.* Ross-on-Wye: PCCS Books.
Patterson, C. H. and Watkins, E. C. Jnr. (1996) *Theories of Psychotherapy.* New York: Addison Wesley Longman.
Proctor, G. (2002) *The Dynamics of Power in Counselling and Psychotherapy: Ethics, Politics and Practice.* Ross-on-Wye: PCCS Books.

Sanders, P. (2002) *First Steps in Counselling.* 3rd edition. Ross-on-Wye: PCCS Books.

Walker, M. (ed.) (1995) *Peta: A Feminist's Problem with Men.* Milton Keynes: Open University Press.

Wilkins, P. (1997) *Personal and Professional Development for Counsellors.* London: Sage.

Journals

The journal of the British Association for the Person-Centred Approach, *Person-Centred Practice,* and the American journal of the Association for the Development of the Person-Centered Approach, *The Person-Centered Journal* (see below for details), are particularly relevant to person-centred counsellors. A new international journal for the wider 'family' of person-centred therapies, *Person-Centered and Experiential Psychotherapies* is to be published from December 2002. In the UK, the leading journal in the counselling field generally is the *British Journal of Guidance and Counselling.*

The journal of the Association for Humanistic Psychology, based in the United States, the *Journal of Humanistic Psychology*, is of general interest to person-centred counsellors. *Self and Society,* is the journal of the British Association for Humanistic Psychology, see below under 'Organisations'.

The journal of the Psychology and Psychotherapy Association (PPA), founded in 1973, The Journal of Critical Psychology, Counselling and Psychotherapy, is available on subscription from the address below. For details of how to join the PPA, write to Chris Pitts, CMHT, 25 Corve Street, Ludlow SY8 1DA.

List of recommended counselling journals

British Journal of Guidance and Counselling: Carfax Publishing Company, PO Box 25, Abingdon, Oxfordshire OX14 3UE.

Journal of Critical Psychology, Counselling and Psychotherapy: PCCS Books, Llangarron, Ross-on-Wye, Herefordshire, HR9 6PT.

Journal of Humanistic Psychology: Sage Publications Ltd., 6, Bonhill Street, London, EC2 4PU.

Person-Centered and Experiential Psychotherapies: PCCS Books (as above).

Person-Centred Practice: PCCS Books (as above).

Self and Society: AHP(B), BM Box 3582, London WC1N 3XX

The Person-Centered Journal: Jo Cohen-Hamilton, Managing Editor, Person-Centered Journal, Department of Counseling and Human Resources, Kutztown University, Kutztown, Pa 19530, USA.

Person-centred organisations in the UK

The main person-centred organisation in the UK is the British Association for the Person-Centred Approach (BAPCA), a registered charity (No.

1044077). BAPCA was formed in 1989 and by 2002 there were over 1000 members. It offers a quarterly newsletter, *Person-to Person*, detailing developments in BAPCA, and various events and workshops, and a journal, *Person-Centred Practice*, issued twice yearly. In 2002, membership cost £30 (£20 concessions) per annum (under review). To subscribe to the journal without becoming a member, write to *Person-Centred Practice*, PCCS Books, Llangarron, Ross-on-Wye, Herefordshire, HR9 6PT, or you can email enquiries@pccsbooks.globalnet.co.uk.

BAPCA also issues a directory of UK person-centred practitioners. Details of this directory, training institutes and other person-centred organisations, conferences and workshops, etc., can be found on the BAPCA website (see 'Contacts' below).

There is also an organisation for person-centred therapists living in Scotland called Person-Centred Therapy Scotland (PCTS). Training and other criteria must be met for full membership, students may become associate members.

Contacts
BAPCA: For membership details, and other information write to BM-BAPCA, London, WC1N 3XX, or telephone 01989 770 948. Or see the BAPCA website: **http://www.bapca.org.uk**
PCTS: For all information write to 40 Kelvingrove St, Glasgow, G3 7RZ, or telephone 0141 332 6888.

Person-centred European organisations

Recently, an organisation called Network for European Associations of Person-Centred Counselling and Psychotherapy (NEAPCCP) has formed to promote the interests of person-centred therapists in Europe.

Contact
Write to NEAPCEPC, SGGT Office, Schoffelgasse 7, CH-8001, Zurich, Switzerland, or contact them through their website: **http://www.pcc europe.org**
More information is also available from BAPCA and vis the BAPCA website (see above).

Person-centred organisation in the USA

In the USA, the main organisation is the Association for the Development of The Person-Centered Approach (ADPCA). This offers a quarterly newsletter, *Renaissance*, and a journal, *The Person-Centered Journal*.

Contact
ADPCA: For details of membership, write to ADPCA, PO Box 3876, Cleveland, Il, 60690-3876, USA. Website: **http://www.adpca.org**

Person-centred international organisation

The World Association for Person-Centered and Experiential Counselling and Psychotherapy (WAPCECP) now invites individuals and organisations to join. Among its goals, this association aims to 'support/facilitate person-centered associations, institutes and individuals in their work, and to further their cooperation on an international level, especially in the field of psychotherapy and counseling', and to establish a 'high-quality journal in the English language'. This new journal, *Person-Centered and Experiential Psychotherapies*, is to be published from December 2002.

Contact
WAPCECP: For all details, write to WAPCECP, c/o SGGT Office, Josefstrasse 79 CH-8005, Zurich, Switzerland. You can also join by completing the online registration form. Website: **http://www.pce-world.org**

Other useful organisations

In the UK, one of the most useful organisations for counsellors is the British Association for Counselling and Psychotherapy (BACP). There are specialist divisions for counsellors working in particular organisational settings (in education, counselling at work and medical settings, for example), and a number of regional groups.

BACP issues a number of very useful information sheets on various topics, including on legal and ethical issues, training and supervision, for example. It also publishes directories of counsellors and counsellor training courses, has a library of films and videos. There is a magazine, *Counselling and Psychotherapy Journal* (ten issues per year), and a quarterly research journal.

BACP has a well-established scheme for the accreditation of individual counsellors. To be accredited, an applicant must satisfy a number of fairly strict criteria concerning training, experience and supervision. Accreditation, if granted, must be renewed every five years. There is also a new scheme created to provide the public with a specific UK standard that recognises counsellors who offer 'safe and accountable practice'. This is the United Kingdom Register of Counsellors (UKRC). Membership is, at present, available to members of BACP and the Confederation of Scottish Counselling Agencies.

The Association for Humanistic Psychology, Britain (AHP(B)), though not specifically person-centred, is useful for anyone with an interest in humanistic psychology. AHP has a journal, *Self and Society*, appearing six times a year.

Contacts
AHP(B): For membership and other details, write to AHP(B), BM Box 3582, London WC1N 3XX, or telephone 0345 0708506. You can also email: ahp@saqnet.co.uk.

BACP: For membership and other details, write to: BACP, 1, Regent Place, Rugby, Warwickshire CV21 2PJ, or telephone 01788 550899. You can also email BACP at bacp@bacp.co.uk. Website: **http://www.bac.co.uk**
UKRC: For details, write to, UKRC, PO Box 1050, Rugby, CV21 2HZ.

Counselling resources on the Internet

There are thousands of pages on the Internet (World Wide Web) dealing with counselling, psychotherapy and counselling psychology. You can easily get lost (and bored) by randomly following the links a key-word search will provide. Keep your eye on the various journals in counselling and psychology: they sometimes list relevant websites. After a while, you will get used to how the system works, and be aware of some of its pitfalls as well as its advantages. In the meantime, what follows is a list of some websites that you might find useful, and which will provide a starting point. Some of them have links to other sites, and you might be surprised by what you find.

For a detailed discussion of counselling resources and the Internet, see Goss, et al. (1999).

http://www.bapca.org.uk
The website of the British Association for the Person-Centred Approach (note be careful not to confuse BAPCA and BACP — see below). Contains lots of useful information for anyone interested in the Person-Centred Approach. News, events, directory of UK person-centred therapists, materials, links to other PCA sites and a sense of what's going on in the person-centred community in the UK.

http://www.bac.co.uk
This is the website of the British Association for Counselling and Psychotherapy (BACP — see above). There is a lot of information there including a list of BACP publications, something about the various divisions of BACP, and so on.

http://www.bps.org.uk
The website of the British Psychological Society. Details of how to join, the various divisions of BPS, publications, etc.

http://www.carfax.co.uk/big-ad.htm
The website of the British Journal of Guidance and Counselling gives lists of contents of recent journals.

http://www.allanturner.co.uk
This is 'Allan Turner's Person-Centred Web Site', a very useful site. You will find links to a number of journal articles that you can print off, a list of workshops, seminars and other events, and a directory of person-centred

counsellors broken down by county (as well as some in the USA, Greece, France, etc). There is also a list of person-centred training institutes, publications, papers, and videos for sale and how to get them.

Useful, too, are links to the website of the British Association for the Person-Centred Approach: http://www.bapca.org.uk and the American Association for the Development of the Person-Centered Approach: http://www.adpca.org.

Allan Turner's Web Page also has links to other counselling resources on the Web, including to the American Psychological Association, and to a separate list of links called 'Counselling Resources on the Net', and one called 'Non-Mainstream Psychotherapy and Counselling Resources on the Internet'

Other useful websites

http://www.apa.org American Psychological Association

http://www.americanpsychotherapy.com American Psychotherapy Association

http://ahpweb.org American Association for Humanistic Psychology

http://wwww.counsellingpsychology.org.uk British Psychological Society: Division of counselling

http://centerfortheperson.org/members.html Center for Studies of the Person (La Jolla, USA).

http://sage1.home.mindspring.com The website of Dr. C. H. Patterson. Some reprints of his most useful articles available here (free).

http://biblion.bib.uia.mx/aiecp/ A huge bibliography of person-centred (and allied) publications.

http://irish-counselling.ie/ Irish Association for Counselling and Therapy

http://www.nrogers.com/ Natalie Rogers' website

http://www.pfs-online.at Peter F. Schmid's website. Some very useful links, bibliographies and downloadable articles (in English).

http://www.bap-psychotherapy.org The British Association of Psychotherapists.

http://bps.org.uk/index.cfm The British Psychological Society.

http://www.psychotherapy.org.uk/ The Council for Psychotherapy (UKCP)

http://counsellingwales.org Counselling issues and organisations in Wales.

http://www.counsellingpsychologycsotland.org.uk Counselling psychology in Scotland

http://www.thefdp.demon.co.uk Foundation for the Developing Person: courses and workshops.

http://www.pce-world.org The website of the World Association for Person-Centered and Experiential Psychotherapies. Details of member benefits and how to join are located here.

References

Barrett-Lennard, G. T. (1962) The mature person. *Mental Hygiene, 46,* pp. 98–102.

Barrett-Lennard, G. T. (1993) The phases and focus of empathy. *British Journal of Medical Psychology, 66,* pp. 3–14.

Barrett-Lennard, G. T. (1998) *Carl Rogers' Helping System: Journey and Substance.* London: Sage.

Barrett-Lennard, G. T. (2002) Perceptual Variables of the Helping Relationship: a measuring system and its fruits. In Wyatt, G. and Sanders, P. (eds.) *Rogers' Therapeutic Conditions: Evolution, Theory and Practice. Vol. 4. Contact and Perception.* pp. 25–50. Ross-on-Wye: PCCS Books.

Baughan, R. and Merry, T. (2001) Empathy: An Evolutionary/biological Perspective. In Haugh, S. and Merry, T. (eds.) *Rogers' Therapeutic Conditions: Evolution, Theory and Practice. Vol. 2. Empathy.* pp. 230–39. Ross-on-Wye: PCCS Books.

Bayne, R., Horton, I., Merry, T., Noyes, E. and McMahon, G. (1999) *The Counsellors Handbook,* 2nd edition. Cheltenham: Stanley Thornes.

Bergin, A. E. and Garfield, S. L. (eds.) (1994) *Handbook of Psychotherapy and Behaviour Change,* 4th edition. New York: Wiley.

Bernard, J. M. and Goodyear, R. K. (1992) *Fundamentals of Clinical Supervision.* Boston: Allyn and Bacon.

Binder, U and Binder, J. (2001). A Theoretical Approach to Empathy. In Haugh, S. and Merry, T. (eds.) *Rogers' Therapeutic Conditions: Evolution, Theory and Practice. Vol. 2. Empathy.* pp. 163–80. Ross-on-Wye: PCCS Books.

Bozarth, J (1984/2001). Beyond Reflection: Emergent modes of empathy. In Haugh, S. and Merry, T. (eds.) *Rogers' Therapeutic Conditions: Evolution, Theory and Practice. Vol 2. Empathy.* Ross-on-Wye: PCCS Books.

Bozarth, J (1993/1998). Not Necessarily Necessary, but Always Sufficient. In J. Bozarth, *Person-Centred Therapy: A Revolutionary Paradigm.* Ross-on-Wye, PCCS Books. pp. 35–42

Bozarth, J. (1998) *Person-Centred Therapy: A Revolutionary Paradigm.* Ross-on-Wye: PCCS Books.

Bozarth, J. (2001) Client-Centered Unconditional Positive Regard: A historical perspective. In Bozarth, J. and Wilkins, P. (eds.) *Rogers' Therapeutic Conditions: Evolution, Theory and Practice. Vol 3: Unconditional Positive Regard.* pp. 5-18. Ross-on-Wye: PCCS Books.

Brodley, B. (1993) The Therapeutic Clinical Interview — Guidelines for beginning practice. *Person-Centred Practice,* 1, (2), pp. 15–20.

Brodley, B. and Merry, T. (1995) Guidelines for student participants in person-centred peer groups. *Person-Centred Practice,* 3, (2), pp. 17–22.

Cain, D. (1990) Celebration, reflection and renewal. *Person-Centered Review,* 5, (4), pp. 357–63.

Cain D. (2002) *Classics in the Person-Centered Approach.* Ross-on-Wye: PCCS Books.

Combs, A. (1989) *A Theory of Therapy: Guidelines for Counselling Practice.* London: Sage.

Cooper, M. (1999) If you can't be Jeckyll be Hyde: an existential-phenomenological exploration of lived plurality. In Rowan, J. and Cooper, M. (eds.) *The Plural Self.* London: Sage. pp. 51–70.

Cooper, M. (2000) Person-centred Developmental Theory: Reflections and revisions. *Person-Centred Practice.* 8, (2). pp. 87–94.

Cooper, M. (2001) Embodied Empathy. In Haugh, S. and Merry, T. (eds.) *Rogers' Therapeutic Conditions: Evolution, Theory and Practice. Vol. 2. Empathy.* pp. 218–29. Ross-on-Wye: PCCS Books.

Dryden, W. (ed.) (1996) *Developments in Psychotherapy: Historical Perspectives.* London: Sage.

Dryden, W. and Feltham, C. (1992) *Brief Counselling: A Practical Guide for Beginning Practitioners.* Milton Keynes: Open University Press.

Dryden, W., Horton, I. and Mearns, D. (1995) *Issues in Professional Counsellor Training.* London: Cassell.

Dryden W. and Thorne, B. (1991) *Training and Supervision for Counselling in Action.* London: Sage.

Duncan, B. L., and Moynihan, D. W. (1994) Applying outcome research: intentional utilization of the client's frame of reference. *Psychotherapy, 31,* pp. 294–301.

Egan, G. (1990) *Exercises in Helping Skills.* Monterey, CA: Brooks/Cole.

Ellingham, I. (2002) Carl Rogers' 'Congruence' as an Organismic, not a Freudian Concept. In Wyatt, G. (ed.) *Rogers' Therapeutic Conditions: Evolution, Theory and Practice. Vol. 1. Congruence.* pp. 96–115. Ross-on-Wye: PCCS Books.

Elliott, R., Greenberg, L. and Lietaer, G. (in press) Research on experiential psychotherapies. In M. Lambert, A. Bergin and S. Garfield (eds) *Handbook of Psychotherapy and Behaviour Change.* New York: Wiley.

Evans, R. (1975) *Carl Rogers: The Man and his Ideas.* New York: Dutton.

Fairhurst, I. and Merry, T. (1999) Group work in client-centred counsellor training. In Lago, C. and MacMillan, M. (eds.) *Experiences in Relatedness: Groupwork and the Person-Centred Approach.* Ross-on-Wye: PCCS Books.

Feltham, C. (1997a) *Time-Limited Counselling.* London: Sage.

Feltham, C. (1997b) Challenging the Core Theoretical Model. In House, R. and Totton, N. (eds.) *Implausible Professions: Arguments for Pluralism and Autonomy in Psychotherapy and Counselling.* Ross-on-Wye: PCCS Books.

Freire, E. (2001) Unconditional Positive Regard: the distinctive feature of client-centered therapy. In Bozarth, J. And Wilkins, P. (eds.) *Rogers' Therapeutic Conditions: Evolution, Theory and Practice. Vol. 3: Unconditional Positive Regard.* pp. 145–55. Ross-on-Wye: PCCS Books.

Friedli, K., King, M., Lloyd, M. and Horder, J. (1997) Randomised controlled assessment of non-directive psychotherapy versus routine general practitioner care. *Lancet, 350,* pp. 1662–5.

Gaylin, N. (2001) *Family, Self and Psychotherapy: a Person-Centred Perspective.* Ross-on-Wye: PCCS Books.

Gendlin, E. (1981) *Focusing.* New York: Bantam Books. Revised edition.

Gendlin, E. (1984) The client's client: the edge of awareness. In Levant, R. and Shlien, J. (eds.) *Client-Centered Therapy and the Person-Centered Approach: New Directions in Theory, Research and Practice.* New York: Praeger.

Goss, S., Robson, D., Pelling, N.J. and Renard. E. (1999) The Challenge of the Internet. *Counselling,* 10, (3), pp. 37–43.

Grafanaki, S. (2001) What Counselling Research has Taught us about the Concept of Congruence: Main Discoveries and Unresolved Issues. In Wyatt, G. (ed.) *Rogers' Therapeutic Conditions: Evolution, Theory and Practice. Vol. 1. Congruence.* pp. 18-35. Ross-on-Wye: PCCS Books.

Grant, B. (1990/2002) Principled and instrumental non-directiveness in person-centered and client-centered therapy. *Person-Centered Review, 5:* 77–88. Reprinted in Cain (2002).

Hackney, H. and Goodyear, R. K. (1984) Carl Rogers' Client-Centered Approach to Supervision. In Levant, R. and Shlien, J. (eds.) *Client-Centered Therapy and the Person-Centered Approach. New Directions in Theory, Research and Practice.* New York: Praeger.

Haugh, S. and Merry, T (eds.) (2001) *Rogers' Therapeutic Conditions: Evolution, Theory and Practice. Vol. 2: Empathy.* Ross-on-Wye: PCCS Books.

Heron, J. (1971) *Experience and method: an enquiry into the concept of experiential research.* University of Surrey: Human Potential Research Project.

Heron, J. (1981) Philosophical basis for a new paradigm. In Reason, P. and Rowan, J. (eds.) *Human Inquiry: A Source Book of New Paradigm Research.* Chichester: Wiley.

Kagan, N. (1984) Interpersonal Process Recall: Basic Methods and Recent Research. In Larsen, D. (ed.) *Teaching Psychological Skills.* Monterey, CA: Brooks/Cole.

King, M., Sibbald, B., Ward, E., Bower, P., Lloyd, M., Gabbay, M. and Byford, S. (2000) Randomised controlled trial of non-directive counselling, cognitive-behaviour therapy and usual practitioner care in the management of depression as well as mixed anxiety and depression in primary care. *Health Technology Assessment, 4,* (19). (Also published in *the British Medical Journal,* 321, (2000), pp. 1383–8.

Kirschenbaum, H. and Henderson, V. (eds.) (1989) *The Carl Rogers Reader.* Boston: Houghton Mifflin.

Lago, C. and MacMillan, M. (1999) *Experiences in Relatedness: Groupwork and the Person-Centred Approach.* Ross-on-Wye: PCCS Books.

Levant, R. F. and Shlien, J. M. (eds.) (1984) *Client-Centered Therapy and the Person Centered Approach: New Directions in Theory, Research and Practice.* New York: Praeger.

Lietaer, G. (2001). Unconditional Acceptance and Positive Regard. In Bozarth, J. and Wilkins, P. (eds.) *Rogers' Therapeutic Conditions: Evolution, Theory and Practice. Vol. 3: Unconditional Positive Regard.* pp. 88–108. Ross-on-Wye: PCCS Books.

Lockhart, W. (1984) Rogers' Necessary and Sufficient Conditions Revisited. *British Journal of Guidance and Counselling,* 12, (2), pp. 112–23.

Macran, S. and Shapiro, D. A. (1998) The role of personal therapy for therapists: a review. *British Journal of Medical Psychology, 71,* pp. 13–25.

Malik, K. (2001) *Man, Beast and Zombie: What Science Can and Cannot Tell us about Human Nature.* London: Phoenix

May, R. (1969) *Love and Will.* New York: Dell.

May, R. (1982) The problem of evil: an open letter to Carl Rogers. *Journal of Humanistic Psychology, 22,* (3), pp. 10–21.

McCulloch, L. (2002). A Person-Centred Approach to Antisocial Personality Disorder. *Person-Centred Practice, 10,* (1), pp. 4–14.

Mearns, D. (1993) Against indemnity insurance. In W. Dryden (ed.) *Questions and Answers on Counselling in Action.* London: Sage.

Mearns, D. (1994/2000) The dance of psychotherapy. In Merry, T. (ed.) *Person-Centred Practice: The BAPCA Reader.* Ross-on-Wye: PCCS Books.

Mearns, D. (1994) *Developing Person-Centred Counselling.* London: Sage.

Mearns, D. (1995) Supervision: a tale of the missing client. *British Journal of Guidance and Counselling,* 23, (3), pp. 421–7.

Mearns, D. (1996) Working at relational depth with clients in person-centred counselling. *Counselling, 7,* (4), pp. 306–11.

Mearns, D. (1997) *Person-Centred Counselling Training.* London: Sage.

Mearns, D. and McLeod, J. (1984) A person centred approach to research. In Levant, R. and Shlien, J. (eds.) *Client-Centered Therapy and the Person-Centered Approach: New Directions in Theory, Research and Practice.* New York: Praeger.

Mearns, D. and Thorne, B. (1988) *Person-Centred Counselling in Action.* London: Sage.

Mearns, D. and Thorne, B. (1999) *Person-Centred Counselling in Action* 2nd edition. London: Sage.

Mearns, D. and Thorne, B. (2000*) Person- Centred Therapy Today: New Frontiers in Theory and Practice.* London: Sage.

Merry, T. (1995) *Invitation to Person Centred Psychology.* London: Whurr.

Merry, T. (1997) Counselling and Creativity: an interview with Natalie Rogers. *British Journal of Guidance and Counselling, 25,* (2), pp. 263–73.

Merry, T (2002). Process Work in Person-Centred Therapy: a review article. *Person-Centred Practice, 10,* (1), pp. 49–55.

Merry, T. and Brodley, B. (2002) The Non-Directive Attitude in Client-Centered Therapy:

A Response to Kahn. *Journal of Humanistic Psychology, 42*, 66–77.

Mill, J. S. (1859) On Liberty. In Lerner, M. (ed.) (1961) *Essential Works of John Stuart Mill*. New York: Bantam Books.

Mowbray, R. (1995) *The Case Against Psychotherapy Registration: A Conservation Issue for the Human Potential Movement*. London: Trans Marginal Press.

Mowbray, R. (1997) A Case to Answer. In House, R. and Totton, N. (eds.) *Implausible Professions: Arguments for Pluralism and Autonomy in Psychotherapy and Counselling*. Ross-on-Wye: PCCS Books.

Natiello, P. (2001). *The Person-Centred Approach: A Passionate Presence*. Ross-on-Wye: PCCS Books.

Nelson-Jones, R. (1995) *Theory and Practice of Counselling*, 2nd edition. London: Cassell

Orlinsky, D. E. And Howard, K. I. (1978) The Relation of Process to Outcome in Psychotherapy. In Garfield, S. and Bergin, A. (eds.) *Handbook of Psychotherapy and Behavior Change*, (3rd edition), pp. 331–81. Chichester: John Wiley and Sons.

Patel, N. and Fatimilehin, I. (1999) Racism and Mental Health. In Newnes, C., Holmes, G. and Dunn, C. (eds.) *This is Madness*. Ross-on-Wye: PCCS Books.

Patterson, C. H. (1984) Empathy, Warmth and Genuineness in Psychotherapy: a review of reviews. *Psychotherapy, 21*, pp. 431–38.

Patterson, C. H. (1985) *The Therapeutic Relationship*. Monterey, CA: Brookes/Cole.

Patterson, C. H. (1995) A universal system of psychotherapy, *Person-Centered Journal, 2*, (1), pp. 54–62.

Patterson, C. H. (1996) Multicultural Counselling: From Diversity to Universality. *Journal of Counseling and Development, 74*.

Patterson, C. H. (1997) Client-Centered Supervision. In Watkins, E. (ed.) *Handbook of Psychotherapy Supervision*. New York: Wiley.

Portner, M. (2000) *Trust and Understanding: the Person-Centred Approach to Everyday Care for People with Special Needs*. Ross-on-Wye: PCCS Books.

Proctor, G. (2002). *The Dynamics of Power in Counselling and Psychotherapy: Ethics, Politics and Practice*. Ross-on-Wye: PCCS Books

Prouty, G.F. (1976) Pre-therapy, a method of treating pre-expressive, psychotic and retarded patients. *Psychotherapy: Theory, Research and Practice*, 13, (3), pp. 290–5.

Prouty, G. F. (1990) A theoretical evolution in the person-centered/experiential psychotherapy of schizophrenia and retardation. In Lietaer, G., Rombauts, L., and Van Balen, R. (eds.) *Client-Centred and Experiential Psychotherapy in the Nineties*. Leuven: Leuven University Press.

Prouty, G. F. (1994) *Theoretical Evolutions in Person-Centered/Experiential Therapy: Applications to Schizophrenic and Retarded Psychoses*. Westport: Praeger.

Prouty, G. F. (1998/2000). Pre-Therapy and the Pre-Expressive Self. In Merry, T. (ed.), *The BAPCA Reader*. Ross-on-Wye: PCCS Books, pp. 68–76.

Prouty, G. F. (2001) Unconditional Positive Regard and Pre-Therapy: an exploration. In Bozarth, J. And Wilkins, P. (eds.) *Rogers' Therapeutic Conditions: Evolution, Theory and Practice. Vol. 3: Unconditional Positive Regard*. pp. 76–87. Ross-on-Wye: PCCS Books.

Prouty, G. F. and Cronwal, M. (1989) Psychotherapy with a depressed mentally retarded adult: an application of pre-therapy. In Dozen, A. and Menolascino, F. (eds.) *Depression in Mentally Retarded Children and Adults*. Liedon: Logon Publications.

Prouty, G. F., Van Werde, D. and Pörtner, M (2002) *Pre-Therapy*. Ross-on-Wye: PCCS Books.

Raskin, N. (1996) Person-Centered Psychotherapy: Twenty Historical Steps. In Dryden, W. (ed.) (1996) *Developments in Psychotherapy: Historical Perspectives*. London: Sage.

Reason, P. (1988) (ed.) *Human Inquiry in Action: Developments in New Paradigm Research*. London: Sage.

Rogers, A. (2001) A Voice of Resistance: in response to BACP's call to accreditation. *Person-Centred Practice, 9*, (2), pp. 74–7

Rogers, C. R. (1942) *Counselling and Psychotherapy: Newer Concepts in Practice* Boston:

References 207

Houghton Mifflin.

Rogers, C. R. (1951). *Client-Centered Therapy: Its Current Practice, Implications and Theory.* Boston: Houghton Mifflin.

Rogers, C. R. (1956). Moments of Movement. *Paper given to the first meeting of the American Academy of Psychotherapists.* New York, New York.

Rogers, C. R. (1957a). The necessary and sufficient conditions of therapeutic personality change. *Journal of Consulting Psychology, 21*, (2), pp. 95–103.

Rogers, C. R. (1957b) A note on the "Nature of Man". *Journal of Counselling Psychology, 4*, (3), pp. 199–203.

Rogers, C. R. (1957c). A therapist's view of the good life: the fully functioning person. *The Humanist*, (17).

Rogers, C. R. (1958) A process conception of psychotherapy. *American Psychologist, 13*, pp. 142–9.

Rogers, C. R. (1959) A Theory of Therapy, Personality, and Interpersonal Relationships, As Developed in the Client-Centered Framework. In Koch, S. (ed.) (1959) *Psychology: A Study of a Science, Vol. 3. Formulations of the Person and the Social Context.* New York: McGraw-Hill, pp. 184–256.

Rogers, C. R. (1961) *On Becoming a Person.* Boston: Houghton Mifflin.

Rogers, C. R. (1963) The actualizing tendency in relation to 'motives' and to consciousness. In Jones, M. (ed.) *Nebraska symposium on motivation.* Lincoln: University of Nebraska Press, pp. 1–24.

Rogers, C. R. (1966) Client-centered therapy. In Arieti, S. (ed.) *American Handbook of Psychiatry.* New York: Basic Books. pp. 183–2000.

Rogers, C.R. (1970) *On Encounter Groups.* New York: Harper and Row.

Rogers, C. R. (1980) *A Way of Being.* Boston: Houghton Mifflin.

Rogers, C. R. (1983) *Freedom to Learn for the Eighties.* Columbus, OH: Charles Merrill.

Rogers, C. R. (1986) Rogers, Kohut and Erickson: A personal perspective on some similarities and differences. *Person-Centered Review*, 1, pp. 125–40.

Rogers, C. R., Kell, B. I. and McNeil, H. (1948) The role of self-understanding in the prediction of behavior. *Journal of Consulting Psychology, 12*, pp. 174–86.

Rogers, C. R. and Sanford, R. C. (1980) Client-Centered Psychotherapy. In Kaplan, G., Sadock, B., and Freeman, A. (eds.) *Comprehensive Textbook of Psychiatry, Vol. 3.* Baltimore: Williams and Wilkins.

Rogers, C.R. and Russell, D.E. (2002) *Carl Rogers the Quiet Revolutionary: An Oral History.* Roseville, CA: Penmarin Books.

Rogers, N. (1993/2000) *The Creative Connection: Expressive Arts in Healing.* Palo Alto, CA: Science and Behavior Books. (2000), Ross-on-Wye: PCCS Books.

Rowland, N., Mellor Clarke, J., Bower, P., Heywood, P., Young, P. And Godfrey, C. (2000). Counselling for depression in primary care [protocol for a Cochrane review]. *The Cochrane Library*, (3); update software.

Sanders, P. (2000) Mapping Person-centred Approaches to Counselling and Psychotherapy. *Person-Centred Practice*, 8, (2), pp. 62–74.

Sanders, P. (2002) *First Steps in Counselling*, 3rd edition. Ross-on-Wye: PCCS Books.

Sanford, R. (1999) A Brief History of My Experience of the Development of Groupwork in The Person-Centered Approach. In Lago, C. and MacMillan, M. (eds.) *Experiences in Relatedness: Groupwork and the Person-Centred Approach.* Ross-on-Wye: PCCS Books.

Seeman, J. (1965) Perspectives in client-centered therapy. In Wolman, B. (ed.) *Handbook of Clinical Psychology.* New York: McGraw Hill.

Seeman, J. (1983) *Personality Integration: Studies and Reflections.* New York: Human Sciences Press.

Seeman, J. (2002) On Congruence: A Human Systems Paradigm. In Wyatt, G. (ed.) *Rogers' Therapeutic Conditions: Evolution, Theory and Practice. Vol. 1. Congruence.* pp. 200–212. Ross-on-Wye: PCCS Books.

Shlien, J.M. (1957) Time-Limited Psychotherapy: An Experimental Investigation of Practical Values and Theoretical Implications. *Journal of Counselling Psychology,*

4, (4), pp. 318–22.

Shlien, J.M. (1961). A Client-Centered Approach to Schizophrenia: First Approximations. In Burton, A. (ed.) *Psychotherapy of the Psychoses*. New York: Basic Books.

Shlien, J.M. (1984/2002). A Countertheory of Transference. In Levant, R. and Shlien, J. (eds.) *Client-Centered Therapy and the Person-Centered Approach: New Directions in Theory, Research and Practice*. New York: Praeger. Reprinted in Cain (2002).

Shlien, J. (1989/2002) Boy's person-centered perspective on psychodiagnosis. *Person-Centered Review, 4* (2), pp. 157–62. Reprinted in Cain (2002).

Shlien, J. (1997/2001). Empathy in Psychotherapy: Vital Mechanism? Yes. Therapist Conceit? All Too Often. By Itself? No. In Haugh, S. and Merry, T. (eds.) *Rogers' Therapeutic Conditions: Evolution, Theory and Practice. Vol. 2. Empathy*. pp. 38–52. Ross-on-Wye: PCCS Books.

Taft, J. (1933). *The Dynamics of Therapy in a Controlled Relationship*. New York: MacMillan.

Thorne, B. (1991). *Person-Centred Counselling: Therapeutic and Spiritual Dimensions*. London: Whurr.

Thorne, B. (1992) *Carl Rogers*. London: Sage.

Thorne, B. (1999) The move towards brief therapy: its dangers and its challenges. *Counselling, 10*,(1), pp. 7–11.

Thorne, B. and Lambers, E. (eds.) (1998) *Person-Centred Therapy: A European Perspective*. London: Sage.

Tudor, K, and Merry, T. (2002) *Dictionary of Person-Centred Psychology*. London: Whurr.

Warner, M. (2000) Person-centred therapy at the difficult edge: a developmentally based model of fragile and dissociated process. In Mearns, D. and Thorne, B. *Person-Centred Therapy Today*. pp. 144–71. London: Sage.

Warner, M. (2001). Empathy, Relational Depth and Difficult Client Process. In Haugh, S. and Merry, T. (eds.) *Rogers' Therapeutic Conditions: Evolution, Theory and Practice. Vol. 2. Empathy*. pp. 181–91. Ross-on-Wye: PCCS Books.

Watson, N. (1984) The Empirical Status of Rogers' Hypothesis of the Necessary and Sufficient Conditions for Effective Psychotherapy. In Levant, R. and Shlien, J. (eds.) *Client-Centered Therapy and the Person-Centered Approach: New Directions in Theory, Research, and Practice*. pp. 17–40. New York: Praeger.

Wilkins, P. (1997) *Personal and Professional Development for Counsellors*. London: Sage.

Wilkins, P. (2001). Unconditional Positive Regard Reconsidered. In Bozarth, J. and Wilkins, P. (eds.) *Rogers' Therapeutic Conditions: Evolution, Theory and Practice. Vol. 3: Unconditional Positive Regard*. pp. 35–48 Ross-on-Wye: PCCS Books.

Wood, J. K. (1999) Toward an understanding of large group dialogue and its implications. In Lago, C. and MacMillan, M. (eds.) *Experiences in Relatedness: Groupwork and The Person-Centred Approach*. Ross-on-Wye: PCCS Books.

Wrightsman, L. S. (1992) *Assumptions about Human Nature*. London: Sage

Wyatt, G. and Sanders, P. (2002) (eds.)*Rogers' Therapeutic Conditions: Evolution, Theory and Practice. Vol. 4: Contact and Perception*. Ross-on-Wye: PCCS Books.

Zimring, F. (2000/2001). Empathic Understanding Grows the Person. In Haugh, S. and Merry, T. (eds.) *Rogers' Therapeutic Conditions: Evolution, Theory and Practice. Vol. 2. Empathy*. pp. 86–98. Ross-on-Wye: PCCS Books.

Zinschitz, E. (2001) Understanding What Seems Unintelligible. In Haugh, S. and Merry, T. (eds.) *Rogers' Therapeutic Conditions: Evolution, Theory and Practice. Vol 2. Empathy*. pp. 192–205. Ross-on-Wye: PCCS Books.

Zinschitz, E. (2002). 'You really understand what I'm talking about, don't you?' Basic Requirements for Contact and Perception in Person-Centred Therapy and the Implications for Clients with Learning Disabilities. In Wyatt, G. and Sanders, P. (eds.) *Rogers' Therapeutic Conditions: Evolution, Theory and Practice. Vol. 4. Contact and Perception*. pp. 133–52. Ross-on-Wye: PCCS Books.

Index of subjects

acceptance 40, 42, 56
accreditation 6, 7
actualisation 21, 52, 53, 54, 65, 69, 112–3, 162
actualising tendency 21–2, 24–6, 28, 32, 34, 56, 68–70, 120, 123, 151
advice 95, 97
anti-social behaviour 22
anxiety 40, 55, 58, 65, 68, 120
assessment 75, 156 (see diagnosis)
Association for the Development of the Person-Centered Appr (ADPCA) 6, 199
attitudes 52, 92, 137, 142, 152
authentic/ity 44, 52, 65, 82, 134
autonomy 50
awareness 45, 58, 69, 123–4
Barrett-Lennard's five-phase model 64
befriending 154
behaviour, attitudes and values 70
belief system 54, 56
biography of Rogers 2, 191
blocks to communication 126
boundaries 8, 181
brief counselling/therapy 152, 158, 161 (see time-limited)
British Association for Counselling and Psychotherapy (BACP) 5, 11, 153, 163, 170–1, 183
    ethical framework 6, 11
    guidelines 171
British Association for the Person-Centred Approach (BAPCA) 6, 198
CD-ROM 191, 194
change/process 41, 70–1, 99
client
    work 157
    -centred phase 13
    not patients 74
communicating 77
    empathic understanding 80
communication skills 151–2
    of the counsellor's empathy 49
community groups 165
companion 74
Component Factor Method 48
conditioned self 27–8, 39, 46, 56, 76
conditions of worth 26, 28, 30, 32, 37, 40–2, 53, 55–8, 68, 70, 113
confidentiality 75, 154–5
configurations of self 33, 38, 108, 112

congruence 40, 45, 49, 52–4, 65–6, 69, 70–2, 82–7, 119, 122, 134, 143, 151, 170, 179
contract 180
    -setting session 75
core conditions 50, 52, 54, 64, 70–2, 83, 92, 93, 101, 119, 170
counselling
    agencies 161
    or psychotherapy? 5
    relationship 56, 93
    resources on the Internet 201
    skills 154
counsellor
    as a person 89
    as an expert 10
    attitudes 100
    values and attitudes 67, 69
    belief system 71
countertransference 83, 170
courtesy 166
creative/creativity 40, 44
cross-cultural communication 165
cultural/ly
    and political context 9
    aware counsellor 10
    diversity 165
    groups 10
    norms 10
daimonic 18
defence 45, 53, 56, 65, 68
denial 39–40, 46, 56, 68–9, 71, 114, 123
diagnosis 51, 75–6, 97 (see assessment)
different approaches to counselling 147
'dissociated' process 86
distort/ion 35, 39–40, 45–6, 68–71, 123
dreams 136
edge of awareness 38, 110–12, 115
effective helpers 54
effectiveness of person-centred therapy 67
embodied empathy 8, 64
emotion 34, 43, 96, 99
empathic understanding 45, 49, 51–4, 56, 65, 71,–2, 77, 79–80, 84–6, 111, 117, 119, 122, 124, 129, 134, 137, 142, 170
    in everyday life 133
    targets for 87
Employee Assistance Programmes 9, 158
encounter groups 124

ethical
    framework (BACP) 6, 11
    issues in counselling 11
ethnicity 10
evidence base/ed practice 7, 12, 67
evil 19
existential 18, 32
    encounter 102
external locus of evaluation 26, 68, 162
family life 68
fees 75
focusing 3
'fragile' process 86
frame of reference 18, 32, 35, 50, 69, 79, 80,
    84, 93, 99
freedom 18, 166
Freud, S. 52
fully functioning person 27–8, 37, 40–2,
    45–6, 56
goals of counselling 52
GP surgeries 153
group/s
    encounter 124
    work 165
    guidelines for personal learning in 167
    guidelines for assisting in 168
    supervision 182–3
HIV/AIDS 153
homeostastic balance 24
human
    nature 16, 17
    potential 20
humanistic psychology 2, 16, 32
hurt 142
identifying 128
    with the client 95
idiosyncratic empathy 86, 116
immediacy 125
incongruence 26, 46, 55, 84 (see also
congruence)
influencing 91 (see persuasion)
instrumental non-directiveness 92
integration 49, 52
internal
    frame of reference 35, 49, 52, 69, 70
    locus of evaluation 26, 41
    supervisor 187
Interpersonal Process Recall (IPR) 146
interpretations 91
introjection/ed values 35, 37, 42, 56
journal, personal 136
journals, academic (resources) 198
judgements 140
labels 76
locus of evaluation 26, 39, 41, 46, 53, 56–7,
    68, 162

external 26, 68, 162
    internal 26, 41
log, keeping a 157
metaphors 125, 131
moments of movement 66, 71
moral values 91
motivation for change 120
mutual/ity 79
    positive regard 40
National Health Service, 9
necessary and sufficient conditions 49, 58,
    72, 84
nineteen propositions 34
non-authoritarian 54, 91, 123, 162
    attitude 91
non-directive 2, 13, 54, 70, 93, 123, 143, 162
    attitude 90, 123
    instrumental 92
    phase 13
    principled 92
non-possessive 81
non-verbal communication 136
norms and values of the society 41
openness to experience 40–1
oppression 10 (see prejudiced)
organismic
    experiencing 24, 113
    self 27–8
    valuing process 27, 32, 42, 52–3
own experiencing process 40
pathology 76
perceptual field 34, 35
person-centred
    books (list) 189, 192
    counselling interview 72
    Expressive Therapy 3
    peer groups 166
    phase 14
person-centred phase 14
personal
    beliefs 54
    congruence 41
    counselling (counsellor's) 163–4
    development 164–5
    growth 134
    indemnity insurance 156
    qualities 142, 152
    resources 120
personality theory 34
persuasion 120 (see suggestion)
phases of the counselling process 64–5
phenomenological approach 18, 32
placement 152
political context 9
positive regard 25, 27, 41, 45, 56

positive self-regard 25, 27, 32, 38, 40–1, 45, 56, 70
power 92, 139
presence 119, 134
Pre-Therapy 50, 77, 88
prejudice 10, 91, 138–9, 151 (see stereo-typing, see also oppression)
principled non-directiveness 92
private practice 153
pro-social behaviour 22
process 32, 37, 52
    conception of psychotherapy 58
    'dissociated'/'fragile' 86
    of change 58
    scale 59, 63
    stages of 59
professional
    and ethical issues 75
    context 6
professionalisation 7
projection 83, 140
psychodynamic model/tradition 52, 170
psychological
    adjustment 27, 36, 40, 68
    assessment 75
    contact 49, 50, 55, 76, 114, 120
    defences 28 (see also defence)
    disturbance 37, 68
    integration 27
    maladjustment 25–6, 36, 69, 75
    resources 120
    safety 166
    tension 36
qualities 52, 65, 71, 92
questions 95, 98
race/racism 9–10, 139
rapport 81, 125
real/ness 52, 82
    being, 52, 82
    self 27, 40, 56
reassuring 96
reflection of feelings 12, 51, 78, 93
relational depth 101
research 48, 67
    effectiveness of PCT 67
respect 80, 137
self 21–4, 35–7, 58, 66, 69, 108, 110
    -actualisation 24–5, 27–8, 32
    -awareness 52, 151, 165
    -concept 24–8, 32, 40, 56, 68–9, 111, 120
    -destructive behaviour 55
    -determination 50
    -development 152
    -disclosure 55, 82, 85, 134, 151
    -discovery 55
    -esteem 26, 44, 52, 120

    -experience 24, 32
    -exploration 55
    -healing 70, 123
    real, 27, 40, 56
    -regard 40, 68, 120
    -regulation 69
    -resources 151, 162
    -structure 25, 28, 35,–7, 56–8, 111–13
    -theory 46
seven stages of process 59
sexism 9, 139
sexual orientation 10
silence 96, 98
similes 125, 131
skills 52, 80–1, 93, 120
social
    and cultural values 9
    context of counselling 5, 20
socialisation 23
society
    healthy scepticism of 44
    norms and values of 41
solution-focused therapy 12
stereotyping 10, 138–9
subjective experiencing 53, 93
suggestion 91, 120
supervisee role and expectations 181
supervision 75, 138, 153, 170, 182
    agreement 181
    arrangements 155
    as 'collaborative inquiry' 173
    co- 183
    images of 171
    peer group 182
    requirements 154
supervisor 143
    developing your internal 187
    role and expectations 180
symbolisation 35, 82, 114
sympathy 122, 127
tape-recording 131, 143, 154, 186
technique/s 50, 52, 81, 93, 149
therapeutic
    alliance 81, 101
    attitudes 84
    change 84
    relationship 78
threat 56, 68
time limited counselling (client-centred) 12, 152, 158–9, 161–3 (see brief therapy)
training 152
    placement 153
transference 52, 126 (see counter-transference)
trust 45, 65, 90, 150
U.K. Council for Psychotherapy (UKCP) 6

unconditional positive regard 27, 40, 44–5,
     49, 52–6, 67, 70–2, 81, 85, 88, 90, 122,
     137, 151, 170
unconditional positive self-regard 68
unconscious, the 113
United Kingdom Register of Counsellors
     (UKRC) 6
unstructured groups 165
values 35, 40–1, 43, 65, 79, 81, 92, 94, 97, 137,
     142, 151–2
value system 26, 37

valuing process 40–1
voluntary organisations 153
vulnerability 55, 120
warmth 52, 80–1, 125
     excessive 81
way of being 41, 93, 81, 119
well-functioning relationship 45
World Association for Person-Centered and
Experiential Therapies 200
woundedness 64

Index of checklists and exercises

Checklists
True or false   15
Human nature, actualisation and the emerging self   32
Self and Person   46
Counselling theory   71
Counsellor attitudes   100
Relational depth   118
Values, skills, personal qualities and attitudes   151
Client work   157
Time-limited work   163
Experiencing groups   169
Supervision   188

Exercises
Your own philosophy of human nature   17
Your conditions of worth   30
Your ideas about the fully-functioning person   42
Staying with the client   94
Your current 'model' or approach to counselling   121
Listening   126
Developing empathy (The empathy lab)   129
Experiencing empathy yourself   130
Using a tape recorder   131
Using metaphors and similes   131
Doing it all wrong   132
Using transcripts   132
Empathy in everyday life   133
Listening to yourself   133
Say how you felt   135
Keeping a journal   136
Non-verbal communication   136
Stereotype bashing   138
Valuing yourself   140
Making judgements   140
Things from the past   141
Hurt people do hurtful things   142
Practice counselling   144
Images of supervision   170
Images of being a supervisee   172

PCCS Books

The largest list of Client-Centred Therapy and Person-Centred Approach books in the world

Client Centred Therapy and the Person Centred Approach
Essential Readers
Series Edited by Tony Merry

Client-Centred therapy: A revolutionary paradigm
Jerold Bozarth

Experiences in Relatedness: Groupwork and the person-centred approach
Colin Lago & Mhairi MacMillan (Eds)

Women Writing in the Person-Centred Approach
Irene Fairhurst (Ed)

Understanding Psychotherapy: Fifty years of client-centred theory and practice
C.H.Patterson

The Person-Centred Approach: A passionate presence
Peggy Natiello

Family, Self and Psychotherapy: A person-centred perspective
Ned L. Gaylin

Rogers' Therapeutic Conditions: Evolution, Theory and Practice
Series Edited by Gill Wyatt

Volume 1: Congruence
Gill Wyatt (Ed)

Volume 2: Empathy
Sheila Haugh & Tony M

Volume 3: Unconditional Positive Regard
Jerold Bozarth and Paul Wilkins (Eds)

Volume 4: Contact and Perception
Gill Wyatt & Pete Sanders (Eds)

more overleaf . . .